Gender, Development and Identity

AN ETHIOPIAN STUDY

To David

HELEN PANKHURST

Gender, Development and Identity

AN ETHIOPIAN STUDY

ZED BOOKS
London & New Jersey

Gender, Development and Identity was first published by
Zed Books Ltd
57 Caledonian Road
London N1 9BU
and 165 First Avenue,
Atlantic Highlands, New Jersey
07716, in 1992

Cover design by Andrew Corbett
Typeset by Opus 43, Cumbria
Printed and bound in the United Kingdom
by Biddles Ltd., Guildford and King's Lynn

A catalogue record for this book is available from the British Library

ISBN 1 85649 157 9 Hb
ISBN 1 85649 158 7 Pb

*Grateful thanks are due to Dr Haddis Gebre Meskel
who kindly set the Amharic poems, using a font
of his own design.*

Contents

Maps

Acknowledgements

My thanks go to all those in Ethiopia and the United Kingdom who made this research possible, fruitful and enjoyable.

The discussions with numerous friends in Gragn, and with Alem, Tigest and Welde Tsadik in Mehal Meda, were seminal during the fieldwork period. My apologies for the monomaniacal scribblings and mumblings about 'work' which seemed to get in the way of friendship.

I would like to take this opportunity to express my thanks to the Economic and Social Research Council of Great Britain, to the Institute of Ethiopian Studies and the Institute of Development Research of Addis Ababa University, to Edinburgh University, to the Canadian International Development Agency, the Baptist Mission and Save the Children UK. My thanks also to the Ethiopian Bus Corporation whose vehicles transported me to and from Menz on innumerable occasions and almost without mishap.

Grateful thanks are also due to Dr Haddis Gebre Meskel, who kindly set the Amharic poems, using a font of his own design.

Hilary Standing and many others at the School of African and Asian Studies, Sussex University, equipped me with the background and stimulated the interests which resulted in this research. Tricia Jeffery and Chris Allen, the supervisors of my thesis, provided invaluable advice and guidance throughout. To them, to Anna and Jessica and to my family I am most grateful for all their help, patience and support.

Notes on Language

Transliteration

The following rules have been adopted to reduce as much as possible the number of diacritical marks used when transliterating from Amharic:
- The seven vowel orders are represented as: e, u, ï, a, é, i, o.
- Glottalized explosives are indicated by an apostrophe after the letter: t', k', ch', etc.
- Letters are doubled where the syllable is stressed.
- Where a different but more common transliteration exists, in particular in the case of the names of people and places, the more common spelling has been adopted.

Dating

In most cases, the Ethiopian calendar is translated directly into the Gregorgian one. However, where an Ethiopian date is given in a direct quote, the Gregorian figure is provided in brackets.

Glossary

A translation is generally used together with all Amharic words. This glossary lists the terms used repeatedly and in more than one chapter.

Arek'ï	Liquor, made out of barley in Menz	*Meher*	Long rains, term used for rain and crop
Awraja	Second tier administrative region		
Bana	Locally made woollen blanket	*Mengist*	Government, state
Belg	Short rains, term used for rain and crop	*Ribbï*	System of renting out livestock
Berberé	Ethiopian spice, based on red chillies	*Shiro*	Ground pulse-based stew, staple food with *injera*
Birr	Ethiopian dollar, almost equal to half an American dollar	*Sira zemecha*	State organized communal or *corvé* labour
Dabbo	Bread, usually made from wheat		
Dego	Highlands		
Fird shengo	Local law courts	*T'ella*	Locally brewed beer, made from barley in Menz
Guassa	Communal pasture land		
Iddir	Burial association	*T'ibbeka'a gwad*	Local police
Injera	Staple pancake bread made from barley in Menz, eaten with *shiro*		
K'olla	Lowlands	*Wereda*	Third tier administrative region, now being abandoned
Mehaber	Religious soul gathering, usually held monthly		

Equivalents

1 quintal = 100 kilos
1 *silicha* = approximately 1/2 quintal
1 hectare = 10,000 square metres
1 *t'ind* = approximately 1/4 hectare

1

Introduction: Stating the Issues

The fieldwork for this book[1] was carried out during 1988–9 in a rural community within Menz, Ethiopia, during the last years of Mengistu Haile Mariam's régime. Two sets of interactions are discussed: first, the relationship between the state and the peasantry, and, second, relations between men and women. The analysis focuses on understanding and explaining the position and the channels of action of the subordinate groups – the peasantry in one case, women in the other.

In Part 1, after an introduction to Ethiopia and the region of Menz, the community's relationship to the state is documented in the context of the activities of various associations, cooperatives, campaigns and ministries. Attention is then focused specifically on one particular policy, the Villagization Campaign, in order to illustrate the complexity of the state's overall impact on a heterogeneous population. Consideration is given to areas of mismatch between government theory and practice, between what the state conceived and what the peasantry understood to be happening, between the impact of the state on men and on women.

Having explored in Part 1 the significant areas of society in which there was state involvement, in Part 2 the book is increasingly devoted to areas of people's lives which the state had not penetrated. Some activities are more visible than others, both to the state and within society. In Menz, ploughing was a male domain which could not exist without crop processing, a female domain. Livestock husbandry, and other work such as spinning and fuel production, show the ways in which women are marginalized, while demonstrating at the same time their vital role in the economy.

The phenomenon of marital instability and the relationship between spouses points to hardship and dissatisfaction. It also demonstrates women's ability to play an active role in decisions that affect their position. Neither state nor church had much success in regulating the forms of contract and number of marriages an individual enters into. Government policies were directed at the household as a single unit, oblivious of the frequency of divorce, the demographic cycle of the household and the stratifications within it.

The identity and valuation of women is established, at least in part, by their reproductive abilities, and life-giving events are firmly within their domain. Yet women's experiences, such as menstruation and pregnancy, were camouflaged; their blood had to be purified through the mediation of a priest. The burdens of biology and the social constructions of womanhood were not considered by the government. Similarly, death is a crucial occasion of great social importance in the society, yet it is an event in which the state was not involved. Despite its goal of radical transformation, life-cycle events were not reconstructed or even scrutinized by the policy makers; government's interests and priorities were focused elsewhere.

The dominant Orthodox Christian religion gives power to men rather than to women, yet it appeared more meaningful to women, who found support particularly in the Virgin Mary. In addition, women prevailed in alternative, socially marginalized and eclectic spirit beliefs. These various manifestations of religion existed despite the conflicting ideologies of a state which was imbued with socialist modernizing values. In Menz, state ideology had little impact on rural beliefs and its local legitimacy rested, in part, on a manipulation of Christianity.

The empirical findings presented in the book are brought together in the final chapter. Interrelationships emerge between different spheres of state intervention, between the household economy, religion, marital relations and life-cycle events. All these considerations combine to show how women were oppressed, but also how women took control; to show how peasants were constrained and influenced by the state, yet also how their lives remained directed by themselves and the battle against desperately scarce resources.

The first of the two sets of issues addressed concerns the peasant–state relationship and especially these questions: In what areas did the state attempt to effect transformations? What were the attitudes towards, and the effects of, state policies on the peasantry? Where the state had little impact, what non-governmental structures and services were operative?

Although the question of how state policies related to society is a major component of this work, the focus here is not on the internal logic of the state itself,[2] nor on the events that took place on a national scale. These issues are dealt with only briefly in Chapter 2. Rather, the aim is to look at how people perceived the state, what services, infrastructures, and ideologies came their way, and how people reacted to them. As Azarya explains:

> [Until recently] scholarly interest still focused on the state itself; it tried to explain what went wrong with the state and the reasons for its weakness. When the society was brought into the analysis, it was usually in order to explain why the state did not function properly. The focus has thus remained state centric . . . relatively little attention has been paid to how societies cope with the state, rather than how the state acts upon the society. . . . State–society relations in contemporary Africa can be studied with greater emphasis on societal responses. This is not a methodological point, nor is it simply a plea for a new research agenda. It raises some substantive questions about the relevance of the state to African social life, which make it imperative to know how the society behaves irrespective of or despite certain state actions.[3]

The term state will not be distinguished from that of government, nor is the state, as a socio-political entity, clearly disaggregated. The focus of this study is not on how different government organs interacted, or how analysts interpreted the history behind particular state actions, but on how the population perceived and was affected by ministries and policies that were, in effect, incarnations of the government. There remains a need for studies which will lead to a more precise understanding of the constantly negotiated power structures within and between different parts of the state apparatus.

Turning more specifically to the area covered by this research, it is easy to be appalled by the social, economic and political record of Mengistu's régime, both in terms of its relationship with the peasantry and in terms of women's position. However, the context is one of 'failure' in much of the developing world and in Africa in particular. Furthermore, war and famine have long plagued Ethiopia, and the complex web of causal factors resulting in hardship is likely to remain in force, irrespective of the particular form of government in power.

The second strand to this book is that of gender relations and the lives of rural women. The data-led research raises questions such as: What is the position of rural women in Menz? What do they do? How do their actions reflect how they see themselves and how they are perceived by men? What are their sources of oppression or subordination and their sources of power and self-expression?

These questions require empirical answers. However, before focusing on women's lives in Menz, it may be useful to look at the contextual literature and theories which can inform case-study observations. In much of the literature on women and development a ubiquitous patriarchy,[4] the capitalist system in general[5] and colonialism in particular have been blamed for women's subordination. Given the inequality and oppression experienced almost throughout the world, an emancipating herald was necessary and, traditionally, socialism was the solution offered.[6] Yet what was the rationale behind the notion that socialist transformation would resolve gender inequality?

Socialism was conceived, theorized and practised as a stage of political evolution. In Marxist theory, political economy was reduced to the social relations of production and the interaction between social relations and means of production. The issue as expounded by Marx and his followers was about class, defined narrowly in terms of a relationship to production. Yet all societies and economies have been, and more than ever remain, divided across lines such as gender, race, ethnicity, age and religion. It cannot be assumed *a priori*, yet theorists persisted in assuming that socialist countries or countries with 'socialist tendencies' were more sensitive to the injustice in all forms of oppression, not merely those based on class and production.

As for religious oppression, the socialist state's response was clear: it banished all religions in one derisive sweep, proclaiming an egalitarian atheism and explaining the emergence and function of religion in class terms – as an ideology used by the powerful to justify their dominance and subjection of the masses. When it came to hierarchies based on age, ethnicity or colour, early Marxist tracts had little to say. Later writings at least developed their analysis in, for example, the debate on the articulation of modes of production, which considered syncretic relations between capitalism and pre-capitalist social formations on the periphery. Even then, the colour and ethnicity issues were barely mentioned and had no causal influence on the theoretical paradigm.[7]

However, what concerns us here is the reaction in socialist theory and practice to the gender divide. When comparing themselves with previous régimes, socialist states often equated their revolution with a transformation in which all oppressed people were liberated, and the category of women emerged as one of the victors. Yet the concern tended to be at a rhetorical level only. The literature on the former USSR, China and Tanzania, for example,[8] suggests that the commitment to gender equality was secondary to that of 'male' socialism, and conditional on not interfering with the dominant agenda. In reality, the class division of labour was reorganized, but not the sexual division of labour.[9]

Similarly, socialist liberation movements were in the vanguard of groups that campaigned for women. Yet, studies of such movements suggest that their awareness of women's issues was largely a result of a labour requirement and the need to galvanize men, women and children into participation in the social, political and military struggle. Personal and private realms were, as much as possible, suspended by the struggle, and after 'liberation' life resumed as before; gender inequalities unchallenged. Commitment to women's issues by socialist movements and governments was limited by an unwillingness to devote political force, time and money to a consideration of the complex and interrelated factors at work.[10] Moreover, the autocratic and militaristic nature of the régimes left little room for abolishing male domination.

The literature on 'feminist' social sciences was central at all stages of this research.[11] Moving beyond the argument that, to counter male bias, women must be included both as subject matter and as theorists, this literature developed into analyses of gender relations, studies of differentiation within 'male' and 'female' characterizations and, in some cases, documentation of areas of gender reversal.[12] Methodologically, such studies have also been in the vanguard of an interdisciplinary approach and rethinking the unbalanced and often exploitative relationship between researcher and informant. With regard to this book, the choice of subject matter, influences thereon, and the approach adopted are discussed more fully in Appendices A and B.

There is a growing literature on women and development which points to the dangers of assuming that economic growth benefits men and women equally. It is now common knowledge that development can be detrimental to women, resulting in greater economic oppression and political powerlessness.[13] Boserup in *Woman's Role in Economic Development,*[14] moved beyond such generalizations to an analysis correlating different forms of agricultural production with their effects on the position of women. The argument was that the world can be divided into an Asian – male – plough-based agricultural system and an African – female – hoe-based agricultural system. In the Asian system, women play a relatively minor role in cultivation, and it is here that veiling, gender segregation and greater restrictions on the mobility and actions of women seems to occur. On the other hand, in the African system, women predominate in agricultural production and have a relatively powerful, though still subordinate, position in the household.

Connected with this theory is that developed by Goody.[15] In *Production and Reproduction: A Comparative Study of the Domestic Domain*, he argued that in parts of the world where the plough is used, agricultural surplus can be produced. This surplus leads towards a more stratified society and one in which inheritance becomes a key to reproducing the social order. Seclusion of women, arranged marriages, and inheritance rules ensure that reproduction can be controlled and is not a threat to burgeoning class structure. In this scenario, women become marginalized. By contrast, he suggests, areas of hoe agriculture are likely to be more egalitarian in terms of both class and gender.

A third theory can be included in the discussion, namely that resulting from research in West Africa by, for example, Guyer and Henn.[16] This theory suggests that development and increased involvement in the market economy have affected the female hoe economy in a way which is detrimental to women. The benefits to be obtained from cash-crop production have attracted men into agriculture, leaving women to continue subsistence domestic production with a reduced economic power and status, working on increasingly marginalized lands.

How do these theories apply to Ethiopia, or Menz? Despite being part of Africa, plough agriculture is practised, as in many parts of the rest of Ethiopia, and women are not the 'dominant' force in crop cultivation. To quote May and McLellan:

> Contrary to common African usage, the Ethiopian male works in the fields, leaving the women to prepare meals, crush the grains which the men have threshed, carry water and collect wood.[17]

Much of Ethiopia, including Menz, thus seems to accord with the Asian rather than the African pattern. Moreover, until the revolution of 1974, the society had the appearance of a 'feudal' political structure. These combined factors fit Goody's Asian category associating plough agriculture with stratification. The problem is that Goody locates the basis for stratification in crop production and, specifically, the agricultural surplus. The literature on Ethiopia, however, clearly points to a hierarchy which was not solely or even primarily based on agricultural production. The nobility was a military one; moreover, control over long-distance trade was an important source of wealth. The sustainability of any one area both in terms of fuel and agricultural production was so low that capital cities often shifted. The machineries of the state, kings and emperors with armies and entourages, were obliged to be on the move, continuously, because of the incapacity of the land to produce constant and sufficient surplus.

If, ignoring this caveat, we accept the correlation between men as the main cultivators, the use of the plough, and greater stratification, then much of Ethiopia conforms to the Asian rather than the African model. The Ethiopian case might then be used to prove the dangers of a simplistic geographical determinism. However, in gender terms Ethiopia does not sit happily in the Asian category, either. The sexual division of labour is not as rigorously upheld as in the Asian model. There is little segregation and veiling, and, as we shall see later, women have the ability to act independently in a way which does not accord with the theory. In fact, wherever the position of Amhara women is documented, impressions are ambivalent. According to Messing,

> Cultural participation of the female is so restricted during her life cycle, that many emotional outlets are denied her. Monotonous daily routine of manual labour, two years of breastfeeding after every birth; denial of active participation in the church; derogatory views of female intelligence on the part of the males....[18]

Yet Reminick, another researcher in the area, observed:

> In learning of the prevailing cultural norms and patterns of authority, one's impression of the superior dominant male appears strong. However, when one examines the rights and duties inherent in the marriage alliance and divorce procedures, the picture becomes more one of equality where the real factors of authority and domination consist in relative wealth, influence and outside support regardless of the sex of the spouse.[19]

> The cultural definition of inequality between the sexes allows for a greater behavioural, acted-out equality.[20]

References to the position of women in Ethiopia are puzzling, and the attempt to fit the country into the general theory proves problematic; either there is some validity in these theories and Ethiopia is an exception, fitting neither the Asian nor the African category, or there is something missing or wrong in the theories themselves.

With the exception of this brief overview, the relevant literature and theory will be integrated with the empirical data in the following chapters. The literature consulted falls into categories which include women's studies, socialist Third World and the peasantry, Ethiopica, and general anthropological, sociological and political works. It is perhaps in the nature of such work that one starts by bemoaning the paucity of relevant studies, and ends up groaning under their abundance. Nevertheless, there is still no single book devoted to the position of women in Ethiopia as a whole, let alone in Menz, and most of the general works have been written by, and focused on, men. [21]

In Part 1, Chapter 2 provides some background information on Ethiopia, then looks at the characteristics of Menz, and finally concentrates on the specific area of study, Gragn peasants' association.[22] Chapter 3 considers the different forms of state presence at the local level, and how these are perceived by the population. Chapter 4 focuses on one particular government policy, that of villagization.

In Part 2, the analysis moves to issues in which the state's presence is increasingly marginal, despite the central importance to people of these issues. Thus Chapter 5 considers the household economy, Chapter 6 marital relations, Chapter 7 the life-cycle, and Chapter 8 the influence of religion and language. The chapter on religion shows spheres in which the society's pre-revolutionary ideas and modes of operation continued, the state altering a few conditions rather than establishing a radical alternative. The state's blindness to women, described in the empirical chapters of Part 1, contrasts with their emergence, in the subsequent section, as significant actors in society. Thus, understanding how women are marginalized while remaining contributors to household and community, we are drawn away from the state to the household, marital relations, the individual life-cycle and religion.

Chapter 9 goes beyond specific issues and the empirical data to bring together the main themes of state–peasant and gender relations. The Epilogue considers some of the changes observed during a return visit to the area in 1992. This is followed by three appendices. The first is devoted to methodological considerations involved in the process of transformation from data to book. The second consists of an anecdotal account of how I came to undertake the research and the factors involved in the selection of the village. The final appendix summarizes the quantitative data used in the various chapters.

Notes

1 H. Pankhurst, 1992.
2 Evans, *et al.*, eds, 1985. In Ethiopia, see Pausewang, 1987.
3 Azarya, 1988: 5–18.
4 There is considerable controversy about what patriarchy means, its origins and historical progression, how it is perpetuated, etc. Analysts like McDonough and Harrison, 1978, attempt to define it in Marxian and psychoanalytic terms; Beechey, 1979, suggests that there is a value in the integration of the two theories, though she argues that the duality leads to confusion and that a materialist analysis is more useful; whilst Eisenstein, 1979, suggests that patriarchy is rooted in biology and women's role in reproduction, rather than in economic or historical factors.
5 Engels (1884), 1972, for example, located the beginnings of female subordination in the introduction of private property relations and sexual divisions of labour that kept women in a static domestic environment whilst men's productivity in the wider economy increased. The implication is that the end of private property would end women's oppression.
6 For example, a publication of the Revolutionary Ethiopia Women's Association stated: 'When socialism was declared as the guiding principle of Ethiopia, a green light emerged for the equality and freedom of women in Ethiopia', Ethiopia, REWA, 1982:14.
7 In the debate on the articulation of modes of production, ethnicity or colour divisions are not perceived as central to the analysis. Rather, the assumption is that social divisions within the pre-capitalist social formation are used to the advantage of the

imperialist capitalist system. Wolpe, 1980; Seddon, 1978.

8 Molyneux, 1981, 1985; Croll, 1981, 1983, 1985; Buckley, 1981; Bengelsdorf, 1985; Alpern-Engel, 1987; Pelzer-White, 1987. There are, however, differences between the experiences of women in different socialist countries, Bystydzienski, 1989.

9 Hartmann, 1979, and Eisenstein, 1979. For a study of the changing attitude of the Soviet state to women's emancipation see Juncar, 1978.

10 Of all the countries, Cuba seems to have put the most political will behind women. Attempts were made to include women in production, to socialize domestic chores and to make men as involved in the domestic sphere as women. However, considerable structural obstacles have not been removed, Nazzari, 1983.

11 See Moore, 1988 and Ardener, 1975, 1978.

12 Studies of gender relations often assume that, ubiquitously, women have a reduced status and political role. For an interesting account criticizing this view on the basis of a case-study of Nigeria, see Amadiume, 1987.

13 For example, Rosaldo and Lamphere, 1974.

14 According to Benería and Sen, 1981:279, probably the most quoted book on women in development.

15 Goody, 1976.

16 Guyer, 1980 (a), (b); Henn, 1983, 1984.

17 May and McLellan, 1970: 487.

18 Messing, 1957: 707.

19 Reminick, 1973 (b): 57.

20 Reminick, 1973 (b): 362.

21 See Cassiers, 1974; Tsehai Berhane Selassie, 1984; Hirut Terefe & Lakew Woldetekle, 1986; Poluha, 1987; Fellows 1987; Fetenu Bekele, 1989; H. Pankhurst, 1989 (b); the papers presented for The Seminar on Gender Issues in Ethiopia, Addis Ababa University, Institute of Ethiopian Studies, ed. Tsehai Berhane Selassie, 1991.

22 In the thesis upon which this book is based, the peasants' association was given the pseudonym of Gera. Since then, the change of government means that there is no need to keep up the fiction. 'False' names have still been given to people within the association, to protect them from possible interference due to the public dissemination of private conversations.

PART
1

The Country
and State Policies

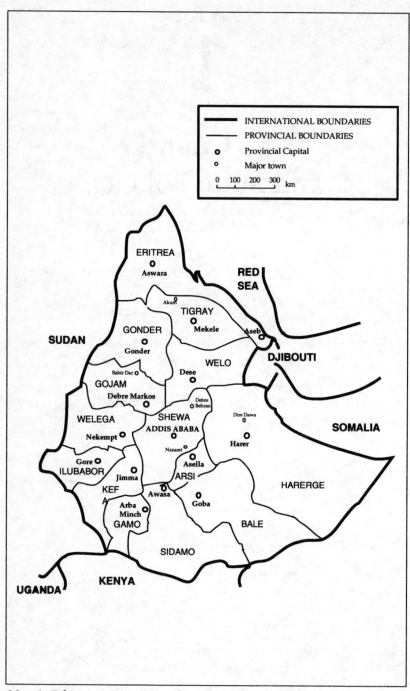

Map 1: Ethiopia – international and provincial boundaries

2

Ethiopia, Menz and Gragn

This chapter establishes the setting for the empirical research by providing background information on country and region. It is divided into three sections, in which the focus narrows from the whole country, through Menz, to Gragn peasants' association.

Ethiopia[1]

Physical geography

Ethiopia is situated in the hinterland of the Horn of Africa, bordered to the north and west by Sudan, and to the south by Kenya and Somalia. To the east it faces the Red Sea coast, Djibouti and Somalia. The country has been described as pear-shaped in appearance, with the stalk facing north. Elevations vary from 100 metres below sea level in the Dallol Depression to 4620 metres on the peak of Ras Dashen in the Simien Mountains. The Ethiopian highlands form a central belt, bordered by lowlands on the east and west. In the south, the highlands are bisected by the Rift Valley, within which lie a series of lakes. Much of the land has experienced considerable volcanic activity and subsequent erosion. Particularly in the north, erosion has often removed tertiary lava to expose limestone and sandstone rock faces.

Ethiopia is located in the tropics. The main rainy season occurs between mid-June and late September; the less predictable 'small rains' fall some time between February and April. Differences in altitude produce considerable regional variations in both climate and vegetation. Traditionally, Ethiopians classify the land into three major zones: *dega*, the highlands, which begin at approximately 2400 metres; *weyna dega*, the lower highlands, between 1800 and 2400 metres; and *k'olla*, the lowlands, below 1800 metres. The great majority of the population live in the *weyna dega* region. The people in the lowlands tend to be pastoralists, whilst those in the middle and higher regions are predominantly mixed farmers engaged in livestock and crop production.

Ethiopia covers an area of 1,251,282 square kilometres. According to the 1984 Ethiopian Census, the population was then estimated at 42 million and was expected to reach 50 million by 1990.[2] Until recently, the country was divided into 16 administrative regions. Shewa, the area in which fieldwork was undertaken, was one of the largest regions, stretching over 85,094 square kilometres. It was also the most populous and the fastest growing.[3] The estimates for Shewa in 1989 were a population of 9,333,735 and a density of 43 persons per square kilometre.

Culture and religion

Cultural and ethnic diversity characterize much of Ethiopia, with periodic migrations and intermarriage of races reducing the homogeneous nature of each community. There are said to be at least 80 population groups, and nearly a hundred languages spoken, many with additional regional or other dialects. The main languages can be divided into four groups, the Semitic, Cushitic, Omotic and Nilotic.

Amharic, a Semitic language, is apparently spoken at home by a third of Ethiopians.[4] It has also functioned as the official language of the Ethiopian state. The centralization of power within Ethiopia, and Amhara dominance, has been a cause of social and political unrest and the so-called 'nationalities' problem is a major consideration in domestic policies. It has resulted in crippling human and financial costs, including civil war, major military expenditure, years of aggravated famine conditions and the loss of government control over large tracts of the country.

The Islamic religion is practised in the lowlands of Ethiopia and, overall, around a third of the population is Muslim. Ethiopian Orthodox Christianity, adopted as the state religion in 333 A.D., predominates in the highland areas of Ethiopia, and is followed by over half the population.[5] In 1986, the Orthodox Church was estimated to have 22 million members. A minority of the population include animists, Protestants, Roman Catholics and *Felasha* or 'Ethiopian Jews'.

In generalizations about Ethiopia, the diversity of cultures and societies tends to be forgotten, submerged by an over-representation of the Christian Amhara. This study is also located amongst the Amhara of Menz, and what is written here should not be taken to apply automatically to all Amhara, let alone to other, more disparate, societies within the country.

Recent history

Modernization began to make an impression at the end of the nineteenth and during the first years of the present century, during Emperor Menilek's reign. In the second half of the twentieth century, during the latter years of Emperor Haile Selassie's rule, those representing modernizing forces clashed with those supporting 'feudal' interests in the society; they criticized the Emperor's autocratic form of government and the slow pace of development. Dissent from Haile Selassie's rule took the form of an attempted coup in 1960, followed by student unrest throughout the 1960s and early 1970s; there were intermittent calls for land reform and denunciations of official corruption. Attempts at reform, such as a landlord–tenant bill, were blocked at the parliamentary stage in 1968. The 1972–4 famine in Tigray and Welo, rapid inflation spearheaded by a rise in petrol prices, unrest amongst the urban population, discontent over proposed educational reforms, guerrilla activity in Eritrea and Bale, and peasant disturbances in the south set the scene for the second and successful coup, dubbed the 'creeping coup'. The remainder of this section briefly highlights the main events since this revolution, in chronological order.[6]

In February 1974 a series of strikes in Addis Ababa and a mutiny in the armed forces led to major changes. Ministers were arrested; the Prime Minister Aklilu Habte Weld and his cabinet resigned, and he was replaced by Lij Endalkachew Mekonen, who was expected to carry out reforms. In June the Coordinating Committee of the Armed Forces, Police and Territorial Army was formed and took direct action resulting in further arrests. Haile Selassie was deposed on 12 September 1974. Power was thereafter exercised by a 'Co-Coordinating Committee' of the Provisional Military Government of Ethiopia (PMAC), also calling itself the *Derg*. A bitter and bloody power struggle led to the rise of Mengistu Haile Mariam as Chairman of PMAC and, eventually, as Head of State.

Meanwhile, the PMAC was increasingly adopting a socialist model of government. On 20 December the country was declared a socialist state and more than a hundred companies and banking institutions were nationalized, and in March 1975 the nationalization of all rural land was decreed. Students were sent out across the country to help organize a Campaign of National Development, the *zemecha* programme. They implemented the reform, setting up locally elected peasants' associations, and organized literacy campaigns. Elective, regional, provincial and district associations were created. The schemes culminated in the first All-Ethiopia Peasants' Association Congress (AEPA), which took place in April 1978. Cooperatives and communal farms were also introduced during the period. Meanwhile, in July 1975, urban land was nationalized and people with more than one house had additional ones confiscated. *K'ebelé*, or urban dwellers' associations, were set up, local and elective in form and with their own militia. Between 1977 and 1978, the years of the 'Red Terror', Ethiopia witnessed a period of unprecedented urban terrorism. Thousands were arrested and many killed in inter-factional fighting.

In December 1979 the Commission for Organizing the Party of the Working People of Ethiopia (COPWE) emerged as the new focus of power, still dominated by the military. In 1980 the Revolutionary Ethiopia Women's Association (REWA) and the Revolutionary Ethiopia Youth Association (REYA) were founded. In 1981 a judicial system based on special people's courts was established. Juries were elected by members of the urban dwellers' associations and peasants' associations. The system comprised tiers of appeal from the sub-regional, *wereda* courts, to the regional, *awraja* courts, the high courts, and finally the supreme court in Addis Ababa.

In 1984 the Workers' Party of Ethiopia (WPE) was inaugurated as the 'Marxist-Leninist Vanguard Party'. It consisted of 135 men and one woman (in charge of women's affairs) full members, and 60 men and 4 women alternative members.[7] The same year drought and famine ravaged the north, affecting some nine million people. Action taken by the government included relief and rehabilitation in the affected areas, and the controversial resettling of 600,000 people as an attempt at a partial long-term solution.

In 1985 the Villagization Campaign was implemented in parts of the country, a policy which will be discussed in depth in Chapter Four.

In June 1986 a draft constitution was drawn up and publicized by the Workers' Party of Ethiopia; a million copies were disseminated, in 15 languages. After supervised debate, it was announced in February 1987 that the constitution had been endorsed by 81 per cent of the 12 million who had voted. On 14 June 1987 elections were held for a National Assembly or *Shengo*, with an 85 per cent participation rate. Lieutenant-Colonel Mengistu Haile Mariam and all members of the Politburo of WPE were returned as deputies. Ethiopia was proclaimed a People's Democratic Republic.

The constitution described Ethiopia as a unitary socialist state under the 'democratic centralism' of the Workers' Party of Ethiopia. It vested considerable power in the President, elected for a term of five years; he was Head of State, Chief Executive, Commander-in-Chief of the Armed Forces, and Chairman of the Council of Ministers, of the Defence Council and of the State Council. The constitution was supposed to grant all citizens freedom of press and of speech. Religious freedom was permitted, provided it was not exercised to the detriment of the interests of the revolution. The constitution also claimed the equality of all nationalities and a degree of autonomy through devolution to unspecified administrative units. It expressed the equality of men and women. Yet the rights of citizenship and theories of equality were seen as little more than empty words. Clearly the constitution was meant to disguise the militaristic nature of the existing power base rather than to transform or widen it.

The 1986–7 period saw the defection of a number of key officials. These included Dawit Wolde Giorgis, head of the Relief and Rehabilitation Commission, Goshu Wolde, the Foreign Minister, and a number of ambassadors. In 1987 a further resettlement programme was introduced, with the aim of relocating 200,000 people, though only a few thousand were in fact resettled. The villagization programme became a nationwide campaign.

Since the fieldwork period, there has been major political change. An attempted coup took place between 16 and 18 May 1989, led by Major General Merid Nigussie, Chief of Staff. Twelve generals involved were tried, sentenced to death and executed in May of the following year. From 1988 onwards resistance movements, and in particular the Tigrean People's Liberation Front (TPLF), increased their hold on many parts of the country. On 21 May 1991 Mengistu Haile Mariam fled the country and a week later the Ethiopian People's Revolutionary Democratic Front (EPRDF), formed by the amalgamation of the TPLF and other liberation movements, took control of the capital and the country. A National Conference on Peace and Democracy held in July endorsed a 20-article charter. The transitional government subsequently set up was headed by the Council of Representatives under the presidency of Meles Zenawi.

The economy

Dominant among the many different means of livelihood undertaken by

Ethiopians is sedentary agriculture in the form of mixed farming. Shifting cultivation in the south, and pastoralism with different degrees of transhumance in the arid lowlands, are also practised. There is a 'modern' urban sector with manufacturing and service industries. Mineral resources, including petroleum and potash, are by and large unexploited.

A summary of the basic economic indicators is given in Table 2.1.

Table 2.1 Basic economic indicators

GNP p.c. dollars (1986)
Low income countries	270		Ethiopia	120

Average annual GNP p.c. growth rate 1965–86 (%)
Low income countries	3.1		Ethiopia	0.0

Average annual inflation %	1965–80	1980–5
Low income countries	4.6	8.1
Ethiopia	3.4	3.4

Average annual growth % in the different sectors (1980–86):	GDP	Agriculture	Industry	Manufacturing	Services
Ethiopia	7.5	4.9	10.6	11.2	6.6
Low income countries	0.8	–3.9	3.8	3.9	5.1

Source: *World Development Report 1988*, Statistical Appendix

Over the centuries Ethiopia has experienced a history of unrelenting famine. The famine of 1985 struck most regions and was estimated to have affected some 11 million people. In many parts of the country conditions have not returned to pre-1985 levels; indeed some areas have suffered drought conditions intermittently ever since.

The figures in Table 2.2 show the predominance of agriculture. The table also suggests that women make up 39 per cent of the labour force, a figure reflecting perceptions about what should and should not be incorporated in the definition of 'economically active'.[8]

It was estimated that 95 per cent of the total cultivated land was farmed by smallholders, who produced 95 per cent of the country's agricultural

Table 2.2. Estimated economically active population

	Male		Female		Total	
Agriculture, etc.	8,164,000	76%	5,877,000	85%	14,040,000	80%
Services	1,547,000	15%	623,000	9%	2,170,000	12%
Industry	960,000	9%	422,000	6%	1,383,000	8%
Total	10,671,000	100%	6,922,000	100%	17,593,000	100%
		61%		39%		100%

Source: Statistical Survey, Ethiopia, *Africa South of the Sahara*, 1990: 463

crops, excluding coffee. Of the remaining land, 3 per cent was taken up by state farms and 2 per cent by collective farms and agricultural settlements.[9] A trend towards minimal increases in state farms and cooperatives characterized the 1980s. State farms received preferential treatment and funding for services and facilities. In 1989 the government also introduced a distinction between high potential and low potential areas, the former receiving more inputs than the latter. Agriculture in the peasant sector is undertaken side by side with the rearing of livestock. Much of the livestock in the country is, however, owned by pastoralists. The years of attempted socialist transformation saw little collectivization of livestock.

Policy declarations made in the year preceding the downfall of Mengistu Haile Mariam's régime showed a movement away from the socialist policies advocated for 14 years, and towards greater economic incentives to the population. This could be interpreted as a response to internal conditions, an attempt to survive in the face of increasing discontent and loss of control over much of the country. Officially it was presented as a realization that earlier policies were not delivering. The changes can also be seen as having external origins. Pressure had been exerted by the West and aid-giving bodies, in particular the World Bank and the European Economic Community, which were funding development schemes in Ethiopia. Finally, the shift can be explained as a response to *perestroika* and the fundamental changes which were occurring in Eastern European countries. The EPRDF likewise appears to have shifted allegiances from a mixture of Marxism and populism to the espousal of a multi-party polity and a mixed economy.

Menz and Gragn

Menz

Menz is situated in northern Shewa, some 300 kilometres north of Addis Ababa. The region, known until 1989 as Menz and Gishe, comprised seven administrative sub-regions, or *wereda*.[10] In 1989, when a new administrative division was introduced throughout the country, the former region of Menz and Gishe was divided into two, Menz Mama Midir and Menz Gera Midir.[11] For the purpose of this study the pre-1989 administrative units will be used.

The area covered by Menz and Gishe was estimated by the Ministry of Agriculture at some 387,000 hectares. Of this, 54 per cent was defined as agricultural land, 16 per cent as grazing land, 15 per cent as forest, 12 per cent as barren, and 3 per cent as settlements. The region's population was estimated at 315,888 persons in 1989, 97 per cent of whom were rural.[12] Mehal Meda, the capital, is a new 'planned' town conceived and, as local people put it, 'opened' by Emperor Haile Selassie when he visited it in 1964. It grew particularly fast, supporting 51 per cent and 58 per cent of the urban population of Menz in 1981 and 1986 respectively. Molale, the former capital, was just under half the size of Mehal Meda in 1981 and not even a third as big in 1986. The official figures for the female urban population in 1981 and 1986 were 47 per cent and 51 per cent respectively. These and other data show a tilt in urbanization towards a greater proportion of women. Furthermore, these figures are likely to be underestimates. Fewer women than men were likely to register as urban dwellers, many of them eking out an existence in the informal and hence less visible sectors of the town and its economy. They squatted with friends and relatives, or in various bars and hostels.

The rural population was based on subsistence production in peasant households who were, in addition, involved in exchange circuits inside and outside the community. In this book, as in other studies of Amhara society, the individual and the household are central concepts while the concept of kin is considered less important. The family unit is rarely mentioned because it has little operative meaning in the society. As we shall see, the household included members who were not necessarily related. It encompassed persons sleeping in the same homestead – usually, but not always, in the same hut.[13]

The high altitude at which most of the population live imposes constraints on the variety of crops cultivated. Barley is the dominant crop, though wheat, beans and lentils are also grown regularly. The population practises a mixed farming system in which crop production complements livestock rearing and handicraft work.

Menz is seen as both the heartland and the backwater of highland Christian Ethiopia. It is the heart because it is in the geographical centre of the northern highlands, an area in which the capitals of the kingdom were located, and which has provided a large proportion of the governing élite. It is considered a backwater because of its isolation and lack of development. More than 60 per cent of the land is in the higher stretches of the *dega* high altitude range, and many of the *wereda* are almost exclusively in that altitude range.[14] Furthermore, to insiders and outsiders alike, the area is synonymous with bleak and cold conditions. During the day, and in the dry months, this reputation seems misplaced as the sun beats down unsparingly. However, at night, and in the morning before the sun has had a chance to warm the air, the highland cold is punishing. When the wind picks up, it is simply chilling, and escape into a hut offers virtually the only protection to be found. Even inside, the temperature at night drops to freezing point, and the households huddle round the hearth for as long as there is a fire going.

The high mountain ranges with their steep eroded slopes have had to support an expanding population. Nonetheless, gradual impoverishment of land and people has also resulted in out-migration[15] which in turn reinforces the view of Menz as a centre, a homeland about which migrants and their descendants reminisce. The area is perceived as having an unusually homogeneous population, compared to the diversity of coexisting cultures elsewhere in Ethiopia. Even in Menz, however, this picture belies the reality of a mixture of social practices which have their sources outside the dominant local culture. Early settlers in Menz are themselves thought to have migrated from the north, and many place names and names of

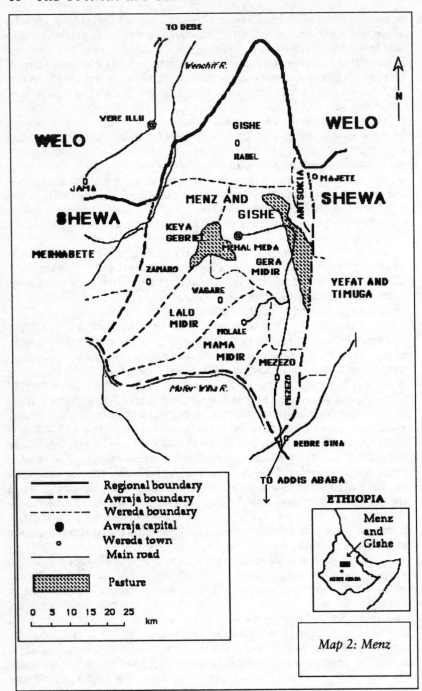

Map 2: Menz

early settlers seem closer to Tigrynya than to Amharic. Although the area was more isolated than much of the Amhara highlands, there are also influences from neighbouring Oromo populations, as well as the mark left by a short period of Muslim rule. Despite having resisted the Oromo encroachment, Menz was overrun in the early sixteenth century by Ahmed Ibn al Ghazi, commonly known in Amharic as Ahmed Gragn or Ahmed the left-handed.[16]

Many of Ethiopia's rulers have had a connection of some sort with Menz. The children of Menilek I and the grandchildren of the legendary Makeda, Queen of Sheba, and King Solomon, were said to have been born and to have settled in the area. Until recently, the name of some early settlers of famous lineage would be invoked in the form of a poem, when somebody died:

እኛቀራ፡የጎለ፡ልጅ፡	Afk'era the child of Golé,
ድብብ፡የፀጋ፡ልጅ፡	Dibibi the child of Tsegga,
ሞረት፡የፀዱ፡ልጅ፡	Moret the child of Tsedu,
ጊሼ፡የአውሳቤ፡ልጅ፡	Gishe the child of Awsabé,
ጊድም፡የለታ፡ልጅ፡	Gidimthe child of Leta
አራድግ፡የአስቦ፡ልጅ፡	Aradma the child of Asbo,
አጋንቻ፡የአምዴ፡ልጅ፡	Agancha the child of Amdé.

Most of these 'names of sons' are now the names by which people refer to specific locations. Thus, the peasants' association of Gragn falls within the vicinity which is now referred to as Aradma. Gragn itself is named after Ahmed Gragn who was said to have fallen off his horse in the area.

A number of early medieval rulers, in particular Emperor Zera Yaqob, spent some time in Menz. He is said to have had in his possession a piece of the cross on which Jesus Christ was crucified. Having first placed it in a number of churches, including one in Gishe, Menz, he was told in a dream that the proper resting place for this 'true' cross should be at Gishen, in present day Welo. Emperor Tewodros, too, was said to have spent some time overlooking Shewa from the highest mountain in Gishe. King Haile Melekot, Sahle Selassie's son, had an affair with a woman in Menz when visiting the area and fathered 'the second Menilek', the Emperor who ruled from 1889 to 1912. Emperor Haile Selassie's father was from the area, and the 1960 coup against him was led by the Neway brothers, whose father likewise came from the region. Menz was, finally, one of the last regions to accept the revolution of 1974, being under the control of *shifta,* bandits, until around 1979; today, people from areas which resisted the changes most vigorously still spend many an evening recounting the exploits of local leaders.

Menz is on the edge of the region that suffered most from the famine of 1985, and was one of the areas from which people were resettled. Endemic poverty, varying with the harvest, has not yet reached the scale of famine experienced in Welo and Tigray. Nonetheless, estimates of livestock depletion in the area, an indicator of famine conditions, suggest that up to 90 per cent of stocks might have been lost during the famine years.[17] In 1989, according to the government's Relief and Rehabilitation Commission, 262,150 households, or approximately 85 per cent of the population, were aid beneficiaries. Aid was donated by the Relief and Rehabilitation Commission, working with UNICEF, World Vision, the Baptist Mission and the Ethiopian Orthodox Church. It came in the form of wheat (and to a lesser extent some other grains), oil and milk powder, though some agencies also occasionally distributed clothes and other goods. In 1989, cash aid and food-for-work projects were common, relief being given in exchange for people's labour in constructing roads, planting trees, building wells, and furthering other development-oriented projects.

In attempting to understand the causes of this poverty, the literature points to different factors. The list includes: neo-Malthusian population growth; inhospitable physical landscape, isolation, ecological difficulties and environmental degradation; the *rist* and *gult* land tenure system; limited technology; poor savings and investment infrastructures; capitalist development or the lack of it; and the nature of the state, blamed either for lack of penetration or, on the contrary, for the exaction of burdensome tributes.[18]

As Vaughan has argued,[19] for most famines no uni-causal explanation will suffice. Undoubtedly, different factors feed upon each other, and it is difficult to mention one without another. I would nevertheless suggest that for Menz, as for other areas of Ethiopia, a central factor is the involvement of a predominantly subsistence-based economy in wider networks such as market relations.[20] A subsistence economy implies a lack of integration in exchange relations. It follows that any disaster is met only with goods produced from within the society. But subsistence also means the absence of both investment and surplus. It is not coincidental that the two meanings are conveyed in the same word. In a subsistence society it is difficult to accumulate. Grain cannot be stored easily and the value of livestock, the main form of alternative investment, is highly sensitive to drought and slow to recover from it.

Amongst the subsistence-based peasant population of Menz, the disquiet with which people react to the occasional need to sell grain in order to meet other needs, shows the primary concern with cultivation for direct consumption and a tendency not to see agricultural surplus as a means of expansion. In Menz, the term *meshemet*, to trade, when used in the context of selling grain, has strongly negative connotations. If you sold other goods to buy grain, it was because the harvests had been insufficient. If you sold grain, it was because you had nothing else to sell and had cash obligations. The situation reflects the absence of a middle peasantry, or a peasantry with urban links feeding back to the rural sector, and hence the lack of an investing sector. The absence of exchange production results from the old tenure patterns, exacerbated by socialist policies and laws restricting trade and capitalist development amongst the peasantry.

Restrictions were applied to trade within single localities, across areas, and across the urban–rural divide. The weak links with other groups in the society and with state extension agents were also a cause of dependence on the 'subsistence' sector, and of the need to look inward for help at times of stress. However, these were not purely subsistence peasants. Involvement in the state and nation had imposed its strains on the economy, such as the *gult* and tax systems of the past, or the tax and other contributions exacted by the modern state. The goods that came from outside the community, such as salt, coffee, spices and kerosene, had also exerted a syphoning effect. These all represented important and increasing costs.

Gragn peasants' association

Gragn peasants' association, covering an area estimated at some 720 hectares, is situated approximately 10 kilometres from Mehal Meda. According to association figures, about 500 hectares of the total area is private agricultural land for peasants' association members, 70 hectares is communal agricultural land, and 30 hectares is recently reforested land reserved for communal ventures. About 15 hectares is inhabited, and the remainder is grazing or barren land.

In 1989 the peasants' association comprised 423 households. According to my research, the household unit consisted on average of 4.4 persons and most households included at least two generations.[21] According to the peasants' association figures, 23 per cent of households were headed by women. Single male-headed households, on the other hand, were extremely rare, accounting for no more than about 2 per cent of the peasants' association. As will be shown in Chapter 6, there was considerable fluidity over time in the members included in a particular household, especially because of the fragility of the marital tie. In addition, the children of either or both parents might leave the household and new workers could be brought in. According to my data, at least 16 per cent of households had a relative's child living with them, and at least 4 per cent adopted a child who was not a relative.

The peasants' association was divided into eight geographical zones, and prior to villagization the number of households in each varied from 43 to 68. Some of the households formed a part of a single relatively large village, or *mender,* of up to 60 households. Most households, however, were more dispersed, dotted about the land in clusters of up to ten households.[22] Villagization was expected to regroup this population into fewer and larger units. The villagized population of Gragn was planned to house 80 households, or approximately 19 per cent of the peasants' association. At the time I carried out the fieldwork, about 60 households were living in the village.

Gragn, unlike some other peasants' associations, did not have a producer cooperative. However, it shared with two other neighbouring peasants' associations a service cooperative, located in Gragn and consisting of a mill, a store, and a shop.

Notes

1 Sources for this section include: Ethiopian Census of 1984; entries on Ethiopia in: *Africa Contemporary Record,* 1985–6 and *Africa South of the Sahara,* 1990; *World Development Report,* 1989; *The African Review,* 1988. Most of the statistics quoted

should be taken only as a rough estimates.

2 The 1984 census, by far the most comprehensive data source to date, was based on access to 85 per cent of the population. It gave an average annual birth rate of 46.0 per 1000 (1970–81) and an average annual death rate of 18.1 per 1000 (1970–81).

3 After Addis Ababa, which was a separate administrative region and the fastest-growing one.

4 Amharic was found to be the language spoken at home by 32 per cent of the total population; however, 28 per cent of the population referred to themelves as Amhara. Ethiopia, Ethiopian 1984 Population and Housing Census, 1991: 48–51.

5 The published figures, excluding rural areas of Eritrea and Tigray, were 33 per cent Muslims and 61 per cent Christians. Ethiopia, Ethiopian 1984 Population and Housing Census, 1991: 56.

6 There are a number of accounts of the revolution. See in particular Lefort, 1981; Clapham, 1988; and Harbeson, 1988.

7 Clapham, 1988: 84.

8 Male labour is generally more visible than female labour, because of bias at the recording stage and the narrow definitions of labour usually used. See Leon, 1984 and White, 1984.

9 Cohen and Isaksson, 1987: 443.

10 Gera Midir, Mama Midir, Lalo Midir, Mezezo, Keya Gebriel, Antsokia and Gishe.

11 The first included the former *wereda* of Mama Midir, Lalo Midir and Mezezo, the second included the former *wereda* of Gishe, Keya Gebriel and Gera Midir.

12 Taking registered population as the criterion, 9682 urban dwellers and 303,277 rural dwellers.

13 Hoben, 1973; Bauer, 1977.

14 Ministry of Agriculture figures collected in the area gave the following percentages: 62 per cent *dega*, 20 per cent *weyna dega* and 18 per cent *k'olla*. The aggregate figure masked the fact that most of the *k'olla* area was accounted for by one *wereda* (Antsokia).

15 See McCann, 1984. In much of the south and in Harerge, for example, some places were known to have a concentration of settlers from Menz. However, the name Menz is sometimes given to an area which extends beyond the regional administrative boundaries.

16 Menz is mentioned briefly in Basset, ed., 1897: 283.

17 Alula Abate *et al*, 1988: 25.

18 *Rist* was a cognatic inheritance system while *gult* were rights of tribute accorded to lords. McCann, 1987: 42–5. On environmental factors, see Mesfin Wolde Mariam, 1984.

19 Vaughan, 1987.

20 Bernstein, 1977. Where such an approach has been taken, for example by Marxist economic anthropologists, the focus has been on theoretical constructs rather than on a grounded local level study. Clammer, 1978, 1987.

21 The peasants' association gave a much larger figure since it estimates the total population to be 2853. However, the average of 6.7 per household is not in keeping with national estimates, and was probably inflated in the hope of gaining more aid. According to my questionnaires, 71 per cent of households were made up of three generations, 22 per cent two generations and 7 per cent one generation. Household sizes ranged from one to ten, with an adult mean of 2.3, a range from zero to five. The mean for the number of persons under 18 years of age in the household was 2.1, the range from zero to seven; see Appendix C.

22 Messing, 1957: 76, writes about the residential unit in Gonder as being the nearest thing to a village, and consisting of between two and a dozen huts, divided into about five compounds. McCann, writing about northern Welo, 1984: 23, suggests that the typical *mender,* which he translates as hamlet, consisted of a cluster of 30 to 40 households.

3

State Structures
and the Peasantry

Studies on the state, like those on other aspects of society, exhibit a distinct schism between authors who concentrate on a particular community and those who interpret conditions from the more general, national, perspective. In the latter case, the workings of the state, the structures themselves and the motives of the power-holders become the focus of attention. Most studies of the post-1974 revolutionary state in Ethiopia have tended to analyse the state from the national viewpoint.[1] It is with such a perspective that the radical transformations undertaken by the socialist government are described, usually as a disaster and exceptionally as praiseworthy. What is attempted here is a study of the local presence of the state.

Local structures

Land reform and peasants' associations

Merét larashu, or 'Land to the tiller',[2] was the slogan of student activists prior to the revolution. After the revolution, the implementation of this slogan was the main legitimizing measure undertaken by the Provisional Military Government.[3] In 1975, land was declared the property of the Ethiopian people, the size of holdings was restricted, existing forms of land tenure and the hire of labour were abolished. Peasants' associations were set up to help with land redistribution.

Land reform implementation was the first state action which had significant repercussions almost throughout the country. These were far from uniform within one region, let alone across the country, and the literature suggests that the most fundamental changes were manifested in the south rather than in the north. Everywhere, however, peasants' associations created by the revolutionary government became administrative entities which transformed a one-off legitimizing event into an on-going link between the state and the rural population.

The reform was introduced in two stages. The first, *idget be hibret,* 'development through cooperation', took the land from the 'lords' and gave it to the tillers. This reform was known locally as *shigshega,* redistribution. In the second stage, known as *merét sizzeregga,* 'when the land was measured out', peasants' associations were formed and the leadership redistributed the land with help from the Ministry of Agriculture. The peasants' associations provided a local structure with which the state could interact. Each association was headed by a chairman, a deputy chairman and a secretary, universally male, and, in Menz at least, a local person. Below them were nine other members of the executive committee, as well as a local militia and a local law court.

In Gragn, attitudes to the land reform were mixed. Inevitably, those who lost were bitter and those who gained, grateful. More than a decade after the event, conversations tended to steer towards current arrangements, rather than dwell on what happened during the reallocation. Respondents suggested that, in the first stage of reform, land was divided more or less equitably, in terms of the quantity received by a household of a particular size. However, there were variations in the quality of land received, and those in power ensured that they, their kin and friends obtained the better fields. Over the years, variations in quality were compounded by variations in quantity. Almost all informants believed that the peasants' association leadership, which controlled reallocation, became increasingly nepotistic.

The number of official independent households in Gragn had decreased from 438 soon after the land redistribution to 423 in 1989. The decrease was explained by household dissolution and resettlement. Though the population was growing and new households had been established, officially, none had been given additional land since the initial land reform. Young householders, in particular, saw themselves as casualties of this freeze. And, although allocations were fixed according to the size of the households at the time of the reform, most households subsequently expanded or contracted with little concomitant redistribution. Allocations, even ignoring other irregularities, no longer correlated with need.

The issue of women's access to and control over land illustrates the problems. The importance of land rights lies not only in their value as a source of income and as an asset, but also as proof of rights to residence and shelter. Some women had visible and direct access to land, others had none. Where they did, these could be either active or latent; they might be held by women as minors or as adults; even where women had active rights as adults, they might be paying the full land tax, half, or none of it. In addition, a woman's yield, and the amount of control she had, were influenced by whether the ploughing was done by a present or former husband, a relative or a friend. In all cases, her land was likely to be ploughed after the male plougher's own land and at his convenience, making it more vulnerable to bad timing and hence poor harvests. Other important variables included whether the woman was living in the area where she had rights to land, or whether she had moved, for example through the predominant virilocal form of marriage. Connected with this was the length of her residence in the peasants' association, or, if she had left, the links she retained in the area. Generally, the longer her connection, the more secure her rights. The presence of children was an important consideration, as children often reinforced a woman's right to a share of the land.

There was thus considerable variation in women's entitlements to land – more so than men's. Some of the configurations follow.

• *Women with complete land use rights*. Many of these were widows who had inherited from their husbands. This land was most likely to be in the same peasants' association as the one in which the woman lived, though she might have moved to join the household of an adult child and therefore have less immediate control over the land. Other women in similar positions might be married or single, and would have inherited land from parents or other kin for a number of reasons, such as the departure or death of the initial male land holder.

• *Women who had inherited half shares to land rights*. This was the case for some women who had rights to land jointly with an ex-husband, the land having been officially divided and each partner paying the full tax. The land might be either in the same or in a different location from the woman's present residence and was often ploughed by the woman's present husband who might, or might not, have land rights of his own.

• *Women who had a latent right*. This occurred where a woman had rights to a share of land from her husband in case of divorce, but, in the meantime, the land remained in the husband's name. This was usually the case if the marriage had been in existence for a number of years, and was always the case if it pre-dated the revolution. The woman thus had potential rights which could be transformed into direct ones in the case of a divorce, providing she could argue her case, or find people to do so on her behalf.

• *Women with a minor's share*. In some cases, young women, who were minors at the time of the land reform, had an adult share of land with their husbands. Others might have retained a latent right to a minor's share of land with the household in which they were living at the time of the reform, though this share might have been lost when the adult share was allocated. The land was not necessarily in the same location as their subsequent residence.

• *Women who had no active or latent land rights*. This could be because rights were ignored at the time of the land reform, because they were lost, for example because the woman left the area, or because she was born after the land reform.

The degree of control that women had over land-related production was highly variable and difficult to quantify. Any confusion over men's relationship to land was negligible in comparison. Women's rights could not be ensured by empty slogans of equality, and there was no clear governmental policy to oppose the reinforcing biases inherent in the social structure. In pre-revolutionary Menz, ambilineal descent systems allowed women some rights to land, though in reality these were less likely to be activated than the rights of their male kin. Use of land was acquired through descent rather than through marriage. Since the revolution, though the bias against women remained, the rights to land use were no longer a simple matter of inheritance. The attitude of the peasants' association leadership and marital status could also have a bearing on whether and to what land a woman could claim rights.

Beyond the issue of land allocation, the peasants' association was conceived of as a 'mass organization' and the primary channel of state administration. In effect, it was the tool of the state and gave people little, if any, autonomy. The leaders of the associations played a crucial role as intermediaries between state and society. They organized, among other things, regular meetings which heads of households had to attend, and which were used to inform members about government directives. The peasants' association leaders, moreover, represented the state and implemented its policies, at the same time as belonging to the society in which they had become powerful.

Corruption and nepotism, illustrated for example in the following rhyming poems, were increasingly visible.

ለቀመንበር፡ውሻ፡	The chairman is a dog
ስራስኳጅ፡መጥግጥ ፤	The administrator is a grabber
እንደው ፡እግዳን፡	Just to save the people
የሰው፡ገንዘብ፡መዋጥ ፨	The money of people they swallow.

	Oh the *Derg* !
እረ፡ደርጉ፡	His own mother and father
እናትና፡እባቱ፡	He is ignoring them
እያስቀረው፡ነው፡	[favouring]
ስራስኳጅ፡ኮሚቴው፡	The executive committee
	[of the peasants' association].

The first poem insults the chairman and peasants' association officials, accuses them of receiving bribes and only then resolving disputes. The implication is also one of 'false' justice. The second poem takes the form of a complaint to the *Derg* about the nepotistic behaviour of the peasants' association leadership. Such complaints were, perhaps, unavoidable after the initial revolutionary enthusiasm had waned, and officials who had to undertake endless administrative tasks without much acknowledged reward created their own recompenses. An explicit summary of the results of land reform was the comment, 'Today land belongs to the committee', i.e., to the peasants' association leadership.

In Menz, as elsewhere in the country, the peasants' association leadership was made up of local male peasants, predominantly from the richer strata of the population, and there were few, if any, re-elections. Rather, the region's leadership structure continued to be based on *balabbat*, 'big men' in the community. The chairman, then in his mid-forties, had attended church school as a young boy and served briefly as a soldier. The secretary, considerably inferior in status yet the second most important figure in the association, was also comparatively wealthy. He was in his late thirties and had more education, having finished fifth grade. Direct coercion and policing within the community was ensured by the *t'ibbek'a gwad*, the local militia, who were trained in the use of firearms by the police force in town. Then, as in the past, military and writing skills were a basis for advancement and differentiation within the peasantry.[4]

The population as a whole was aware of the difference in position and wealth between themselves and the new leaders, but there had always been a tradition of such a division. The *dej t'inat*, the traditional waiting at the gate to obtain favours, had returned within a new framework and by all accounts with greater force. People expressed a pragmatic realization that unbalanced patron–client relationships were inevitable. At the same time they feared the repercussions of complaints or disclosures. Discourse about inequality within the community was therefore usually carried out in veiled terms. In Gragn, the leadership was even rumoured to be involved in political rape – men taking advantage of their power to conduct affairs with unwilling women, silenced by fear.

All forms of state action discussed in this chapter were introduced to the community via the peasants' association. Regular meetings, usually outside the service cooperative building, or alternatively adjacent to the peasants' association chairman's home, were the means by which state directives were passed down. The communication of suggestions or complaints from the local community to regional or national state administrators was almost unheard of. Women generally did not take part in any discussion. When I drew this to the attention of one, who regularly attended meetings as head of her household, she confessed that 'like the other women, I am scared to catch even their eyes [the leadership's], let alone to get up and speak if I have a problem.'

According to Reminick,[5] the annual tax paid in Menz before the revolution was between 1.50 and 4.00 *birr* (Ethiopian dollars). Wood[6] gives similar figures of 1.50 *birr* plus dues and services to village leaders. With the land reform, this fee increased to 3 *birr* and then to 7 *birr*. Payments which the population defined as tax increased to 20 *birr,* and then 40 *birr* in 1989, though the government divided this into different components: land tax, agricultural income tax, some administrative costs. There were also additional payments for association membership and donations 'for the motherland' during the famine and for the war. The increase can be explained partly by general inflation, but for a community with severe constraints on production, and therefore on access to cash, the increases were nevertheless real. In addition, the tax was fixed at a single level in most parts of the country, including Menz. Socialist notions of equality notwithstanding, it was therefore a regressive form of taxation.

Fird shengo, the law court

One of the structures introduced under the peasants' association system was the *fird shengo*, the local law court, used to settle most internal disputes. There were two branches of Ethiopian law for cases settled at the local level. The first, concerned with *wenjel,* crime, settled disputes about insults and stealing of livestock, grain, cattle feed, etc. The second, *fìthabihér,* literally 'judgement of people', considered cases in which people had not met a commitment, for example where they had not paid back money or returned borrowed goods. In Gragn more than half the cases were in the first category, the total number being about ten a month. Most of these, though by no means all, were brought by male litigants, and, as we will see in Chapter 8, the usual assumption was that women needed a man to speak for them.[7]

The peasants' association *fìrd shengo* consisted officially of five men, though of these only one judged and two served as secretaries. The judge, a 50-year-old man of average wealth, was generally regarded as just and impartial. Significantly, in the only legal case involving foul play which occurred during research, the peasants' association leadership was suspected. The case, which involved accusations of murder, was heard by the regional and not the local court. The local courts were, in theory, separate from the executive, the peasants' association leadership. However, the legitimacy of the courts depended on that of the peasants' association for which the courts acted. Furthermore, in practice, important disputes were likely to go directly to the association leadership rather than to the courts.

If the link with the executive arm was stronger than might be expected, the link with a Christian ideology was even more entrenched. Despite its revolutionary stance, the local state relied heavily on Christianity in the up-keep of law and order. Thus the oath taken in the local courts was:

ምስክር፡በተቀመርኔበት፡ነገር፡   For that about which we have
በእውነት፡እንመስክራለን፤   been called as witness,
በሃሰት፡ብንመስክር፡   We will give evidence in truth.
በሰግፀም፡በምድርም፡   Should we give evidence falsely,
ክርስቶስ፡ዐፈለየን።   In heaven and on earth too
    May Christ not abandon us
    [forgive us].

The theme of surviving religious ideologies and the use that the socialist state made of Christianity is discussed further in Chapter 8.

Though this was the formal method of resolving disputes, it was costly, involving the expense of paper and the initiation of a court case in addition to any reparation fees. Moreover, when a single active judge bore the entire burden of legal disputes, the procedure was time-consuming. Working in parallel with this form of law and order was the much preferred traditional *béte zemed,* 'house of relative', used by the law courts themselves in the case of marital transactions. More generally *ch'ewa* or *shimagilléwoch,* elders, were called in to settle disputes. Before there was recourse to any of the above, an even more informal and impromptu dispute-settling procedure would be set in motion, in which friends and relatives would try to reconcile the various parties. As Mammit, an informant, noted wryly:

It is in the interest of those closest to you to settle disputes amicably; as for the officials, why should they care what decision is made as long as they can move on to the next case?

Sira zemecha

In the past, peasants were expected to provide tribute to the ruling aristocracy in grain, livestock and labour. These tributes continued into the period under review, though the form and the recipients had changed.[8] Overwhelming in its continuous impact on life was the contribution of labour in the form of *sira zemecha*, work campaigns, or *corvée* labour. These could take place at the national and regional levels, though they mainly consisted of labour within peasants' associations. The availability of 'free' labour made possible help to individual households regarded as vulnerable in consequence of contributions to the state such as military service, and was the basis of development work requiring labour, such as villagization, improving water supplies and road-building.

The amount of time spent at peasants' association meetings and doing *corvée* labour was greatly resented. People generally encapsulated their attitudes to such work in the term *dingay*, stone, with little need for further explanation. Most of the labour indeed involved the transporting and cutting of stones. Standard comments were 'tomorrow is stone again', 'did you do stone?', and the universal complaint 'the stone is killing me'. For a twelve-month period my diary gives fifty-eight entries, an average of just under five 'stones' per month, each one usually lasting most of the morning, if not the whole day. The aggregate masks considerable seasonal variations; during the fieldwork period, the peak was between October and December. Although this is the slack agricultural period, it is time for essential income-earning and maintenance work.

The 'stone' undertaken was almost always a response to policies from outside and above, even if the community was to benefit. Thus, most of the labour was part of the food-for-work relief scheme through which development programmes were undertaken. This included re-constructing the road, which, every year, was partly washed away during the rainy season, levelling a runway used by the Baptist mission for the distribution of aid to the remote area of Gishe, tree planting and working on a number of water points under the aegis of a UNICEF programme. A number of wells were constructed, using cement moulds, one working with a tap, another with a pump. Time and effort were also spent on the construction of the new villagized huts, and, towards the end of my stay, a school.

Most of these activities were, indeed, 'developmental' in nature, with results that the community valued. The level of antagonism to the time and work was therefore puzzling. During the fieldwork I never confronted anybody with this directly, though I remember wondering about the considerable disjunction between an appreciation of some of their products and a constant refrain against the labour that made them possible. The resentment was always there, ready to resurface.

In retrospect there are several points to be made. The first is that gatherings were held at the behest of the leadership; inevitably, for some people, the time chosen was inconvenient and a disruption. Furthermore, time and energy had to be spent on the *sira zemecha* when people wanted to get on with their own pursuits. Occasional non-attendance would not be punished if a good reason was offered; however, repeated absences incurred a fine. Communal labour also involved a considerable amount of waiting around until everybody had assembled, or until the chairman and other officials decided to start the proceedings. It also involved being registered and counted 'like sheep', having to justify absences and, in general, being at the beck and call of the leadership. Thus, because of the binding context within which the work was being undertaken, the purpose of the labour was forgotten, even when the community accepted its probable usefulness. The dislike was inevitably exacerbated when the product itself was resented or irrelevant to the community. By and large, this was, as we shall see, the attitude towards construction of the planned village.

The women's association

The Revolutionary Ethiopia Women's Association (REWA), established in 1980, was a nationwide organization with the stated aim of enhancing the political and economic position of women.[9] The rationale for the organization lay in a socialist ideology which acknowledged the need for women's emancipation. Other considerations, however, were involved. REWA, like other associations set up to organize unpoliticized groups, could widen the basis of power and decrease the relative importance of the former holders of authority. In practice, as we shall see, it operated only at the level of rhetoric because, like the youth association, it lacked real power. REWA acted as a magnet for all issues regarding gender, thus removing them from the central political domain. Because of lack of clout and the administrative inefficiency of the organization, such issues came to nothing once sidetracked in this way.

The association had branches at all levels from the national to that of the individual peasants' association. Membership was supposed to embrace all adult women. In 1989 Gragn had 371 members, less than one woman per household. Once a woman joined, she was obliged to continue payment, though because of mobility, inefficiency or nepotism, a few women escaped membership. At first, payment was made on a monthly basis, but it was later collected annually and amounted to three *birr*, having increased from an initial annual contribution of 1.80 *birr*. This payment, together with all others introduced since the revolution, was usually made by the male head of household, and, within the household, was not considered the women's responsibility. In theory, half of the subscription money raised was used in the community, the remainder being sent to the regional capital, Mehal Meda, or beyond.

The objectives of REWA were defined in the official propaganda:

- To propagate to women the theory of scientific socialism with a view to raising their political consciousness and cultural standards;
- To prepare women to occupy their appropriate position in society and to participate actively in productive social activities;

- To make every effort to ensure that the rights of women as mothers are recognized and they, as well as their children, are well cared for;
- To liberate women from political, economic and social dependence and prepare them to join hands with their class allies and fully participate in the struggle to build socialist Ethiopia.[10]

At the local level these words had a number of practical repercussions. Membership could, in theory, have been used by women as proof of residence in a peasants' association. In fact the system of identity cards was not established for women's associations although it had been for both peasants' and youth associations. Furthermore, although the women's association leadership could provide a paper confirming residence in lieu of an identity card, this never occurred. If a letter was required, for example because a woman wanted to travel and needed personal documentation, then the peasants' association leadership was more likely to be approached for this.

The fact that the women's associations did not function effectively also had repercussions on women's entitlements to land. The theory was that when a woman left her peasants' association for another, at the time of marriage for example, she was given proof of her initial residence, and any rights she had there were transferred to her new location. Thus, land rights could be transferred from one peasants' association to another. In practice, once again, any such transfer occurred through the peasants' association leadership and not through the women's association structure. Furthermore, the absence of a clear policy resulted in women having very tenuous rights to transfer. As I recorded in my diary, Zewdé's experience was an example of a woman's inability to activate her rights:

> Zewdé tried to avoid paying the three *birr* women's association membership fee on the grounds that she was not given any land when she came to Gragn, so she should not have to pay as if she were a resident. The women's association leadership sued her for not paying, using the local law court, the *fird shengo*. The judge decided that she had to pay, saying that women's association membership fee had nothing to do with rights to land and that she or her husband should put their complaint about not getting land to the peasants' association leadership. Zewdé's husband had tried doing so several times over the last two years, but without success.

Documented membership was the channel through which resources, in particular land and aid, were distributed. In effect, for women, the link to the state through the allocation of resources and citizenship was restricted because most of them were not direct members of a peasants' association and the indirect channel, the women's associations, did not function effectively. This provides a clear example of the state's tendency to see the household in terms of a single, male, household head. Since, by definition, household structures were complex and fluid, the straight-jacket could not be made to fit, and a token and inoperative measure was introduced to deal with women and mobility.

The outlook when it came to 'raising consciousness' or the educational side of the women's association was equally unsatisfactory. In Gragn there were no general meetings. There had, however, been training schemes for selected women. One woman was trained to make earth-based seats for the village. She built two, but then gave up because she did not want to be looked down upon as a lowly artisan and had other things to do; moreover, people were not particularly interested in the kind of seats she had been taught to make. The same woman went on a training programme with classes in nutrition and a pottery-making course in Holeta, not far from Addis Ababa. She felt she had learnt something, through the experience of travel if nothing else. Another woman was trained in midwifery, but left subsequently, when she got married to someone outside the peasants' association.

A few years before my stay in the village, money from the portion of the women's association membership fee retained over the years for use within the community had been used to buy a sewing machine. One of the women had been trained to use it, but had never put her training to use. Although averse to the idea of the training, she had been chosen for the project by the peasants' association and was obliged to attend the classes. By the time I arrived she had had a young child and this gave her an excuse not to use the machine; she told me that she had, in any case, forgotten most of what she had learnt.

The machine was, however, generating an income, as it was rented at 15 *birr* a month to a man who sewed clothes at a somewhat cheaper rate than the tailors at Mehal Meda. I was told that the money collected from the rent was only spent when demands for money came from the national or regional branches of the women's association.

During the period of research, the following activities were also undertaken by the women's association:

- For a number of years, they had attempted to raise money by growing garlic on a plot of land not far from the river. This involved women's labour for a few days: planting one day, weeding on one or two occasions, watering slightly more often, and then gathering the crop. In 1988, approximately 8000 garlic bulbs were harvested and sold in the peasants' association. It was, however, difficult not to notice that the work held no interest for the women, a reaction similar to that resulting from *sira zemecha*. The planting was not repeated in subsequent years.
- For the anniversary of the revolution, in September, the peasants' association chairman encouraged all able persons to attend the ceremony in Mehal Meda, and the 50 or so women who turned up formed a separate line, as the women's association contingent.
- The women's association officials in the village occasionally received letters from the regional women's association leadership in Mehal Meda. These letters directed the local association to celebrate International Women's Day on 8 March, or some other such event. The messages were usually not understood, and tended to be ignored.
- When youths were selected for military service, the women's association officials were asked to arrange for some food to be brought to them for

a couple of days. To do this, the women's association leadership met and, through the peasants' association leadership, demanded that each household contribute some food. This system of feeding conscripts had been in place for a number of years.

• During the period of fieldwork the only time there was an attempt to bring all the women together was to pay their contributions, and even this was stretched over several months; most women were represented by their husbands or other male members of the household.

In Gragn, as in most other peasants' associations, the women's association was run mainly by women in female-headed households with land rights in their own name who were born and remained in the area. In terms of wealth they were not as much above the average as was the case of the peasants' association leadership, though the chairwoman of the women's association, at the time in her fifties, was the daughter of a former rich landlord, and her son was the chairman of the service cooperative. Unlike the rest of the leadership, which was illiterate, the secretary successfully finished fourth grade before giving up school. There had been little change in the leadership which was chosen at a meeting called by the peasants' association soon after it was set up. This ossification was because re-elections were not organized and not because the women had any vested interest in their status, since there were few benefits from the job.

Unlike the peasant's association structure which had an enforcement arm, the women's association had no direct way of ensuring compliance, except by appealing to the peasants' association leadership or to the local law courts. The head of the women's association needed to ask the chairman of the peasants' association to organize payment or to hold other meetings, as she had no direct legitimacy. The main activity in which the organization showed some conviction was the extraction of the obligatory annual membership cost. In more than a decade, the garlic and sewing ventures were the only schemes with some benefit to the community, at an outflow of over 10,000 *birr*.[11] Apart from some money kept in a bank in town, the rest of the money was 'donated' to state ventures, or was used in women's association schemes at both the district and the regional levels.[12] In addition, some money was undoubtedly lost in the form of corruption.

Given such a record, it is easy to sympathize with the standard comment: 'Oh, for us, it is just another expense, there are no benefits'. The element of coercion, and the form in which policies were conceived and brought in from outside, discouraged local interest. Not only was the women's association not perceived as a channel of support to women in the community; worse still, it was equated with state oppression.

These findings are depressing, but were they inevitable? Why was the women's association structure unable to improve the lives of women? It had, after all, a nationwide remit, and, as stated in its pamphlets, existed for the social, economic and political advancement of women. Turning to the literature, it is clear that in China, at least, the Women's Federation set up by the state in the early years of the revolution made a positive contribution. It campaigned to provide younger generation women with an independent income and supported them against family and kin in their attempt to break such traditions as early arranged marriages.[13]

However, in a comparative survey of the position of women in socialist countries, Molyneux[14] has shed doubt on the emancipatory value of state-organized women's associations. She suggests that they tended to reproduce the official policy, reinforcing the ideology based on class struggle. Where they did touch on issues pertinent to women, they reinforced gender stereotypes as well as diverting women from demanding fundamental change. This might have been the case at the national level in Ethiopia and in some ways also at the local level. As seen earlier, the association in Gragn had no political power – it was a front, a pretence, used to portray an image of gender consciousness. The activities it undertook were rarely geared to the interests of the community, let alone to the specific needs of women. Yet, I would argue that the failure of women's associations in Ethiopia was not a result of a misconception of gender issues, nor a fear of women's emancipation. The Revolutionary Ethiopia Women's Association never advanced far enough to challenge and hence threaten patriarchy or the primacy of class-struggle. The failure of the women's associations was essentially an administrative one, paralleling the failures of the youth associations and cooperatives. The absence of an understanding of how to approach women's emancipation was part of governmental mismanagement. The administrative problem resulted from the failure to gauge social responses to imposed change, and in part from intractable problems of planning and execution at both local and national levels.

The youth association

The nationwide Revolutionary Ethiopia Youth Association was formed in 1980. By 1981 there were 182 rural and four urban youth associations in Menz, with a total membership of 23,734 of which 17 per cent were women. By 1988, there were 43,946 members, an increase of 85 per cent, in membership, of whom 31 per cent were women. The data for Gragn shows a membership of 210 in 1980, increasing to 403 in 1988. Much of the increase was accounted for by greater female participation, from 25 in 1980 to 145 in 1988. It would seem likely that this development resulted from a change of policy, probably in the form of directives from the national body alerting regional ones to the gender bias in the figures. There was no simple definition of who should be considered as a 'youth', since there were some people over 40 years old who paid, and others in the 15–30 age range who did not. The only obvious pattern was, once again, the attempt by each household to ensure that no more than one person contributed.

People reacted to the youth association and the women's association in similar ways. At an annual cost of 3 *birr* for a head of household and 1.20 *birr* for dependants, the youth association was perceived as another form of tax. It had achieved little. In the past, its members had paraded in Mehal Meda on Revolution Day, which involved making a uniform and teaching people to march. No other activity was mentioned, and the association appears to have been even less active than the women's association. This was probably because youth were already accessible to the state through the provision of education and military service, discussed below.

Producer cooperatives and state farms

At the time of the land reform, state farms were established to take over large commercial farms where these existed. Since there were no such farms in Menz, there were likewise no state farms. Producer cooperatives were conceived of as smaller than state farms. They were rural production cooperatives, in which the means of production – principally land – was held communally. Three stages of cooperation were envisaged: *melba*, *welba* and *weland*, representing progressive increases in joint ownership of the means of production, the last stage involving a larger scale of operation and the inclusion of livestock as a socialized resource.[15] In theory, producer cooperatives were eventually to supersede peasants' associations as the institutions with which the state interacted. The setting up of producer cooperatives was voluntary, those willing to join being given incentives of various kinds, including better land and preferential access to state inputs and extension services.

Menz had been none too enthusiastic about setting up producer cooperatives. Contrast the official view of progress in which the peasant in a cooperative lies at the heart of a new 'technological' world with the local parable. The official view is taught in a school song:

እራሹ፡ገበሬ፡	The ploughing farmer,
እምራቸ፡ገበሬ ፤	The producing farmer,
ሶሻል፡ኢትዮጵያን፡	Socialist Ethiopia
ይገነባል፡ዛሬ ።	Is being built today;
በምድር፡ቢኽhርኩሩ፡	Even if they drive on the land,
በሰማይ፡ቢበሩ ፤	And fly in the air,
እንተነህ፡ገበሬ፡	You are the farmer,
የልታና፡ግንሬ ።	The lynchpin that holds us together![16]

The local version tells how a hyena, a cat, a stork and a pheasant bought an ox jointly. They took turns minding it. When it came to the turn of the hyena, he took the ox and ate it. As the hyena was eating, the stork saw him and returned quickly to tell the others. The cat and the pheasant lamented at the news. When they went to look, they found the hyena finishing his meal. It was the end of the cooperative venture; the wealth of the four had been consumed by the one.

In 1989, there were nine producer cooperatives in Menz, four of these in Antsokia, the remainder in Keya Gebriel and Lalo *wereda*. In total, according to the regional peasants' association, there were only 269 household members, cultivating 836 hectares between them. The producer cooperatives amounted to 0.4 per cent of the total rural household population in Menz. This compared with a national average of more than seven times this figure.

Producer cooperatives all over Ethiopia allocated an 'income' to their members based on a work-points system. In general, the head of the household, usually a man, earned the work points. The proportion of female-headed households in producer cooperatives was lower than that in the country as a whole. As a consequence many women, more than in the overall peasant population, were dependent on men for access to resources. More generally, women's contributions to the household and to the community were not valued, since they were not allocated points for activities which were necessary to the society. Furthermore, those women who were heads of households, or managed to gain work points as an additional member of the household, were likely to be rewarded with fewer points per unit of labour time, since physical strength, contribution to 'production', educational background, and military prowess were the criteria employed in the scale allocating points to different tasks.[17]

Looking beyond Ethiopia, the general history of cooperatives is one of disasters, especially where cooperativization is a response to a state initiative rather than arising from the dynamics of the community. In Ethiopia, not only was the cooperativization call taken up only by a small minority, but the stories circulating by the end of 1989 were that an increasing number of these producer cooperatives were suffering from internal feuds. Some were disbanding and returning to peasant production systems, a process officially sanctioned in March 1990. Before this admission of failure, the elders of one peasants' association, in Arsi, are said to have explained their decision to the officials from Addis Ababa through the following parable:

> Once a upon a time a hare came upon an elephant. 'My friend', said the hare, 'why are you eating this poor grass when there are fertile lands beyond. Come with me and I will show you places where you can eat until you say "enough".' Hearing these words the elephant was tempted, his pasture was indeed very poor, yes, he would go to better lands. So the elephant accompanied the hare. He walked on and on, following the hare, day after day, month after month, scrounging the most meagre of meals on the way, getting thinner and hungrier all the time. At last the elephant, hungry and exhausted stopped. 'Friend', he said to the hare, 'I cannot go any further. I know that there are richer lands beyond, but getting to these places is killing me. That's it, I have had enough. I would rather return to the parched grass I left behind.'

Service cooperatives

Service cooperatives were a vehicle for bringing infrastructure and services to rural communities. Through a nationwide government organization, the Ethiopian Domestic Distribution Corporation, service cooperatives were provided with goods allocated on a rationed, fixed-price distribution system. In theory, the service cooperatives could procure crop extension services; market the produce of their members as well as produce imported from outside the region and the country; give loans; and provide storage, milling and craft facilities. Cooperatives could also be used to collect contributions required of the population by the government. Membership was by household and was voluntary, the use of some of the facilities being denied to those who had not paid their membership fee. The extractive arm of the association was the enforced sale by peasants' association members to service cooperatives of a quota of grain at state prices. This affected the whole population, irrespective of membership. A policy change was declared in March 1990 to alter this so that the Agricultural Marketing Board thereafter had to buy on the open market.

In Menz as a whole there were 50 service cooperatives by 1989, out of which 14 were in Gera Midir. In total, 203 out of the 206 peasants' associations in Menz had access to service cooperatives and, on average, four peasants' associations shared one.[18] The service cooperative used by Gragn joined two other peasants' associations. In 1989 it had a membership of 824 households, about two-thirds of the total households in the area. The cooperative was estimated by the Ministry of Agriculture, to have a capital of 103,692 *birr*. Nominally, the cooperative was run by a committee of 24, though in fact a smaller number were actively involved.

Of all the structures provided by Mengistu's government, the service cooperative was probably the most popular, both in Menz and more generally throughout Ethiopia. This was because it often installed and ran a mill, and sold a few goods more cheaply than anyone else. In Menz, the shops were valued because they sold salt, a basic good, and sugar, a luxury, at almost half the market price. Distribution of the scarce goods occurred on a quota basis whenever they were brought in, theoretically once a month, in practice much less regularly. The ration was usually about 1.5 kilos of salt and 1 kilo of sugar per household. Distribution was regulated by records kept in a booklet, though preferential treatment and misappropriation were common. The entry in my diary, after my first visit to the cooperative reads:

> Went to visit the *agelgilot* [service cooperative] shop for the first time. It sells boots, razors, matches, pens, note-books, soap, two umbrellas hanging from the ceiling, a few sheets of corrugated iron. People were buying note-books for the new school year and soap which has just come in. No salt or sugar. Queues. Preferential treatment for scarce goods which are kept aside. I was told I could probably get salt if I asked. Booklet system with the rationed goods is a sham.

The mill was much appreciated, but was out of order half the time because of mechanical failure or because it ran out of diesel. Inefficiency, particularly in the accounting and transport systems, and corruption were major problems for the cooperatives. In Gragn more than 28,000 *birr* had 'gone missing', the leadership was highly distrusted and the patronage networks were sources of budding social stratification.

In much of Ethiopia, the goodwill gained by the service cooperative as a source of provisions had been eroded by its role in forcing people to contribute a quota of grain at prices invariably below market prices. This system provided the state with a marketable source of agricultural produce which it could extract from households. In Menz, however, the Agricultural Marketing Corporation kept a low profile because of the area's acknowledged poverty and the series of bad harvests. In Gragn, for example, contributions had been requested only occasionally. In 1989 I was told by the peasants' association leadership that 72 quintals (17 kilos) per household were demanded. Even then, the extraction was eased by using the harvest from communal lands to fill the quota, rather than asking households to contribute from their own supplies.

Extension and extraction

Ministries of Agriculture, Health and Education

The Ministry of Agriculture was involved in development schemes in agriculture and livestock improvement, afforestation and 'home economics', a term which gave half-hearted recognition to women's economic role and tended to focus on food processing. The Ministry collected statistics[19] and liaised with aid agencies involved in various relief schemes, and it implemented campaigns or new policies launched by central government. Land reform, the different forms of associations, cooperatives and villagization had all been introduced through the Ministry of Agriculture. In Menz, its personnel were based in town, and called in the peasants' association leadership whenever it came to implementing policy. Most peasants had little direct contact with the Ministry, and therefore little to say about it.

The Ministry of Health had eleven clinics or health stations in Menz, most of them located in the towns. From these bases, nurses made occasional forays into the rural areas. Complaints from those working in these clinics included shortages of personnel and medicine. There were no facilities for any type of surgery in Menz, and serious cases had to be referred to the regional capital at Debre Berhan, some five hours away by bus, or directly to Addis Ababa, though even in these larger centres the hospitals were severely strained.

More impressive in terms of direct intervention in the area were the activities of the non-governmental organization ALERT (All African Leprosy and Rehabilitation Training Centre), which focused exclusively on leprosy, and over the years had made a concerted effort to reach even the most isolated areas, and to keep track of patients. People also remembered with affection an American Baptist doctor and his family who lived and worked in the area in the 1960s. The legend of his ability to cure was passed on to younger generations. Just before I left, there was talk of the clinic in Mehal Meda being upgraded to a hospital by the aid agency Médecins du Monde. This is not to say that suspicion towards 'modern' medicine did not exist; rather, people believed in it as an alternative or an additional option to traditional cures.

The literacy and education programmes of the Ministry of Education were seen as one of the cornerstones of the revolution, even winning international recognition with the UNESCO literacy prize in 1980. In 1970 the literacy rate for those ten years of age or older was estimated at 13 per cent for the nation as a whole, and even lower for the rural population. By 1983 this had allegedly increased to 65 per cent. The literacy programme made use of 15 languages and involved all sectors of the population, irrespective of age.

Literacy
In Gragn, the National Literacy Campaigns took place inside huts with mud-based benches at three sites, the last one located near the new village and close to the administrative centre. There were two literacy 'rounds' per year, each lasting five months. In 1989 the Campaign had reached its twenty-first 'round'. In the early literacy 'rounds' there was a system of fines for non-attendance, still theoretically operative but no longer levied in practice. Classes took place in the morning from 7 to 9 a.m., and in the afternoon from 1 to 3 p.m. Equipment available to the teachers consisted of a couple of blackboards, chalk, a poster displaying the characters of the Ethiopian alphabet, and a few other manuals. Students bought their own notebooks and pens. There was no other direct cost, though one *birr* of the annual peasants' association membership fee was said to be allocated for the Literacy Campaign.

The teachers, all men, were local peasants with some education. For example, the teacher at the village site had finished fourth grade, and the other teachers in the peasants' association had similar qualifications. In return for this service to the community, they tended to be exempt from the *sira zemecha*, and the peasants' association leadership ensured that they were lent an ox in times of difficulty, or given help with such tasks as the pounding of their grain.

During the fieldwork there were 142 students at the village site, and a total of about 300 students registered in the three locations. At the village site, 76 adults and 66 children were registered.[20] Approximately 20 per cent of these students attended regularly, most of them young children; among the adults, most regulars were women. Each session was divided into two groups in a hut partitioned by a low mud wall. The larger group recited the alphabet, while the smaller moved on to such subjects as arithmetic, health and 'politics'. There was also a third, higher-level group which was supposed to attend on Thursdays and Sundays, but rarely did so.

The overall attitude towards the Literacy Campaign seems to have been one of good will. The value of education was not challenged, nor was it seen purely as a political tool of the government. The results were, however, disappointing. Most of the population remained illiterate, or at best only able to spell out an inaccurate version of their names. Reasons for this failure amongst the elderly were sickness, poor eyesight and old age itself. Women referred to pregnancy and infant-care which interrupted attendance; men put the blame on lack of time and illness, adding frequently 'there is no point, it does not enter', 'we just don't understand'. The reasons given for children's absenteeism were ill health and the extreme cold which kept them huddled at home in the mornings, whilst during the day they were engaged in minding livestock. The comment was often made that some people knew 'a bit' and then forgot, exemplifying the fundamental problem of follow-up.

School

In February 1989 Gragn had competed successfully against a nearby peasants' association to have a school built on its grounds. Construction had begun on a primary school some fifteen minutes' walk from the village. The work was supervised by four men who were paid from funds accumulated for the purpose by withholding one month's instalment of aid. During the fieldwork year, from the 423 households, only 37 children went to school. Nine attended a school built with Swedish funds, over an hour's walk from Gragn, six attended the government-built primary school in an adjacent association, and 22 continued beyond sixth grade walking to Mehal Meda.

Non-attendance at school was partly due to financial problems. The cost, which had to be found in cash, increased from two *birr* per annum in first grade to about eleven *birr* in twelfth grade. Children occasionally contributed through their own schemes, for example, by breeding chickens and selling eggs. The cash constraint was a problem at the beginning of the year when many parents, though theoretically in favour of their child being educated, found themselves hard up and reluctant to part with the money required. In fact, for this and other reasons connected with the harvest, schools rarely started in earnest in the appointed month of September. Instead, increasing numbers of children drifted to school in the course of the following month. More important as a deterrent was the opportunity cost, the loss of contributions to the pool of household labour resulting from school attendance. This was summarized by the often repeated comment 'we have yet to wake up', expressing a consciousness that education was a good thing, a means towards development, but that individual households did not have the determination or energy to make sacrifices for it.

Appendix C provides some data on the school nearest to Gragn. It shows that the majority of students were boys. The percentage of female attendance, 35 per cent, was not as low as might be expected, although it fell to 8 per cent in sixth grade, the highest primary class. The reasons for the surprisingly high percentage of female students in the primary school were peculiar to the time at which the questionnaire was administered, when there was a fear of military service round-ups of boys which had taken place in schools. Female attendance in secondary school fell off very quickly. Overall, the age range of the students in primary school varied from seven to 22, the average being 14. This was probably significantly higher than the ages of students in towns. Rural children's labour was more likely to be called upon, interrupting school and leading to high rates of failure; and age itself was a reason why most students did not continue their education beyond primary level.[21]

In answers to my question, 'Why do you come to school?' most gave the answer 'for knowledge' or 'to learn'. Others added 'to help my family' or 'my country', and some 'to find a job'. Another common answer was to learn about cleanliness, *nits'ihinna*. This was because of the emphasis on scientific explanations for germs and diseases which children learned at school, together with the lessons on combating these through hygiene. To the question 'What do you want to do in the future?', most mentioned continuing their studies and 66 per cent wanted to become teachers. The next most popular ambition was to become a pilot. Of those questioned, 5 per cent wanted an office job and the same number aspired to become doctors. Other careers mentioned were car or bus driving and one boy said he wanted to become the *awraja astedadari*, the regional administrator. More than 65 per cent of the students specified that they wanted to live only in a town, many of them setting their sights on Addis Ababa.

The answers pointed to the desire to move away from agriculture, and the importance of role models. The students came from rural households and were aspiring beyond the peasant life. The contact that they had with people in the 'modern' sector was mainly with teachers; particularly for girls, the teacher was almost the only model. The school lay on the flight path of planes flying from Mehal Meda to Gishe with grain deliveries for the Baptist Mission, hence the awareness of planes and pilots. The children would have seen car and bus drivers in the region's capital, Mehal Meda. The boy who chose the regional administrator as his role model was probably influenced by the fact that this official was a man from the region.

Relief

The situation of drought, poverty and recurrent famine has already been touched upon in the previous chapter. Here the discussion will centre on famine relief projects. In Menz, there were stories of some aid being distributed before the revolution. However, it was soon after the Resettlement Campaign of 1985 that distribution of monthly rations began and soon came to be relied on. Credit schemes, such as loans with which to buy oxen, were also introduced on occasion by some of the aid agencies operating in the area.

Viewing distributions through the eyes of the population, there was an arbitrariness about who received relief, when, and in what form. Sometimes the donations were perceived as free, while at other times work had to be carried out in exchange. Sometimes it was money that was given (and this was by far the most popular form of contribution), sometimes it was grain of various kinds and quantity, and occasionally other goods, such as oil or even clothes. Not knowing whether a family would receive assistance, and, if so, when or how much, contributed to the insecurity in people's lives and to difficulties in planning.

Despite these uncertainties, the relief was greatly appreciated. At the best of times, in terms of quantity, the donations were able to feed the household for one to two weeks in the month. No other achievement of the *mengist* 'government' was valued as highly. People use expressions like, 'That is why we are still standing', '*Yederg dabbo*', the bread of the *Derg* (The Provisional Military Government) and 'We are living by [thanks to] God and the government'.[22] Appreciation of the relief was, however, tinged with a sense of the futility of the fight, for, as one woman put it, 'What is the use, we get aid all year, we have become beggars, but it does not help us stand tomorrow, it does not pull us out of this poverty.'

A study of aid distribution in different parts of the country by Yeraswork Admassie and Solomon Gebre found that corruption was particularly rife in Menz.[23] During the fieldwork period I often heard complaints such as: *belayé sew ch'emmerubign*, 'they added someone on top of me'. It was never clear to me, however, whether what was happening was actual corruption, or whether people were expressing the confusion they felt about the distributions. The various suppliers and distributors of aid each came with their own rules about who should receive aid and how much they should be allocated. My own sense of not being able to keep track is noted in my diary as follows:

> Aid. It is all so patchy, so uncertain, so many complaints. Could blame everyone: aid agencies with their own changing priorities, funds and supplies fluctuating; peasants' association officials because they control and alter who is and who is not a beneficiary; officials in Mehal Meda and higher up, who parcel up the areas and make plans that have no bearing on local conditions; the people themselves for their high expectations. And everybody sees the distribution from their own angle, crying out against dependency, inefficiency, or unavailability.

Resettlement

Resettlement was the name given to the movement of populations over large distances, mainly from drought-affected areas of the north to areas assumed to be more fertile and less densely populated in the south and west of the country.[24] In Menz, four *wereda*, Gishe, Gera Midir, Mama Midir and Mezezo, were areas from which people were recruited for resettlement, mostly on a voluntary basis, though I also heard accounts of pressurized and forced migration. The area in which all people from Menz were resettled was in the lowlands of Metekel in Gojam. According to the Relief and Rehabilitation Commission figures, 1341 households (22 per cent of which were female-headed), or a total population of 7431 (46 per cent female) were moved. From the questionnaire I administered in Gragn, 37 per cent of respondents replied that they had at least one close relative who had been resettled.[25]

There were stories of people having left the area to be resettled, often leaving relatives behind. Some told their relatives of their decision, others disappeared without a word. Dessita and Yematawerk' told their stories as follows:

Dessita

This child, Gebeye, is my own but the mother who gave birth to her went to Gojam for resettlement. I knew her from meeting her on market days in Mehal Meda. She used to sell onions, and then '77 [1985] came. She told me she could not cope any more and was going to leave. Somehow I ended up telling her I would look after the girl who was then about two years old. So, one day I returned from the market with a child! The other mother, who knows, she might be alive somewhere, but she has never been back.

Yematawerk'

I got married to Cheré Gebré's son and they made me a beautiful house. We had been together, then he decided to go to resettlement, sold all the grain that was left. He wanted me to go with him, but I refused. We had been together two years when this happened, his land was given over to the peasants' association leadership, but they left me my land that I had from before I married him, and aid distributions started soon after.

Feelings about the famine conditions and resettlement were also expressed in rhyming verse, as in the two following examples.

መ7ን፡ሰበ፡ሰባት፡	Oh '77 [Famine year of 1985]
?ሰፈኸው፡ኽፈ፤	The things you brought about!
ግግኹን፡በመሞት፡	Half [you took] to their death,
ግግኹን፡ሰፈፈ፨	The others to resettlement.

ወይ፡ንዴት፡ወይ፡ንዴት፡	Oh anger, oh anger [I feel anger],
ብር፡በነበረ፤	If only there was money [to buy food],
?አገፈ፡ልጅ፡ሁሉ፡	All my country's children
ጎጃም፡ተሻገረ፨	To Gojam have crossed over.
	[i.e. have left for resettlement there]

Whilst I was in Gragn, there was also talk about settlers returning. Some would send word to relatives in Menz, asking for travel money, telling them that although there was grain to eat, there was no money for clothes or other goods, and expressing fears about malaria. Indeed, a number of funeral wakes took place, the families in Menz mourning those who, having left for resettlement, survived the famine and the initial unsanitary conditions, but succumbed to malaria once their troubles seemed to be over.

In 1989 those who returned did so unofficially, seeking employment in the informal sectors in Addis Ababa, Mehal Meda or other towns. Sometimes they even came back to their rural homes knowing that they could not expect to be reinstated as members of the peasants' association since they had lost their land. Wherever they went, they feared being punished, fined, or sent back to resettlement. Orphans were the exceptions, the only returnees to be recognized. They were helped by a Relief and Rehabilitation Commission programme aimed at reducing the number of young children in state orphanages by locating family members who had remained in their homelands, and, if these members were willing to accept responsibility, returning the children to them. K'achilé, a thirteen-year-old who came from a peasants' association nearby, told me his story:

> I used to live with my mother, one brother and two sisters; I was the oldest.
> I do not know about a father, we never had one, and the land belonged to
> my mother. There was nobody to help us, so, in February, she decided to
> try resettlement. It took three days to get there. Many of us came from here,
> all being fed on the way. We were in Pawé, *ket'ena* 2 village 11 [name of
> location]. There were about 500 households from Welo and Shewa. It was
> all right there, there was help with the work and we were given food.
>
> My mother did not remarry. The following year she died; we lived one
> year in another woman's hut, but she died too; they said it was malaria.
> Then in '79 [1987] they put us in an orphans' home. My brother and sisters
> died too, only I was left. In June I was returned here to my grandmother, I
> had written to her on behalf of my mother while she was alive, but we had
> not heard from her then.
>
> Returning to Menz was difficult too. It is so cold here, and school was
> much nearer there; also I will have to repeat third grade at school, since we
> were moved before the end of the year; I had nearly finished the year.

It was usually the most vulnerable households that turned to resettlement. This was both because those unable to support themselves were
more willing to take their chance, and because the selection procedure
carried out by the Relief and Rehabilitation Commission was aimed at
convincing or 'volunteering' those least able to survive in Menz. Thus, the
state took on the responsibility of finding a solution for the hardest hit.
Yet, post-resettlement, orphans, without any social ties in their new locality,
in other words without a family, were considered a problem. Ironically,
the solution undertaken was to return the children to dependence on
traditional kinship support systems.

Consciously or not, because of the erosion of kinship and other traditional forms of support, the revolution itself had contributed to the creation
of a section of the population dependent on it. Thus the land reform took
land allocation away from the household and community and increased
the role of local state representatives, whilst both cooperatives and
associations provided new forms of resource allocation. The social
transformations that the state was attempting inevitably weakened existing
social structures. When the famine occurred, the society facing it had, to
some extent, been changed; vulnerable groups in society were less mobile
and less able to turn to previous forms of support. Likewise, we will see
in the next chapter that some of the more vulnerable sections of the society,
with lessened possibilities of traditional action, found themselves more
involved in the new structures and services introduced by the state.

Military service

In 1990 Ethiopia was nominally a republic ruled by the Workers' Party of
Ethiopia, although many of the leaders of the party were members of the
junta which had carried out the revolution of 1974. There is an element
of continuity in the importance of the military, given that the traditional

Ethiopian state was largely held together by a military aristocracy. In former, as in recent times, a soldier's life provided some men with a means of escape from home. Writing in the mid-nineteenth century, Parkyns commented: 'The whole country was always more or less in a chronic state of war.'[26] Nearly a century later Weissleder wrote:

> Today, as in the past, a history of military achievement and renown is still the most direct and promising road to any position of real consequence. [27]

More than 20 years later, despite the political changes in the interim, the comment was still applicable, from the national level right down to that of individual rural communities.

The military history of Menz included resistance to the Italian invasion, and to the revolution. Though the rebellions against Mengistu's régime were concentrated further north, in Eritrea, Tigray, Gonder, and Welo, there were isolated rumours during my fieldwork of active rebellion in this part of Shewa. Most of this discontent reared its head at the time of call-ups. In 1989 there were two recruitment drives in Menz. In one of these, the quota for conscription for the region of Menz was estimated to have been 500.

There were in fact two types of soldiers. The first, nicknamed, *weddo geba*, 'having wanted he entered', were those who volunteered to join and were given an income by the state. In Gragn numerous *weddo geba*, often young boys, joined up over the years, on their own initiative, usually on the spur of the moment, in anger or frustration and against the wishes of their families. The second group were 'volunteered' from the area to serve their country, and it was the increase in these round-ups that was bitterly resented, and gave rise to feelings aired in poems such as those presented later in this section. The peasants' association leadership were given a quota that they had to fill, and the association was responsible for the upkeep of the household from which this person was chosen. The association members thus ploughed and harvested the land of the recruit, such labour being one of the duties of the *sira zemecha* work campaigns.

There were rules about who could and who could not be called up, with criteria of age and fitness, and not more than one person could be chosen from a single household. In 1989, five people were selected from Gragn in the first of the two Campaigns. Two of these were brothers, but since they lived in different households the rule about not taking people from the same household was not technically violated. Of the five, two were attending school in fifth and eighth grade respectively, and one was married. All five were rounded up by the peasants' association leadership and held overnight in the association's offices, watched over by the local police, the *t'ibbek'a gwad*. In the middle of the night we heard shots fired by the guards when they woke up to find that one of the youths had escaped through a window. News of the successful escape spread quickly and was greeted with quiet joy.

One estimate, by Bek'ele, a man from Gragn who had returned with a leg injury after eight years as a soldier, suggested that at least 100 people had done military service from this peasants' association since the revolution, and 59 per cent of my respondents answered that they had a close relative who had, or was, undertaking military service.[28]

There was a heavy sense of disruption and loss when the young boys and men decided to sign up or were taken away, especially as recruitment had been going on, at intervals of a year or less, for more than a decade. Furthermore, it was young men who were recruited: some were from households that had been supporting them through school; others were married, with elderly or young dependents. The distress was augmented by social tensions in the community and talk about nepotism or bribery in the selection procedures, all of which not infrequently resulted in exchanges of blows, not only between the local leadership and its members, but also between different members of the local leadership. During the recruitment drives many peasants' associations had a story to tell. In one case the peasants' association chairman and his brother were shot by the relative of a boy who was chosen; in another the leadership itself came to blows.

There were many commonly known stanzas that expressed the distress caused by military service. They include the following two:

ኢትዮጵያ፡እገሬ፡	Ethiopia my country
እፈረድሻለሁ ፤	I shall judge you!
ጀግናች፡ወንድሞቼን፡	My heroic brothers
ገብሬልሻለሁ ።	I have given you in tax
	[Have died for you].
የወንድ፡ልጅ፡እናት፡	The mother of a boy,
ታጠቂ፡በገመድ ፤	Tie your stomach with rope
እጥሬ፡ነው፡እንጂ፡	[So as not to give birth];
እደቀብረው፡ም፡ዘመድ ።	It will be a vulture,
	And not a relative, that will
	bury him.

Overall, it seemed as though the national issue was submerged under the local disruption it was creating. There was little concern over the validity or otherwise of the underlying causes: national unity and the legitimacy or otherwise of the government. There was never any question as to whether or not the population had to fight 'to preserve the Ethiopian nation'; nor was conscientious objection an option. Most of the discussion was about how many, when, and who it would be this time; in other words, about the direct impact on the society. Mammit, one of my friends in the village, who had a seventeen year old son said to be mad and possessed by a spirit, commented:

They say this world of ours is healthy/sane, *t'énegngna,* yet I have a son who is not healthy/in a proper state of mind; were he sane I would have lost him to military service. This is what is called sanity.

Conclusion

This chapter has covered a number of separate, essentially administrative, structures which form the basis of the peasant–state relationship. It would, perhaps, have been more interesting to adopt a more avowedly analytical approach, dropping some of the empirical detail and presenting the actions of the state in terms of concepts such as social reconstruction, control and legitimization. This would, however, have required a lengthy attempt to justify the analytical categories, and would have resulted in the loss of a grassroots understanding of how people viewed specific policies. Furthermore, though initially I was interested in abstract notions of power, the 'whys' and 'wherefores' of state action, my respondents were not. They were confronted on a day-to-day basis by the particular and the concrete, and it was these – the 'this' and 'therefore' – with which they had to live.

A number of factors nevertheless emerge which summarize the relationship between peasants and state. The first is that it was not as developed as might be assumed from the rhetoric of radical transformation. Massive campaigns and talk of revolutionary policies amounted to little in the face of the daily struggles of the peasantry. In particular, there was little engagement between women and state. On the points of contact between state and peasantry, the latter perceived the relationship as intrusive, unbalanced and extractive. When offered, the state's help tended to be acknowledged, but such inputs were submerged by the costs they imposed.[29] In the words of a respondent, 'the government with one face is kind, with the other cruel; but the cruelty has become too much for us.'[30]

The relationship between peasantry and state was mediated through local officials, who were almost automatically elevated beyond the others in the community by their administrative role. In the past there had been a hierarchy of lord and peasant, while such influence as government had was structured through a patronage system. In later times, the representatives of the socialist government and its institutions were the local 'lords'. The only difference is that there was a somewhat greater, though similarly hierarchical, 'interference' by government.

Looking at the policies in theory and practice, there was clearly a gap between what the government thought it was doing and what was perceived by the people to occur; what the government wanted to do and what it actually achieved. The scene was one of universal, though usually latent, discontent. In an analysis of people's complaints, two of the main problems with government policy can be described as the *tabula rasa* fixation and the campaign method. The former summarized the desire to recreate society in a modern and scientific mould. No value was set on existing structures, such as social and religious associations, which could have been built on for development purposes. The population therefore suffered from a kind of schizophrenia: the need to accept new structures of which they were suspicious, and to reject existing social and economic beliefs that had proved their worth in the past. Moreover, as seen in some of the discussion of new services in this chapter, the government's assumption that objectivity would automatically follow from the new structures ignored the existing forces, the ties and the feuds inherent in social formations, which were merely reshaped during the so-called 'radical transformation'.

The campaign method[31] resulted from the state's desire to create radical transformation – fast. To do this, all efforts were marshalled on the one issue. However, the speed of change inevitably resulted in distress and, where actions were not sensitive to individuals, tended to be antagonizing, irrespective of their potential worth. In addition, the result of such methods was usually superficial rather than fundamental transformation. Thus the source of discontent was not always, or even predominantly, a rejection of concerted action by the state, but rather the consequence of institutional failures and the methods adopted.

Another theme, perhaps not visible enough in the foregoing text, is the complexity behind the uniformity of discontent. The overall impression of discontent hides a much richer situation, in which reactions could be observed which reflect a variety of interests at particular points in time. If a whole chapter were devoted to each policy, these differences would emerge as strongly as they do in the detailed analysis of the policy of villagization in the next chapter.

Notes

1 For example, Schwab, 1985; Clapham, 1988; Harbeson, 1988.

2 In ox-drawn cultivation, the tiller is universally a male figure, and in Amharic the masculine is used for 'tiller'.

3 For the history of land reform in Ethiopia, see Dessalegn Rahmato, 1984; Cohen, 1981 and 1984. For problems with the implementation of the land reform, Mengistu Woube, 1986, Dawit Bekele, 1982. Also, for the situation before the revolution, Dunning, 1970.

4 A. Pankhurst, 1992: 156, writing about resettlement in Welega, comments: 'Most of those who obtained key positions in the Peasants' Association knew how to wield either a pen or a gun, preferably both'. For a similar story of the new socialist peasant leadership in Guinea-Bissau, see Rudebeck, 1988.

5 Reminick, 1973: 74.

6 Wood, 1983: 529.

7 In this book, there is no separate analysis of legislation with a bearing on the position of women in Ethiopia. Such legislation is only relevant to the urban scene, and it is of symbolic rather than practical value. It includes the 45 days paid maternity rights and the Labour Proclamation of equal pay in 1975.

8 With a few changes, Messing's writings could describe the current situation. 'At any moment, authority could decree that a bridge was to be built, a church to be constructed or repaired, at an appointed time and place. Thereupon every *gabbar* [peasant] would have to appear, carrying his own tools, to work under the direction of the feudal officer, governor or his lieutenants. Heavy fines punish failure to appear for this labour.' 1957: 240.

9 For comparative data on the position of women *vis-à-vis* the state see Afshar, ed., 1987.

10 Ethiopia, Revolutionary Ethiopia Women's Association, 1982: 25–6.

11 The figure is for the total contributions since the women's association was set up. It includes the initial two years' payment at 1.80 *birr* per person, and the remainder at

3.00 *birr* per person; the population is estimated at 375. The total figures do not include the rent derived from the sewing machine, nor costs incurred by the ministries for the training.

12 This is so in rural Menz as a whole. In the towns, there is more going on. In Mehal Meda, a cafeteria and a bakery were run by the women's association.

13 Croll, 1981 (a), 1983, 1985.

14 Molyneux, 1981, 1985; see also Urdang, 1984. For contradictions in women's associations in a non-socialist framework in the case of Kenya, see also Wipper, 1975.

15 See Tegegne Teka, 1988; Poluha, 1987, 1988, 1989.

16 Literally, the last line refers to *walta*, the central pole in the hut from which the roof is constructed and *mager*, the bark or rope with which the thatch is held together.

17 For similarities with the Chinese experience of discrimination in work-points, see Stacy, 1979: 328; Diamond, 1975: 388.

18 The figure given by the Ministry of Agriculture on households having access to service cooperatives was 51,434; 14 per cent of these were female, a marginally lower percentage than that of female membership in peasants' associations. This was probably because many female-headed households were amongst the poorest and therefore the least likely to afford the initial costs of joining, though see Chapter 7 for differences within the category of female-headed households.

19 Respondents were often not told for what particular reason they were requested to take part in a questionnaire. After the event rumours competed with each other. In one case, a Ministry of Agriculture/UNICEF questionnaire, which was aimed at an assessment of conditions subsequent to the setting up of improved water facilities, included questions about the kind of bed people slept on. One of the most humorous interpretations given locally was that people were going to be given cotton mattresses, and people joked about what they would use these for. More seriously, however, I became very conscious both of how much of an intrusion the questions could be and how poor the data collected in this way usually was.

20 See data in Appendix C, village literacy site.

21 In the nearest primary school, 36 per cent of the children had repeated at least one year.

22 A note from my diary: 'Wheat has been distributed, more than usual and talk of a regular food-for-work programme starting. Also salt and sugar at the service cooperative. The reaction is such that good-will seems to extend to the government. Two weeks ago I was getting only complaints, right now it is all different.'

23 Yeraswork Admassie & Solomon Gebre, 1985.

24 For accounts of resettlement see A. Pankhurst, 1989(a),1989(b), 1992.

25 Sample size, 92. I used the term *yek'irb zemed,* 'close relatives', but did not define this, leaving the judgement to the respondents themselves. From a sample of 34, 104 relatives went to resettlement, a mean of three per household.

26 Parkyns, 1868: 21.

27 Weissleder, 1965: 61. In Ethiopian history women, too, have played a role in war. A few aristocratic women were known to have fought alongside men, until Emperor Haile Selassie decreed a prohibition on women's enlistment in 1935. Tsehai Berhane Selassie, 1984, also Weissleder 1965: 67. The northern rebel movements have made a point of involving women in the fighting. In Gojam, there was also one rebel group said to be led by a woman with a personal vendetta against the government because of deaths in her family, in particular her father's.

28 From a sample of 93 questioned, 53 had close relatives who had been on military service.

29 Such comments echo much of the literature on state–peasant relations and trends of disengagement, Rothchild & Chazan, 1988; Scott, 1985. They also return to the older literature on the 'rational' analysis of integration made by the peasantry: Lipton, 1968; Popkin, 1979.

30 The expression used was: *'Mengist band fit deg, band fit kifu new, kifunnetu bezzabin inji'.*

31 For a critique of this method, see Clapham, 1988: 192

4

Villagization: To Move or Not to Move?

Overview of villagization

The Ethiopian Villagization Campaign began in late 1985. Its aim, announced the following year, was to move the majority of the rural population into the new villages by 1995. The policy was part of the revolutionary government's drive towards agrarian socialism in an underdeveloped, predominantly peasant-based, rural society. Although the physical focus was on creating a new spatial structure, moving people closer together into a grid-patterned village, the change was intended to have a radical and uplifting effect on the economic, social, and political life of the population.

Broadly speaking, villagization increased the size of rural communities and located the population in a planned physical setting, thus simplifying the task of service provision, tax collection, and control over the population. The villages were also supposed to create non-exploitative and highly productive farming groups, while increasing peasant involvement in the wider society and nation. More specifically, the aims of villagization, as laid down by the Ministry of Agriculture and formulated in its publication *Mender,* were:

1 To ensure that basic development infrastructural facilities and services are provided for the enhancement of the livelihood and socio-economic upliftment of the rural masses.

2 To enable the rural population to develop the tradition of 'familyhood', or sense of community, self-help, and the coordination of efforts towards the solution of rural problems.

3 To ensure that the rural population, in close cooperation and collaboration with local organs entrusted with the tasks of education and agitation, raises the level of its consciousness and discharges to the full its role in the nation's socio-economic life.

4 To provide the means for enabling the rural masses, more particularly the peasantry, to safeguard local peace and security as well as protect their own property.

5 To help arrest misuse of the nation's valuable natural resources, a tendency galloping out of control, and to make judicious utilization of the same.

6 To create conditions whereby expert advice and the benefits of the latest technology to promote agricultural productivity are brought within easy access of the peasantry with a view to improving its livelihood.

7 To create the means whereby the rural population is able to get maximum access to basic infrastructural services like roads, irrigation facilities and dams, which are vital for transforming the quality of rural life, but which, in the present stage of economic underdevelopment, cannot possibly be created through individual means and resources.

8 To create the opportunity for the peasantry to channel its exploitation-free produce to service cooperatives, and to obtain industrial products and commodities needed to uplift its livelihood, thereby narrowing the current imbalance in the urban–rural exchange of goods and services.[1]

The rationale behind villagization was seen differently by Cohen and Isaksson, authors of a Swedish International Development Agency report on villagization in Arsi, and a Survival International team who wrote a short document on resettlement and villagization.[2] These commentators, amongst others, saw villagization as part of a continuing revolution aimed at increasing the power of the state and extracting resources from the peasantry. For example, in terms of economic and hence political control, the villagization policy resulted in parallel illegal markets becoming more visible, and hence more difficult to operate. In general, villagization increased the extent to which the peasantry was homogenized[3] and integrated into the economic and political system.

Two sets of experiences in the south-east of the country provided the background to the nationwide programme. The first was the villagization of Bale (1974) and Harerge (1984), carried out for strategic reasons in response to the Somali invasion and the guerrilla activities of liberation fronts. The second was the resettlement of peasants evicted from lands transformed into state farms in the Wabe Shebelli valley, involving the creation of show-case villages organized into producer cooperatives. Villagization became a nationwide campaign in September 1986, though First Secretaries of the Party in a number of regions, including Gojam, Arsi and Welega, had already started local campaigns, allegedly in response to Mengistu Haile Mariam's approval of developments in Harerge.

Unlike the introduction of the new constitution, which was preceded by directed consultative procedures throughout the country, villagization was based entirely on decisions by senior government and party officials, without any consultation with the population at large.[4] To quote Cohen and Isaksson:

> The Villagization campaign was designed and implemented from the top down. The Guide-lines were formulated centrally in the National Planning Commission and the Ministry of Agriculture, under the direction of the country's senior government and party leadership. The authors found no evidence that any regional Committee members were involved in conceiving, justifying, or designing the overall programme. Once formulated, the objec-

tives and the guide-lines were then communicated to local officials and peasants in the target areas through the Agitation and Propaganda Sub-Committees.[5]

Tanzania and China probably provided the inspiration for villagization, but there is little evidence that the experience of those countries was evaluated, though it is reported that some villagized communities in Tanzania were inspected.[6] The absence of debate during conceptualization, and the mere cursory glance at the experiences of other countries, contrasts with the more considered research that preceded the drafting of the land-tenure reforms, some studies of which even pre-dated the revolution.[7]

The villagization programme was administered at three levels: national, regional and local. At the national level, it was directed by the National Villagization Coordinating Committee; similar structures existed at each level, down to the peasants' association. The first phase of villagization stretched over a period of four months. It started in December 1985 and covered eight regions, the focus being on Shewa, Arsi and Harerge. The programme involved 5530 peasants' associations and approximately 4.6 million peasants were housed in 4500 completed villages. By late 1986, 12 per cent of the rural population had been moved into new villages. In Arsi region alone, the population was housed in 856 villages, with nearly 1 million, approximately 75 per cent of the region's population, being villagized. At the same time, and on a smaller scale, villagization started in Gojam, Sidamo, Welega, Kefa and Ilubabor. Villagization never gained momentum in the northernmost parts of the country, where the Derg lacked effective power. Thus the issue of security seems to have hastened villagization in areas in which the government needed defensive measures to bolster its control (Harerge and Bale), whilst the government's inability to maintain an active presence in other areas (Eritrea, Tigray and Northern Welo) almost completely ruled out the possibility of implementing villagization.

Villagization began in areas cultivating annual grain and pulse crops rather than those in which cultivation involved long-term crop investments. The regions covered by large-scale villagization were, at the same time, the most important ones in terms of national agricultural production. Accounting for 33 per cent of the farming population, they produced 40 per cent of the nation's cereal crops and 55 per cent of the state-run Agricultural Marketing Corporation's grain purchases.[8] Arsi, in particular, was one of the major grain-producing areas. By 1987, at the end of the second phase of the programme, there were twelve regions in which villagization had occurred and the goal was set to gather 1,012,320 households in 9438 villages (see Table 4.1 for a regional break-down). The policy continued to receive attention in 1988, and estimates in 1990 suggested that 40 per cent of the rural population had been villagized.

According to the first English edition of the journal Mender, which included data up to September 1987, the average number of dwellers already resident per village was 1106, if we follow the text, though the Table in the same publication gave a lower average figure of 755.[9] The plan subsequently proposed by the National Villagization Coordinating

Table 4.1. Villagization. Regional breakdown of percentages of heads of households, and percentages of the population villagized, July 1988

	% Heads of household	% Population
Arsi	70	78
Bale	67	93
Kefa	59	61
Gojam	57	59
Harerge	51	61
Ilubabor	51	54
Shewa	40	25
Welega	31	28
Gonder	38	39
Gamo Gofa	12	15
Sidamo	11	11
Welo	3	3
Tigray	0.2	0.2

Source: *Mender* Vol. 2: 16

Committee in 1986–7 was to create villages with an average population of 500 households.[10] According to the second Amharic issue of *Mender*,[11] the national average for heads of household in the new villages for 1988 was 122 per village, with an associated resident population of 570. This data would suggest that the average size of the villagized communities had been falling, both in the plans and in the actual settlement pattern.

Villagization should not be confused, as it sometimes is both by Ethiopians and by the external media, with policies of resettlement or the establishment of producer cooperatives, both of which involved a more drastic transformation but affected a much smaller population. The link between the three policies is that they all represented attempts to rationalize the economy by reducing rural vulnerability whilst increasing productivity and, at the same time, establishing a structure for rural socialism. However, villagization was primarily a change in settlement pattern, carried out to induce future economic, social and political transformation. This was unlike the resettlement and cooperative schemes which, from the outset, involved a change in the relations of production. Ethiopian villagization, unlike its equivalent in Tanzania, did not involve any change in the ownership of resources, or in the social relations of production.

The reason for the confusion between villagization and producer co-operatives lies in the view that villagization was undertaken as a first step towards future collectivization. However, the two policies must be distinguished and assessed on their own, the more so since only 2–3 per cent of the rural population had been collectivized, whereas in many parts of the country the majority of the rural population had been villagized. In 1989, towards the end of the research period, it was still unclear whether, in the future, villages would be collectivized, or whether collectivization policies would be shelved and the new, tighter spatial structure would be used to bolster market forces and encourage trade, petty commodity and service production.

The village in Gragn

The figures for the region of Shewa in 1988 show that 40 per cent of the population had been villagized, with an average of 75 heads of households, and 295 dwellers per village. The villagized population in the *awraja* of Menz and Gishe was considerably smaller than the Shewan average. Gragn, for its part, had a single villagized community which was one of the largest in the *awraja*.

For Gragn, the issue of villagization was first raised early in 1986. During two peasants' association meetings, Ministry of Agriculture and party officials from Mehal Meda spoke about the value and advantages of the policy, set up a villagization committee in the peasants' association, and asked people to raise their hands if they were willing to take part. A large number of the population did so, and by the second meeting, a list was drawn up. The Ministry of Agriculture officials then decided that a village of 80 households would be feasible, and the villagization committee, together with the officials, began considering sites, measuring out plots (40 by 25 metres for each household), and allocating people to them.

Work on village construction was then started with *corvée* labour. The main thrust was to build a maximum of main houses, though a smaller quantity of secondary huts were simultaneously erected. Work brigades were based on the eight zones of the peasants' association with eight huts constructed at a time. In addition, a neighbouring peasants' association in which villagization had not begun was recruited to construct a further eight huts. Once the stone walls had been constructed, the individual for whom the hut had been allocated was to provide wooden poles, thatch and other materials, such as rope, nails and doors, with which the structure could then be completed, still using communal labour. When the hut was finally finished, the workers would be invited by the owner to have some bread and beer, as part of the traditional house-warming ceremony. Sometimes, however, the building of the hut never progressed beyond the erection of the stone shell.

Principal huts

The majority of the principal huts were circular, a few others being rectangular. The huts were, by Ethiopian standards large, stone-walled and thatch-roofed constructions varying in diameter from 4.5 to 6 metres. Occupation of the huts started in 1987. Another village some twenty minutes away was also planned, with 30 huts due to be constructed in 1990. This second village was not erected, since the making of secondary huts in the existing village and the building of a school took precedence over the construction of another new village.

The construction of 80 main dwellings in Gragn implied that about 20 per cent of households had been villagized. However, many of these had not yet abandoned their old settlement area to move into the village. At least 36 households, almost half, had not destroyed all their old huts. The fact that so many old homes were still standing and being used suggests that, for a large proportion of the 'villagized' population, the break from the old homestead had not yet been completed. The case was even clearer for 19 households, or 24 per cent of the potential inhabitants, who had constructed a hut in the new village but had never lived in it. In 13 households, or 16 per cent of the cases, this was allegedly because the new hut had not been completed, and for the remainder, the primary reason given was the absence of a secondary hut in which to put the livestock.

In a number of cases some members of the household occupied the new huts, whilst the rest stayed behind, the two units either remaining closely tied or using the situation to distance some household members from the others. The new house thus provided a place to put an unwanted mother-in-law, or a solution for a couple divorcing, one person setting up a new household in each homestead. An example of a couple splitting up was that of Gétachew's household, which initially lived in one zone. Gétachew's wife refused to join him in the new village, and he married another and moved in. Likewise, Taddese retained contact with his old wife and household in another zone in Gragn, whilst living with his new wife, Sindé, and her daughter in the village. Sindé in turn kept her ties with her old home, in another zone, currently occupied for her by a male relative. In other cases, the owners did not occupy their huts, but allowed others to do so. This arrangement was often sanctioned by the peasants' association leadership; for example, three female-headed households – a single woman regarded as somewhat senile, a poor woman with three dependents, and myself – were all given the use of a hut in this way.

Though an empty abode was traditionally frowned upon and taken as a sign of calamity, some huts in the new village remained uninhabited when their owners moved out of the peasants' association because, for example, of marriage or marital disputes. Almaz closed her hut after her husband, with whom she had quarrelled and who had left, abducted her again. She was living with him and his parents elsewhere in Gragn, although she told me that she planned to come back. The mobility of individuals was not specific to women. Mulatu, for example, closed his hut after living there for only a few months and went to live with his wife in her old house in another zone. Another case of a hut remaining empty after initial habitation was when Ayele's wife died. The widower closed his home in the village and took his infant son to live near his mother, until a new wife was found from another zone. At this point he returned with her to the village.

Secondary huts

One of the theories behind villagization given by officials was that, for reasons of sanitation, people should be encouraged to have separate living quarters, kitchens and cattle-sheds. Villagers conceded that it would be cleaner to have the three huts for different uses, but, during my stay, the existing kitchens and cattle-sheds had not been used for the intended purpose. Moreover, as we shall see, the people had their own reasons and logic for subverting national exogenous plans.

Kitchens

The separate kitchens erected behind the houses were generally smaller, and circular in form. Eleven had been built, but none of them were used as kitchens. This was because fuel was far too expensive in Gragn for people to afford the cost of two fires: one for cooking in the kitchen, and the other in the main dwelling for protection against the bitter cold.[12] Furthermore, household and guests gathered together over meals and coffee, and the isolation of cooking and eating from living was unacceptable. For example, coffee drinking is a lengthy process involving not only drinking, but also eating a snack, incense burning and much sitting around talking to neighbours and friends, often whilst women spun wool or cotton and attended to children. The separation of socializing from consumption on a daily basis was inconceivable. As a result 'kitchens' tended to be used as store huts, cattle-sheds or additional living areas.

There were various uses of the 'kitchen' as extended living areas. Felfelé's sister's daughter quarrelled with her husband and came to Felfelé's to give birth. She was given the main hut whilst Felfelé and her adopted daughter moved into the kitchen. Another case was that of Teshome's household, or rather households. He lived in the main hut with his then current wife, Zewdé, who had recently given birth, an adopted son, and Zewdé's daughter by a previous marriage. His ex-wife, Shewazab, lived in the kitchen with her adopted daughter. The Zewdé and Shewazab units of the household were economically linked since Teshome was the only official land owner, and there was constant communication, friendly or otherwise, between the two units, as well as the sharing of tasks and equipment. When Zewdé gave birth, it was Shewazab who looked after her for the *aras* period, the first few days of convalescence discussed in Chapter 7. Perhaps a similar situation might have developed in Taddese's household, where Taddese's wife Sindé, who had land in her own name, wondered whether the villagization policy would continue or be abandoned. If it was going to continue, she was going to pay for the construction of a kitchen, in case she quarrelled with her husband. In the eventuality of a divorce, this would allow them both to have a place in the village and reduce the squabbling over who should move.

Cattle-sheds

Six rectangular cattle-sheds were erected in the village. Each was for the use of two neighbours, and was therefore subdivided into two compartments. Although three of these huts were completed by the time I left, none were being used for animals. Livestock was kept in the main hut, in the 'kitchen', or in the old huts where some of the household remained. The reasons given for not using these sheds were that they were too cold, that hyenas would eat the cattle, or more generally that the animals were vulnerable in the cattle-sheds, because they were somewhat removed from the principal huts. The dislike of sharing was undoubtedly the main factor behind the non-utilization of these sheds and the preceding arguments primarily rationalizations of distrust for such a scheme. Completed sheds were used, in a couple of cases, to store fodder. Sometimes, as in Zegene's case, the kitchen had been built and was used to house sheep, whilst the humans and a cow resided in the principal hut. Another strategy adopted by Taddese and Sindé's household was to use the empty main hut of neighbouring Tesfayé to keep their sheep and those of Ayele, another richer neighbour for whom they minded some sheep under the *ribbï* arrangement discussed in the following chapter.

Though additional huts were desired, none of the kitchens or cattle-sheds were used for the purposes envisaged. The externally perceived rationality behind the proposed division was understood, but the planned allocation of space was not found to be as practical as other options. The result was that a different strategy was adopted – one better suited to the local situation and to the needs of individual households.

Composition of the village

In 1990, there were 56 household heads in the village, with a total resident population of 218, an average of four persons, ranging from one to seven, per household. If those allocated a hut but not yet resident in the village are included, the figure increases to 73 heads of household, and a population of 356. No data were available on another eight households, and one resident died before he moved in. The population of 73 households also gives an average of 4.9 per household, suggesting that those outside the village had larger households, thus pushing up the average.

It would be satisfying if a clear pattern emerged as to who chose or was forced into the village, and who remained outside. In some parts of the country the logic was a simple spatial one, whole areas being depopulated and communities moved one by one. In Gragn, however, there was no simple rationale, and the decision to enter the village was determined by a combination of geographical, social, and material factors, some attracting people towards the move, others acting in the opposite direction. In all cases the heads of households, who were predominantly men, made the decision. Given the amount of cooperation within households, it might seem surprising that almost all did so without significant consultation with women household members. For this the framework in which the policy was introduced was mainly responsible. The state communicated its ideas to heads of households, most of whom were men, and expected them to endorse the policy. The campaign operated in the political public domain which men regularly attended and in which they made the necessary decisions.

Geographical factors

The people who had been living near the current villagization site were specifically mentioned and given more encouragement to 'volunteer' for villagization. It was argued that it was in their economic interest to move into a village near their land and current assets, rather than be forced to move, in a few years' time, into a second villagized site which would be at a greater distance from their current homestead, and therefore more inconvenient. A considerable proportion of the population in the villagized community therefore came from the nearest zones within the peasants' association which, correspondingly, were the zones most clearly depopulated by villagization.

Social factors

In coming to a decision whether or not to move into the village, family links and ties of friendship had a role to play. Many people had close consanguineous relatives outside their immediate household, but still within the village, a not uncommon situation in other parts of the peasants' association where close neighbours were often related.[13] The decision to move was sometimes influenced by the fact that some other relative had chosen to be villagized, or the motive could work in the opposite direction, influencing the decision of some households to keep away. Thus, there were people who joined the village to escape old ties. One man left a wife in his old hut with their children and married a woman who joined him in the new one. They quarrelled, and he continued living there, with someone else. In another case, a poor couple were living with the wife's very demanding relatives. Villagization provided an excuse for reducing their dependence on these relatives and setting up an independent household.

Status and authority within the peasants' association

Those who began building in the village at an early stage included the chairman, secretary, service cooperative chairman and shopkeeper, women's association chair and secretary, one member of the local law courts, several peasants' association committee members and two of the local militia. To these can be added the literacy teacher and three priests. All these people were encouraged to set an example. Ironically, given the prevalent aversion to the villagization policy, this is a case where power in the community, correlated with greater wealth, was seen to have its disadvantages.

Wealth and poverty

As mentioned in the section on principal huts there were a number of poor and vulnerable people who had been given a place in the village, such as Dessita and Yilfu who were in households lacking a supportive social network. Others, mainly female-headed and other vulnerable households, came to the village on their own initiative, attracted by the greater security of village life, as well as by easier access to labour. Bek'ele, who returned with a leg wound after eight years as a soldier, and for whom the peasants' association ploughed and performed other duties, is another example.

The richer households were those least likely to want to move to the village as they had more capital invested in existing locations, such as a larger number of houses, trees, grain-storage facilities and mills. Further-more, peasants who were better off than the average, feared close proximity to poorer households because of the pressures to lend and fears of envy, theft, and so on. However, the richer households were also those more likely to be able to afford the expense of building the new hut. The result was that there were a number of richer people who had started or even finished building their huts, but did not yet inhabit the village. Most of the unoccupied finished huts in the village therefore belonged to the comparatively better off.[14]

Condition of existing huts

In a few cases I have heard the comment that an old house was falling down in any case, and that it was just as well to build in the village directly, rather than take the chance and have to rebuild twice, doubling the cost, work and time if the villagization policy continued.

Miscellaneous

Some people moved because they were attracted to the idea of change rather than motivated by suspicion of it. Thus, a person with an outward-going character was more likely to 'give it a try' than a cautious individual. Others felt that if they were going to toil on the building of huts for others, they might as well have one for themselves, whilst still others believed that since villagization was inevitable, they might as well 'follow government's orders'.

Evaluation

Having attempted to set the context and to describe some of the attitudes of the population, there remains the task of a generalized assessment. Such an assessment was not directly voiced by the population affected, who, like Ethiopians throughout their long recorded history, tended to recognize that the state had the power to impose its will regardless, and feared that debate on the 'pros and cons' of government policy would be tantamount to sedition. Though it was not always visible, peasants in the country operated in a longstanding coercive framework. Though the impact of villagization was a subject of conversation, there was an element of caution when critical opinions were expressed and a 'why talk about it' type of fatalism resulting from a belief, no doubt justified, that their opinions were, in any case, irrelevant in the wider framework of government decisions.

Most government policies have wide-ranging effects, and side-effects, with varying implications for different individuals and households. In this chapter we have attempted to look at how people made decisions when faced with villagization. In general, there can be no question that most people did not like the idea, but proceeded with it when instructed to do so. In the words of one farmer: 'if the government tells you to throw yourself in a gully you do so'. In veiled terms and using *double entendre*, the following two poems also express a dislike of villagization.

ብበላም ፡ ባልበላም ፡
ጥሬ ፡ ነው ፡ እራቴ ፤
እደሱ ፡ ከተማ ፡
ጐራኝ ፡ ነው ፡ እቤቴ ።

Whether I eat or do not eat,
My dinner is uncooked [food]
The new town,
My house is at Gragn.

ዶሰራዋል ፡ ስራ ፡
ዶቀቀለዋል ፡ ወጥ ፤
ደጥም ፡ እደረገም ፡
ታዶተም ፡ እደታወቀ ።

Work`is done
Stew is cooked
And it will not be repeated
Nothing like it has been seen before.

The first poem picks up on the dislocation to daily existence caused by villagization. The implication is that you cannot even get a proper meal in your new homes because everything is topsy-turvey. The second poem draws attention to the fact that villagized communities appear to be clones that cannot be differentiated one from the other.

There was considerable variation in the density of population within Gragn prior to villagization. It is clear that the changes resulting from villagization were greatest for those previously living in isolated homesteads and unused to village life. Another distinction seems to be that because of the time they had lived in their existing homestead, and a greater attachment to it, the elderly tended to have a more unfavourable attitude to villagization than the young, while the children tended to be quite positive about it, since they could play or carry out their duties in the company of friends. In general, it should be emphasized that complaints were more often heard about increased labour on *sira zemecha* work campaigns, and time thus lost for income-earning and leisure activities, than about villagization *per se*.

Costs and complaints associated with villagization

The mismatch between government's and peasant's perceptions can be summarized by a linguistic illustration. The rationale behind the grid pattern was the government's sense of needing to establish an order and clarity in the physical layout of the rural settlement. The people of the area, however, used the term *kimichit* to refer to the new villages. The word carries connotations of piling up, 'haphazardness', confusion. Thus to the local population, the new straight-lined villages were chaotic whilst the old hamlets had a logic connected to the micro-ecology of the area, and the demographic or social connections between households. On the other hand, to outsiders it would seem that the old villages, with huts seemingly illogically jumbled together, should be called *kimichit*.

The cost of the whole exercise in joint and individual labour time, effort and material was generally resented. Grass needed for thatching involved a day's walk to the area from which it would be brought back by donkey on the following day. Wood often had to be bought, and doors and other fixtures made. Nails, hinges and other items had to be purchased at the market or service cooperative. The average cost for a new house in monetary terms was 300 *birr*, about the equivalent of the cost of an ox. This was without including any measure of labour or opportunity costs, or taking into account such things as the inevitable breakage of household equipment or goods left behind during the move. In the building years 1987 and 1988 the cash burden was, however, considerably lightened by a UNICEF Cash for Work aid programme then in operation.

One of the first points people in Gragn made when questioned on the matter was that living in the village disrupted their way of life. In particular, it increased the distance to grassland and created problems in livestock management. This was because there was no area in the village where livestock could graze under the watchful eye of a household member. If left unsupervised for a moment, the animals were likely to trample over a neighbour's territory and eat grain left out to dry. Under the new arrangements, the grassland allotted to a particular household was likely to be up to half an hour's walk from the village, sometimes on the other side of a river which became impassable for livestock during the rains. Furthermore, it was difficult to ensure that other people did not graze their livestock on private land, and the distance and time taken to get there meant that it was sometimes not worthwhile herding. The passageway to the huts in the village was, moreover, often too tight: the way this was put was that there was no room for the livestock to 'enter and exit'. The feeling of being hemmed in was vividly summarized by the following poem:

መሬት፡ምጣድ፡ሆና፡	The ground having become a stove,
ሰግይ ፡ እክንባሉ ፤	The sky a lid;
መጧቋጧቅያው ፡በረት፡	The place of quarrelling [is] the cattle-sheds,
መውዱ ፡ መገቢያ፡ጧፍታት፡	Having lost the way in and the way out,
ይፉተጋስ፡ፍጥረት ።	Created beings are battling against one another.

The problem of 'entry and exit' was aggravated during the rainy seasons when all the trampling contributed to a muddy terrain from which lambs, in particular, regularly had to be rescued.

As already mentioned, livestock owners were faced with greater problems, the size of which increased with the size of the herd. Worries included where to put the animals and, for the better endowed households, a fear that their livestock would be made more conspicuous by the novelty of the arrangements and the higher density of population in the village. This fear of 'being seen' was expressed in traditional terms of the evil eye, as well as in an open acknowledgement of the difficulty of resisting pleas from impoverished neighbours and relatives. The mirror image of this problem was pressure on poorer sections of the population who felt obliged to do as their neighbours did. For example, during festivals and other occasions it was much easier to know exactly what livestock and how many were slaughtered by a particular household. Where economic differences were more visible, there was social pressure on the poorest to show that they could keep up appearances.

In the general perception of villagization and in the literature, increased distance from agricultural land is often considered the primary economic cost.[15] This was not often mentioned as a problem in Gragn – perhaps because the traditional pattern of *rist* land holdings was characterized by fragmentation into dispersed plots, because people's previous homesteads had not been far from the village, and because the actual time spent in the fields was comparatively low.[16]

Fuel, in the form of dung and wood, was almost always mentioned as a major problem. As we shall see in Chapter 5, the dung economy was jeopardized by the move – a result of the problems already mentioned in connection with livestock. Because dung could no longer be collected in the vicinity, the household's supply dwindled.[17] In terms of wood supplies, there was the problem of the distance from trees planted around the old compound, with the added possibility of theft when there was nobody to keep a watchful eye. A comment made in this context was that villagization would not have been such a problem if everybody had moved, as was the case in many other parts of the country. Tension and fear of theft resulted from a situation in which one household moved to the village whilst neighbours stayed behind, thus obtaining free rein over the whole area.

There were three main reasons why wood shortage increased after villag-ization: many reserves were exhausted in the building of new huts, living trees could not be uprooted and taken to the new settlement, and saplings were particularly vulnerable to theft. Timber was used for pillars, doors and the roof beams on which thatch was laid, and occasionally for windows.[18] Much of this wood was found by cutting down trees belonging to the household rather than moving parts of the old hut, either because of the strategy of keeping a foothold in the old location, or because the hut was old, its wooden components decayed and unsatisfactory as the basis for a new structure. In the meantime, people were slow to plant new trees, because of a sense of dislocation, a policy of 'wait and see', and also because constant supervision was required to protect seedlings from people and livestock. In order to encourage the tree-planting, the peasants' association provided some households with eucalyptus saplings, nursed within the peasants' association. Few of these survived the unusually heavy long rains of 1988, the subsequent dry season, and the trampling. There was no attempt to grow other types of trees that surrounded former compounds. This suggested that there might be a danger of a decline in the variety of flora, as well as the loss of some plants of value for medicinal and other uses. Deforestation was widespread across the country, but in the vicinity of the new villages the almost total absence of any tree or shrub was starkly evident. Not surprisingly, the population concentrated in one location worked outwards to forage anything that would burn.

During the rains, some households formerly grew garlic and cabbages in a garden plot within the homestead. In the same way as tree-planting was interrupted during villagization, the practice of vegeculture was also discontinued in the first two years. By the third year, however, two families had resumed the practice, and the number of vegetable growers seemed likely to increase in the future.

Other complaints voiced around the village concerned the huts themselves. These were often made too quickly, with the emphasis on speed rather than quality: leaking roofs were the result. The walls were made of stones held together only with mud. Traditionally, dung and ash were added to the latter to make a better cement. Some of the newly constructed walls had to be rebuilt, having caved in, and many already showed unhealthy signs of damage. Complaints were also rife about the 'coldness' of the new huts as opposed to the old huts, *yemok'e bét,* or warm huts. The distinction in heat applies firstly to a psychological component caused by the barren-looking new location and the heart-wrench of moving from an old and perhaps long-established locality, and secondly to a real component which included the location of the village on open terrain, and the absence of protective fences and trees. Also, prolonged occupation, and more specifically soot from the cooking fires, had yet to impregnate and thus insulate the buildings. Finally, the setting of the village was also criticized. A group consisting of local and regional Ministry of Agriculture and Party personnel, in consultation with the peasants' association leadership, decided on the new site on account of its proximity to the river, the service cooperative and the road; the site was, however, disadvantageous in that the land was muddy, even waterlogged in the rainy season, and damp seeped into the huts from the ground.

Fears attendant on the densely constructed new structures included fire and disease. A fire could spread through the settlement in minutes. Contagious diseases could likewise sow havoc. This latter fear surfaced early during my stay in the village, when one man was suspected of having typhus, a disease spread by fleas. People remarked that the denser the population, the greater the hazards, and there were no improved sanitation facilities, such as latrines, with which to counteract this problem. Despite the embarrassment caused, everyone was obliged to defecate in public view, between huts or on the outskirts of the village. There were, theoretically, plans to build latrines and three projected ones already existed in the official peasants' association statistics for 1988, though there was no sign of them on the ground.

A complaint from some people with vested interests was that the area on which the huts were built was agricultural land, and those who previously had plots there complained that the land allocated to them as compensation was insufficient or of worse quality. The following poem voices the disturbance felt during the parcelling out of plots.

	Where Gragn was established,
ግራኝ፡እምስረታው፡	In Geremew's [the chairman's]
በገረመው፡ሰፈር፡	neighbourhood,

ፍሪዳ፡ተጥሎ ፤   Having laid down the ox
እንቢ፡አለ፡ቢላዉ፡   [to be slaughtered],
ልብ፡አልቆርጥም፡ብሎ ።   The knife said 'No',
                         Saying it would not cut the heart
                         [of a created being].

This poem is elliptical, with double entendre. Couched in terms of the slaughtering of cattle for meat, the hidden reference was to the unhappiness caused by the division of land into different plots when the village was first laid out.

Another special case was that of people living near, but not in line with, the new huts, who were made to rebuild them within the rigid grid system. Similarly, given that villagization aimed to bring the population closer together, those already living in a comparatively large traditional settlement saw little point in everybody having to move to a completely new location. The issue was more than purely geographical, since groups already existing in social and cooperative units tended to be devalued as a result of the emphasis on the 'modern' units.[19]

There were other problems with villagization as policy and process. The first concerns the rigidity of the structure. It was cast in a mould which did not have built into it the dynamics of social units or the physical wear and tear of buildings. Traditionally, at the peak of the demographic life of a household, children would split off to form their own households. Often sons, and to a lesser extent daughters, would form an adjacent, autonomous, but linked unit. In the village, there was no room for such an expansion next to the first unit. Unless sufficient households left the area, vacating their huts, new households could only be tagged on at the extremities of villages. In the village under review, this meant increasing encroachment on agricultural land. Furthermore, a common sight in the old settlement pattern was an abandoned hut next to a used one, many of the stones of the former having been used to build the latter. Had the villagized huts needed to be rebuilt, maintaining the rigid adherence to the grid formation, the operation would have been particularly difficult.

A second point concerns policy implementation, which was, characteristically, ambitious and quantity oriented. One line of criticism outsiders tended to make was that, instead of bringing people to an empty and potentially more backward environment, the state should have first installed the necessary huts, accompanying compound boundaries and a few services as incentives, offering people a carrot rather than threatening them with a stick.[20] The government's reply was that such a policy required time and money, and that if people were first brought together in villages, their integration itself could be more easily harnessed towards development. Yet, the attempt to speed up the pace of change caused considerable hardship. It showed a lack of consideration for the problems of individuals and communities, thereby invalidating the stated goal of improving the people's conditions of life.

Despite these problems, in Gragn, there was no significant open opposition to villagization. This was not only because of the acceptance of higher authority, but also, as already argued, because there was a clear association between the government's provision of services and aid, 'them helping us', and the government's extraction or other interferences, 'them taxing us and telling us what to do'. To put in another way: 'Even if we don't like it we will do whatever the government asks since they are helping us to "stand', to "survive".' In particular because of the aid the peasants received and expected to receive, most were not willing actively to oppose the villagization policy; they were bound by rules of patronage and were not disposed to disobey, though large numbers 'opted out' when given a chance.

Reports from other areas suggested that people feared that villagization was the first step to collectivization of land or cattle. No such fears were expressed to me in Gragn, nor was the question of loss of independence ever discussed. For most people, there were enough direct repercussions from the policy on daily life, without worrying about other changes which the state might subsequently decide to implement. However, many people explained their initial decision to be villagized partly in terms of the belief that those that did not would be discriminated against in the unpopular selection of people for resettlement. Villagization seemed the lesser of two evils.

Benefits

The population waxed less than lyrical when it came to discussing the positive side to the new villages. I was given vague answers, like *shegga new*, 'it is nice', or more specific ones, such as 'it brings people together', and 'awakens them.' In general favourable comments about villagization referred mainly to a potential for improvement and development with dreams of a clinic, electricity and other facilities being provided to the village in the near future.

Provision of water, nearer and cleaner, education in the form of the literacy hut nearby, and the school under construction in 1989 were already visible changes. Households were also nearer the mill, the service cooperative shop and the administrative centre, where various registrations occurred and where the infant vaccination and feeding programmes occasionally took place. Valuable facilities had undoubtedly come to the peasants' association, yet these had not been part of villagization as such, but rather part of the general and preceding state policies, discussed in more general terms in Chapter 3.

Associated with the view of villagization as part of the 'modern' way of life was the evidence of people abandoning some traditions. On Wednesdays and Fridays, some women were in the habit of burning tobacco outside their huts as a way of honouring the *adbar* spirit which is discussed in Chapter 8. In the new village of Gragn, I was repeatedly told that the custom was not practised and that 'it is good that the area has not learned the tradition'. 'Only if a compound is accustomed to having the smoke, does it bring bad luck to stop the custom' and 'moving to an area where you don't have to bother is good.' Another example was the reduction after villagization of ceremonial slaughtering of livestock. It seemed as if the move to the villagized settlement tended to be used as an excuse to give up a custom seen by its practitioners to be outmoded. Men and women in the village talked about the abandoning of such practices in a positive light and interpreted it as a gain in liberty. However, as we shall see, since the spirits were primarily a form of support to women, where a loss was felt, it was by them, rather than by men. Furthermore, the change was probably more an economizing measure as a consequence of impoverishment, than a positive reaction to the government's policies.

For those formerly living in relatively isolated forms of settlement the positive aspects of villagization were nevertheless significant. The social and economic benefits of a denser population were particularly important to smaller households that would otherwise have fewer choices, essentially because of labour shortage. For the community as a whole, villagization increased the speed with which distress could be dealt with, a point made in the context of the 1985 famine when aid distribution in more scattered settlements in other areas of Ethiopia was hampered by inaccessibility. Any call for help was more likely to be heard and people were easily available when someone was ill, or a woman was having difficulties during childbirth and had to be carried to the clinic in Mehal Meda. This was an immense benefit for female-headed households whose members were otherwise particularly vulnerable. Villagization was likewise perceived as reducing the dangers of such factors as thieving by those outside the community, and as discouraging hyenas from attacking livestock.

Information was also more quickly shared and passed on. The villagers were often the first to know about a new policy or event affecting the whole peasants' association, for example when officials were due to visit the area, when there were changes in the rules governing the use of the communal pasture land, or when new stocks arrived at the service cooperative shop.

In terms of communal work campaigns, people in the new village benefited in that they usually had less distance to travel to the work area. This was because the village was near the administrative and geographical centre of the peasants' association, and, increasingly, the services for which labour was needed tended to be established for village use. Also, in terms of the meetings preceding the work, instead of coming early and sitting around until all the others had arrived, villagers could get on with their own lives until the roll call, then slip in with the others. I often heard bantering between those inside and those outside the village, the former mocking the latter for having to hang around, and those outside, for once, bemoaning their fate and the distance back to their huts.

There seemed to be much more borrowing and informal trading taking place in the village than previously, even when compared with the old village communities. This included the borrowing of household goods, such as a kettle[22] for pouring beer, a Chinese teacup[21] for a guest at coffee time, and food or spices when your neighbour had just made some and yours had run out. The change was partly a function of need, since the necessary equipment often had not reached all households, some being retained in the old settlement; but whatever the reason, it increased interaction. There was also increased sharing of tasks: helping each other with the milling, leaving the children next door when collecting dung or water, getting a neighbour to buy onions at the market.

Furthermore, if pressed, women admitted that as a result of villagization they were more likely to meet people, and drink coffee with others, rather than remain alone. Spinning came to be undertaken by small groups of women. The potential of the close settlement was appreciated, and there was even talk of starting an internal women's *ik'ub*, a sort of club in which each member in turn buys enough cotton or wool to make one garment, allocates the raw material to her fellows, and hosts a weekly social gathering.[23] The difference in lifestyle brought about by villagization was clearly greater for women than for men, who formerly had more possibilities for socializing than women whose lives revolved more closely around their own homes. As a result of the new settlements, women were less likely to be isolated and enjoyed getting together. The reverse of the coin, however, was the danger of a greater amount of friction resulting from closer living. I once heard an Ethiopian official observe that, given the Menz people's reputation of affection for sticks and fights, villagization was 'like bringing fire next to a mountain of kindling'.[24] In addition, socializing did not always increase, and some women in the village rarely communicated with more than a few neighbours.

Some forms of household also seemed to be made more stable by the change. For example, for a man whose wife would go to her relatives to give birth, it was easier to survive alone in the village than in a more isolated social structure. He could rely on a larger network of neighbours as well as relatives, and reduce the pressure on his wife to give birth in the village, away from her kin. It could equally be argued, however, that increased social contacts contributed to social stress and, therefore, to the break-up of households. This occurred, for example, because of the greater possibilities of infidelity and its greater visibility. It was not clear which way the change was working, and any aggregate conclusion would fail to take account of the variety of individual experiences.

Villagization increased the income-earning possibilities of some households. Though there were attempts at prohibiting activities associated with enterprise and resulting in social stratification, trade took place regardless. As we shall see in Chapter 5, some women earned money by producing and selling *arek'i*, a distilled alcoholic drink made from barley, or the simpler and cheaper *t'ella*, local barley beer. Some also bought *arek'i* in town and sold it by the glass in the village. Such activities went on in the old settlements, but since the new village had a denser population the trade was more lucrative. There were no craftspeople such as blacksmiths, potters, or even weavers, and the village relied on Mehal Meda and neighbouring peasants' associations for such services – here as elsewhere, however, villagization might have led to the emergence of local artisans.

One of the results of villagization, and no doubt a component of the logic behind the policy, was its tendency to reduce differences in the number, size and quality of houses owned by rich and poor people. Some differences nevertheless remained, and it was not difficult to guess which was the chairman's abode. Finally, and perhaps flippantly, it could be said that abandoning an old house for a new one also had a number of health-related advantages, namely that many bugs were left behind and it took time for the migrant bug population to reproduce in quantities approaching those in areas inhabited for a long time. All agreed the flea population was smaller in the villagized huts than in the older ones.[25]

In summary, during my stay it was too early to tell what the long-term social effects of the villagization policy might have been. An increase in both socializing and friction could be observed. Which way the balance would have tilted was difficult to evaluate for the individual, let alone for the community. My observations suggest that on a day to day basis, and even more so in emergencies, the benefits of close and numerous neighbours was appreciated rather than resented. On the other hand, it could not be claimed that a feeling of close unity or community had been formed. Cultural events were still celebrated by the old groupings. There was no single village bonfire lit to honour the day of the Finding of the True Cross, *Mesk'el*, which most villagers celebrated in their old localities. Likewise for Christmas, the villagers did not get together to buy one ox or cow for slaughtering. Instead, those living in the village bought a part of the ox or cow slaughtered in the area in which they previously resided. The peasants' association *corveé* labour was also still organized in the old zone system. It should be emphasized, however, that the village was still only in its third year, arguably too young for group consciousness to have developed.

The politics of villagization and the question of coercion

The polarization of opinion about the *Derg's* policies was nowhere more extreme than on questions concerning the use of coercion. The conventional Western view conjured up the bleakest picture of physical and psychological coercion, whilst government publications spoke only of popular actions and voluntary decisions, labelling any discussion on coercion as counter-revolutionary.

It is important in this context to remember that the machinery of control and coercion[26] existed within the peasants' association structure – it was not a factor which could be attributed specifically to villagization. Furthermore, since villagization at the local level was organized by the peasants' association rather than by cadres or other outsiders, the policy was implemented with some consideration towards the population's feelings, since the peasants' association administrators themselves had to abide by the new directives and were its first victims.

There were considerable variations in the methods adopted throughout the country. They depended *inter alia* on the peasants' association structure and the freedom with which the association could act.[27] In Gragn, there was a policy of encouraging the population to take part in the new scheme, and people willing to fill the 80 houses were found with only a limited amount of pressure. The whole hut-building procedure was, moreover, slower in Menz than in most areas, because of the tradition of building walls out of stone rather than wood and mud: replacing stone walls was a time-consuming venture[28] and the scale of the campaign in the area was therefore smaller. Since most people were not to be settled in one go, those particularly antagonistic to the policy kept away from it, though they did not thereby escape *corveé* labour.

In terms of psychological pressure, it was reported that at the initial meeting on villagization in Gragn, the officials from Mehal Meda used the threat of resettlement against those who refused to villagize. In addition, an enforcement problem arose in the area during the settling-in stage of the programme, with people refusing to occupy the new houses and a few fines of 30 *birr* being meted out. The strategies for delay and obfuscation were numerous. As we have seen, lack of cattle-sheds was given as a reason by many; furthermore, some specialized in a pretence of occupation when necessary. They visited their villagized huts, sweeping them out and leaving some objects inside. Should, for example, the peasants' association leadership learn that a Party official was to view the area, an even greater pretence of occupation could be orchestrated. Other households had someone, related or otherwise, in occupation. Another strategy adopted by at least two people was to take their time over the roofing of the huts, the delay and exposure of the half-finished building to the weather resulting in part of the wall collapsing and further delays.

During my stay in the village I never witnessed the use of physical coercion in the villagization context, and no complaints along those lines were made to me. This was perhaps not surprising in that the chairman himself was more often than not in his old house, and others, amongst the peasants' association officials, had not even made an appearance in the village: they were therefore not in a position to put pressure on others. The awareness that they 'should' be there nevertheless remained, and discomfort was felt by those 'not obeying the government instructions', whilst those who had settled sometimes mocked and jibed at the absentees.

Conclusion

A villagization programme coming from within the society would be inconceivable because of the considerable initial and perhaps even long-term costs to individuals. The policy could only have come from outside the society. Villagization was but one in a series of rural programmes undertaken by the *Derg*. In keeping with the historical record on such matters, it was a paternalistic, top-down policy conceived of for the rural population, by urban officials. Yet it also showed the power that these officials managed to wield. According to Clapham, it provided 'the most striking evidence of the Revolutionary regime's capacity to re-order life in the countryside.'[29]

Reaction to the villagization policy by the population was almost universally unfavourable, in particular because of a perceived incompatibility between the livestock economy and dense human settlement. Most complaints, however, centred around short-term dislocation and the way the programme was implemented, and many households were involved, by and large successfully, in delaying and 'wait and see' tactics.

There was, nevertheless, a belief that villagization could bring with it an improvement in life-style, and in Gragn some benefits were materializing, though the gap between the goals as presented by the government and the gains as perceived by the population remained. Some people expressed a will to believe in its future beneficial potential, and for them there was a disjunction in time between perceived costs and benefits. This was summarized to me by the comment *yemminimotew, lijjochachin indïnoru new* – 'we are dying so that our children may live'. A reversal of opinion over time also took place within sections of the community. In the initial building stages, the comparatively better off could more easily afford the change, while the poorer households found the burden of construction greatest. Once the work was completed and the cost expended, however, the comparatively wealthy had the most to fear, and the poorest the most to gain, or the least to lose, from the closer density of settlement.

The change was greatest for women, who tended to be particularly isolated, more so than men, because of their domestic duties. Some commented favourably, arguing that socialization had increased, others complained about increased friction. Female-headed households, in particular, felt the benefits. To list but one final pattern, the policy was resented least by young people who found numerous companions, and most by the elderly who had strong emotional and material attachments to their old homesteads.

As we have seen, in assessing the impact of villagization it is important to set this policy in the context of other actions or omissions of the state, and to disaggregate the population. At the time of fieldwork it was unclear whether in the future the distinction between villagization and collectivization would be erased and whether all villages would be collectivized, or whether collectivization would be shelved and the new spatial structure used to bolster market forces, and encourage trade, petty commodity and service production. Subsequent developments in the country and the fall of the Mengistu régime have clarified the situation. Villagization is no longer state policy. How much, if anything, of the villagization experience will remain in the future is difficult to predict, though clearly differences will emerge between regions and within communities. Brief observations on my return visit to Gragn are recorded in the Epilogue.

Notes

1 Ethiopia, National Villagization Co-ordinating Committee, *Mender*, 1987: 14. The draft constitution summarizes the aims in Article 10, clause 3, which states: 'The state shall encourage the scattered rural population to aggregate in order to change their backward living condition and to enable them to lead a better social life.'

2 Cohen and Isaksson, 1987(a) and Survival International Report, 1988.

3 Ironically, given the subsequent Villagization Campaign, in a preface to a book on the different types of houses in different parts of Ethiopia, Fisseha Geda, Commissioner of COPWE and Central Committee Member, wrote: 'Dwellings are an expression of the life, the culture and the environment of the people who live in them ... the homes of the Ethiopians are nearly as varied as the costumes they wear and are another important aspect of cultural expression which the Revolution is dedicated to preserve and develop.' Last, 1981: 1.

4 Cohen, 1981, Clapham, 1988.

5 Cohen and Isaksson, 1987(a): 450. See also Clapham, 1988.

6 For villagization in other countries, see, for example, Coulson, 1977; De Vries & Fortmann, 1979; Hyden, 1980; Mittelman, 1981; Mwapachu, 1979; Thiele, 1986.

7 See for example, Dunning, 1970; Aster Akalu, 1982; Mengistu Woube, 1986.

8 Cohen and Isaksson, 1987(a): 437.

9 Ethiopia, National Villagization Coordinating Committee, *Mender*. The text stated that there were 5,725,530 dwellers in 5176 villages, page 28, whereas the table (page 30) gave 3,899,634 dwellers in 5164 villages.

10 Ethiopia, National Villagization Coordinating Committee, *Mender*, page 29.

11 Survival International Report, 1988, used a resident population figure of between 500 to 2500, but no source was given.

12 If fires were lit in both huts, they would both become kitchens, *ch'is bét,* literally 'smoke huts', since dung, in particular, produces considerable smoke.

13 At least three intra-village marriages occurred during the fieldwork. In addition, given the large number of re-marriages, it is not surprising to find a number of ex-spouses within the village. The issue of marriage and divorce will be treated more fully in Chapter 6.

14 Note also the earlier comment about the size of households within the village being smaller. It should not be assumed from this that *all* larger households were richer; a number of cases in Gragn clearly illustrated that some of the largest households belonged to the poorest section of society.

15 Cohen and Isaksson, 1987; Thiele, 1986; Mittelman, 1981.

16 In many areas of the country, crops need to be guarded against wild animals that destroy or consume the harvest, see Berihun Teferra, 1988. In this part of Menz, however, wild animals are not a problem, see Chapter 5.

17 In other regions, where dung is used as fertilizer, people were complaining that the labour involved in collecting it and transporting it is an increased burden; in some cases households have decided to forgo the custom and villagization has thus contributed to a drop in land fertility.

18 Windows are unusual in Ethiopian huts. In Menz, some huts have windows which consist of openings with no glass, and are closed by wooden shutters.

19 As we will see in the case of male *mehaber* in Chapter 8. Also see Dore, 1971 on the difficult relationship between socialist and traditional forms of cooperation.

20 The same type of logic induced the Relief and Resettlement Commission in its first Resettlement Campaign to move men first, thinking of preparing the ground for later settlement by their families as a whole; however, this policy was later abandoned because of its hardships for single men and because of settlers' sense of dislocation. A. Pankhurst, 1989(a).

21 In this part of Ethiopia the local beer is commonly poured out from metal kettles, used almost exclusively for this purpose.

22 Small handle-less teacups made in Taiwan and China are used as coffee cups.

23 For more on *ik'ub* and a comparison with *mehaber* and the state-run women's

association see H. Pankhurst, 1990 (b).

24 On views about this reputation of the Menz peasantry, see Levine, 1965; Reminick, 1973.

25 Though, in this respect, churches were the greatest offenders. Communicable diseases were, furthermore, a greater danger in the more densely populated new villages.

26 Coercion was no new factor in the lives of peasants in Ethiopia, R. Pankhurst, 1961, 1965.

27 The Survival International Report, 1988, divided its findings into two: the villagization programme in 'stable' areas, and that in 'war zones'. It was much more critical in its findings in the latter area. The point about different experiences is also discussed by Clapham, 1988.

28 Stone provides a better protection against the cold. In any case, the shortage of wood in the area would have prevented a change to walls made of wood. As it is the shortage of wood, even when used only for roofing, caused problems.

29 Clapham, 1988: 177.

PART
2

Women's Work and Women's Lives

5

Household Economy: Beyond the Plough and Ox

The first two empirical chapters considered the state on the basis of its infrastructural and administrative interventions. One of the conclusions reached was that, at the local level, radical transformation had not been achieved. I now move on to a description of the central activities and attitudes of the society, discussing the impact of the state only where relevant. All activities mentioned after the initial section on cultivation were central to the household, yet tended to be ignored in studies and policy formation. Not surprisingly, it was in these issues, located away from the male preserve of cultivation, that women's labour had a key role.

In Menz, as in much of Ethiopia, the household retained a primary economic and social role. Production, reproduction and consumption were all oriented towards the household unit, and much work took place around the homestead. Chapter 2 introduced some of the features of households in Menz; this chapter develops these with regard to the economic scene, how people met their needs, and the resources on which their livelihoods depended. The rationale for adopting households as the unit of discussion lay in their endogenous centrality as social and economic units in society. This is not to say that households were not disaggregated into various components, in particular in terms of men and women.

Where numerical information is provided in this chapter it is based on the analysis of my questionnaires. Appendix C provides the raw data, which should be treated with caution: inevitable distortions result from the suspicion that people feel when asked to measure their resources. Furthermore, they communicate these in terms of local, subjective values, while the researcher is looking for universal objective ones. For example, the answer to the question about what a household had harvested in the previous year was often a vigorous 'nothing', with a gesture of frustration or despair. In fact this 'nothing' could be translated to mean a different quantity of grain depending on speaker, year and expectations; after some discussion we could usually put a more specific figure to 'nothing', which could be used in my attempts at comparative data.

Arable land: cultivation and processing

In Gragn, land holdings per household varied from around 0.75 to 3.2 hectares, with a mean at 1.4 hectares. These holdings were fragmented into between two and thirteen plots, the average being six.[1] Peasants relied predominantly on one cropping season a year, and, breaking the usual pattern in Ethiopia, this was the *belg,* or short-rains crop. The importance of the *belg* crop was repeatedly emphasized in conversations; all was well so long as the *belg* was good. Nonetheless, some land was also reserved for the *meher,* long-rains season. Furthermore, if the short rains failed, the land was reploughed and sown for the long-rains crop. In addition, if the short rains started early, double cropping was attempted by planting one or two plots with a relatively fast-growing crop, such as lentils. Under favourable conditions, this could be harvested and the land made ready for the second crop sown at the beginning of the long rains.

Averaging good and bad years, such strategies resulted in an estimated overall figure of 55 per cent of land holdings sown for the short rains, the yield of 60 per cent of the harvest being proportionally greater.[2] Tables 5.1 and 5.2, based on the questionnaires, give the areas sown and yields obtained in 1988, a bad year, compared to what respondents would expect from past experience in a good year. The data show the cumulative for 88 respondents. Areas are given in *t'ind,* about a quarter of a hectare, and yields are measured in *silicha,* a sack, weighing approximately half a quintal.

The main crops in the area were, in decreasing order of importance, barley, wheat, beans, lentils, peas and castor oil seeds. By far the majority of peasants relied only on the first three, barley being the single most

Table 5.1. Area sewn in *t'ind,* during short and long rains

| | Area sown, 1988 | | Area sown , 'good year' | |
	Short rains	Long rains	Short rains	Long rains
Barley	284 (85%)	71 (25%)	322 (80%)	82 (26%)
Wheat	29 (9%)	96 (34%)	46 (12%)	100 (31%)
Beans	4 (1%)	95 (33%)	10 (3%)	100 (31%)
Other	18 (5%)	22 (8%)	22 (5%)	38 (12%)
Total	335 (100%)	284 (100%)	400 (100%)	320 (100%)

Table 5.2. Yield in *silicha,* during short and long rains

| | Yield, 1988 | | Yield , 'good year' | |
	Short rains	Long rains	Short rains	Long rains
Barley	279 (84%)	76 (33%)	1405 (86%)	362 (30%)
Wheat	30 (9%)	86 (37%)	158 (10%)	329 (27%)
Beans	8 (3%)	58 (25%)	31 (2%)	426 (36%)
Other	14 (4%)	10 (5%)	31 (2%)	79 (7%)
Total	331 (100%)	230 (100%)	1625 (100%)	1196 (100%)

important and basic requirement for subsistence. In 1988, barley accounted for an estimated 84 per cent, wheat 9 per cent, and beans 2 per cent of the short-rains harvest. The figures for the long-rains crops were: barley 33 per cent, wheat 37 per cent and beans 25 per cent.

Three varieties of barley, called *ferké, mawgé* and *t'emej*, were still cropped in the area. *T'emej* had the largest grain, and would be reserved for roasting and eating as a snack. It was also the most temperamental of the three crops and was no longer grown in Gragn because of the gamble involved. The sowing of *mawgé* was likewise becoming rare with the result that most of the barley crop was now of the *ferké* variety. *Ferké* and *mawgé* were often contrasted in the following ways: *mawgé* is white, sown mainly in the long rains, and needs careful treatment, in particular it is often grown on the *dej-merét*, the garden plot on which ash is sometimes strewn as a form of fertilizer. *Ferké* is black, more reliable, and though it is normally sown in the short rains, it can grow in either season. *Mawgé* is preferred for uses such as the preparation of *dabbo* (bread), *injera* (savoury pancakes), *injera* sandwiches (called *annebaberro*) and *besso*, a kind of crumble or dough made from barley. *Ferké* is less highly prized and of lower value in the market. It is used to make *t'ella*, the local beer, and for the previously mentioned dishes when there is no *mawgé*. There was thus a clear trend towards fewer strains of the most important crop and increased dependence on the most reliable, though the least preferred, of the varieties.

A similar picture emerges when we look at beans and wheat, the main supplements to a barley diet.[3] The bean crop, though needed in smaller quantities, was the complement to barley in subsistence consumption. Beans were ground and then used as the basis for *shiro*, the sauce with which the barley *injera* was consumed; lentils could be used for the same purpose.[4] Beans were also eaten fresh, roasted, or dried and then boiled or roasted; however, in times of scarcity their use was reserved for *shiro*. Wheat was considered a luxury, reserved mainly for use in bread for ceremonial occasions. Respondents suggested that fewer beans were being sown because plots were reserved for the more vital barley crop and less wheat was sown as it was the dominant form of food aid and could therefore be obtained without cultivation. Subsistence cultivators were therefore finding themselves increasingly reliant on a single variety of a single crop.

Land was ploughed for the short-rains *belg* crop in February or March after two to five days of rain, and in June or July for a *meher* crop. It took a man and his oxen under a week to plough a field of approximately a quarter of a hectare. Oxen were preferred, though other livestock, such as horses and cows, were sometimes used because of impoverishment and the consequent shortage of oxen. The use of other animals for ploughing does not feature in accounts by nineteenth-century travel writers[5] and was a source of amazement to those visiting the area from wealthier regions.

Work'u, a neighbour of mine, commented that with a pair of oxen he could have had his land ready in two weeks, but that with a horse and an ox it took him an extra week. The plough consisted of a wooden shaft with a metal tip, needing to be sharpened each year by smiths in Mehal

Meda at a cost of 1 *birr*. Eventually a new plough was bought, costing about 15 *birr* during the research period, and the old one was recycled to make a hoe. Together with a sickle, an axe and a threshing fork, these were the main agricultural implements used by men in Menz.

Men ploughed and, in Menz, it was unheard of for a woman to do so. The seed grain, about half a quintal per quarter hectare, was measured and put in a sack, usually by a woman. The sowing itself was men's work; feeding and giving water to men and livestock, in the fields and at home, was women's work. Peasants in Gragn had comparatively little work to do on the crops between sowing and harvesting. Unlike other parts in the area, Gragn had no monkeys to ward off, and the absence of trees relieved the pressure from birds. Mice and porcupines were the major field pests, but no measures were taken against them. High altitude resulted in minimal plant growth and there was therefore little need for weeding. Only the bean crop allowed weed growth, and this tended to be pulled out by both men and women, around February, for use as fodder.

Most harvesting was from June to July (*belg*) and November to December (*meher*). The harvesting of barley and wheat was an exclusively male activity. Harvesting of beans, peas and lentils could involve women, though it was predominantly conceived of as a male activity. Threshing of both crops was often delayed until the winds picked up, around December. However, if the household was suffering from food shortages before the long rains, some of the *belg* harvest would be threshed immediately. Men were the main threshers, though women could help with activities such as driving the livestock over the grain. Once threshed, the grain was put into a separate granary outside the owner's hut or taken inside. Traditionally, men put the threshed grain in large granaries called *gotera* or *rik'*. When requested, they transferred grain from these stores to *dibignit*, small granaries located inside the hut, which the women in the household controlled. I was told that the tradition was no longer upheld because there was not enough grain to necessitate such a division. Usually, the grain was stored directly in the hut under the auspices of the head woman in the household.

Processing and cooking were almost exclusively women's work. Only the tasks leading up to cooking will be discussed here, including setting out the grain to dry, washing, pounding and grinding. All these activities were undertaken in the hut or just outside it. On sunny days grains and spices were set out to dry on a sack outside the doorstep, while somebody inside kept a look-out to protect the food from marauding hens and other possible mishaps. The grain was then pounded, sometimes by two women working together. When men pounded, this was only for *gésho*, the leaf used in brewing beer.

Milling was, undoubtedly, the most laborious of household tasks. Women would get up early in the morning and bend over a grinding stone for at least an hour, a couple of times a week. Here are two *ingurguro*, milling songs expressing the women's desire to finish quickly.

ወፍጮዬ ፡ መጋሳ ፡	My grinding stone,
ተሉ ፡ ተሉ ፡ ብለሃ ፡	Be quick, be quick!
እንገላገል ፤	Let us be rid of this,
እንተም ፡ ይሻስሃል ፡	For you too it is better
ሳትወጣ ፡ ጸንበር ።	Before the sun rises.
እረ ፡ ተው ፡ መጋሳ ፡	Oh come on stone grinder!
ወፍጮዬ ፡ መጋሳ ፤	My grinding stone,
እንተም ፡ እጄ ፡	You too, my hand,
ቢመሽ ፡ ለምንዴ ፡	Why should it get late?
ቢነጋ ፡ ለምንዴ ።	Why should it dawn?

The service cooperative mill was increasingly used to mill barley. However, the mill could not be relied on. It was not always functioning and regularly ran out of diesel. In addition, poorer households found the few cents required too expensive, and still relied on the labour of women. Other crops, beans, lentils and spices were always milled by hand.

Both men and women were involved in the minimal vegeculture of the region. Garlic and cabbages were sometimes planted at the beginning of the rains. Garlic, used in the preparation of the chilli-based spice *berberé*, could be eked out to last the year. Cabbage served for a couple of months around September. The sexual division in vegeculture was not strict. Usually men prepared the land with hoes, and women took over from there. In addition to these vegetables, the diet was supplemented a few times a year with nettles collected by women and made into a smooth sauce.

Most agricultural work in Menz was carried out by the household, appropriate tasks being allocated by age within the overall gender division. However, in addition to household labour, neighbours and kin were also brought in throughout the cycle of food production. The fact that many households did not possess a pair of oxen resulted in various sharing agreements, usually in the form of two households taking turns to lend each other their ox; the sharing of human labour could also be part of the agreement. Livestock were also pooled when it came to threshing. For example, in the case recalled by Wesené, six households shared the use of livestock:

> The threshing took us three days last year. Work'u, Tafese and Wendwessen each put in one donkey, T'ilahun contributed his horse, we had two calves, and Belet'ew two oxen. When each person had done his grain, he passed on the animals to the next one, until we had all finished.

Whether the constraint was in terms of labour or capital, households cooperated in different ways, as and when the need arose. Most of this cooperation was informal, small-scale and along gender demarcations. Thus a man asked for the help of another in harvesting; a woman for help in milling. More rarely, whole gatherings of people could be called in to help. In the case of Zenebech, a woman organized a group of men to do the harvesting for her, because her husband was absent.

> He [husband] was not here when the harvest was ready, this was in 1978
> [1986], he had gone to work in Debre Berhan. I brewed beer, made some
> food and asked people to come and help – that is called a *debo*. We know
> who we can call on, and they remember too. Sometimes in the past it was
> up to 20 people who came, not recently though. It is good when everybody's
> crop is ripe at the same time, since you can get the work finished quicker
> this way, but it is generally organized only if you are in difficulties.

Thus, households relied essentially on their own labour and the sharing
of tasks with a few other friends, relatives or neighbours. Large scale
cooperation organized from within the community was increasingly
unusual, although it still occurred to help households through emergencies,
as in the case above.

In Gragn before 1988, only 2 per cent of the peasants interviewed had
ever used chemical fertilizers and, as we shall see, the use of natural fertilizers
in the form of dung was severely constrained. Soon after I arrived in Gragn
a meeting was called to announce that fertilizer had been allocated to the
service cooperative and every household had to buy 5 *birr*'s worth. Despite
this edict, only half the households used the chemicals on one or two
furrows. Most were suspicious and antagonized by having to pay for
something in which they had little confidence. This was not because they
were unwilling to believe that fertilizers could increase yields, but because
of the bullying involved, and because money was scarce. Furthermore,
given the high possibility of crop failure, the quantity of fertilizer needed
to make a difference to the yield was hardly worth the investment.

Rotation was a common feature of the agricultural system in Menz,
both with regard to which crop was grown on a particular plot, and which
rainy season was used. In particular beans, nitrogen fixers, were never
sown on the same plot twice in succession. Rotations were decided upon
according to the timing of the rains, taking into consideration the
characteristics of the particular plot and consumption needs. To the
uninitiated, the explanations and decisions were difficult to follow. Arega,
for example, told me:

> I have five pieces of land. At the moment one is sown with beans and two
> with wheat. Two have been left for the *belg*. If the *belg* is good, I use it all,
> but this year the *belg* did not come so I planted three of them for the *meher*
> season. If it rains in January, I use the bean land for lentils, otherwise I leave
> it until the next June and alternate it between beans and lentils. It is the *belg*
> that we need.

Land clearing or burning between crops was not practised, although in
the past land was sometimes kept fallow. This is no longer done for more
than one year because of land scarcity. If land was left unploughed, this
was because of rain failure, lack of labour or oxen during the ploughing
season, or a change in use pattern (for example, from the short to the long
rainy season). Most land was sown regularly once and sometimes twice a
year. As with natural fertilizer, the benefits of keeping land fallow were

well known. Nonetheless people had no choice, given land shortage and poor harvests. These conditions were increasingly forcing them into continuous cultivation, and uncultivated land was associated with crop failure. My questions on this subject were often answered with bitter comments such as, 'Do not talk to me about fallow land, it is no longer our choice, we are forced by these conditions to keep *all* our lands fallow!'

Terracing, though a long-established practice in parts of highland Ethiopia, was not much practised in Gragn, respondents suggesting that, unlike areas in the immediate vicinity, the land in Gragn was not steep enough to require it. Some plots were terraced by *sira zemecha* campaign labour, soon after the revolution, and a revival of terracing initiated by the Ministry of Agriculture to reduce soil erosion seemed to be under way just before the end of my fieldwork. At the same time the practice of bunding, to reduce gully formation, was also being introduced. Irrigation of crops was also known in Ethiopia, but rarely practised in the area. Where it existed, it amounted to hand-watering of vegetable plots and tree seedlings, both those of individuals and those grown communally by the peasants' and women's associations.

The land of a Gragn household was rarely all in one place. As mentioned previously, a household's land could be subdivided into as many as thirteen plots. Given the limited size of land holdings, this degree of fragmentation seemed to be a problem, and indeed increased the work involved in taking the oxen to the plots which required ploughing, and decreased the amount of time likely to be given to each piece of land. At the national level, the extent of land fragmentation was seen by agriculturalists, economists and planners as a severe constraint.[6]

However, to the question 'would you prefer your lands to be less fragmented?' only 27 per cent of my interviewees said they would. The vast majority preferred their land to remain fragmented, because of the benefits to be derived from micro-ecological variations in soils and climate. Indeed, even among those who voiced a preference for less fragmentation, the reason given was that they were getting old and tired, and they conceded that otherwise it was safer to have the land in as many different plots as possible. Fragmentation was preferred both to maximize the chances of obtaining some kind of harvest, and for diversification in good years, since some plots were more suited to certain crops. A policy such as land consolidation would not be appreciated in a community like Gragn – another example of how 'progressive' notions can be vulnerable to local critiques.

In Menz, the record of impoverishment was stamped on everything and everyone, and not least on crop cultivation trends. Mammo and Ishetu explained their troubles as follows:

What can I tell you, you see the way we are. . . . We are poorer now. Before, in good years, I would harvest 15 to 20 sacks [1 sack = approximately 1/2 quintal], now little more than one sack. Even if you have the land it is useless.

Only in '79 [1987] did we have some respite. Still, '77 [1985, the drought year] has not cleared up, it has not let us go. In '80 [1988] there wasn't even enough for the livestock. First not enough rain, and then too much when it was time to harvest. I harvested only three sacks of barley, no wheat or lentils.

Almost everyone had painful stories to tell. At the aggregate level, the responses to my questionnaires allow a comparison between a good and a bad year, in terms of the amount of land sown and the yield. For the crops of the short and long rains, the aggregate data suggest that although in a bad year only 14 per cent less land was sown, the harvest was around 80 per cent lower.[7] The fact that the difference between good and bad years was mainly visible in terms of yield shows that the problem was one of rainfall rather than constraints at the time of ploughing and sowing. In a bad year, most people planted, but had little to show for it; the loss was therefore also one of investment in grain and labour. The summary data also suggest that the difference in yield between a favourable scenario and reality in 1988 was a factor of five. Even in a good year the harvest was insufficient to cover nutritional needs, let alone other household expenses. In a bad year, it could only support a household for a few months and, increasingly, other income-earning activities and aid had become crucial.

The population saw the plight of Menz first and foremost as the outcome of rain failure and land degradation. However, there were a number of other hazards to which land was susceptible. During the period of research, the barley suffered from an infestation of worms which were said to appear under dry conditions. When the rains did come they were torrential, leading to flash floods and the loss of harvested grain for those who had piled up their grain near river banks. Most households also found that the rains started when the *belg* crop was ripe but had not yet been harvested, resulting in much of the crop sprouting. This grain was used for beer, but could not easily be made into *injera* (when it was, the taste was disliked). The reasons behind crop failure were numerous: to mention one last one, bean crops could fail because of one night's frost.

Some households were undoubtedly richer than others, though the degree of stratification was considerably less than in the past. Before the revolution the difference between rich and poor could be measured in hundreds of sacks, now it was less than a factor of ten. To this, however, had to be added new sources of stratification, such as uneven access to aid and other services associated with greater state penetration.

Livestock and grazing land

Livestock has always been a key element of the economy in the mixed-farming systems of northern Ethiopia. Moreover, it could be argued that the importance of livestock increased as a consequence of the closer control exerted by the revolutionary state after the land reform. Land was redistributed, livestock not. The state collectivization of land was conceived of as the first stage of cooperativization, that of livestock only at a subsequent, higher level of collectivization. Independently, the role of livestock in subsistence strategies increased because of poor crop cultivation. It is nevertheless important to stress the close relationship between crops and livestock in the production system. Livestock need to be fed from land and its products; land needs to be cultivated with livestock. The dung of the livestock fertilizes the land and the yield from the land is threshed using livestock.

The discussion below will focus on grazing and access to fodder. However, the issue of animal care is considerably more complex. Apart from feeding and drinking, there is the general care of livestock. In all these activities a sexual division operates, one in which women participate fully in the work, but only very partially in ownership and rights. In this sphere of work, tasks are not rigidly allocated, although, where there are men and women in a household, most of the dirty work is generally done by women. There were four sources of fodder available to households: private pasture lands, direct feeding of stubble after the harvest in which private crop land became communal pasture, private fodder from harvested crops, and communal pasture lands.[8] Each of these will be discussed in turn.

At the time of the land reform, most households were allocated small grass plots as well as significantly larger agricultural plots. In Gragn, according to the peasants' association secretary's estimates, the grass plots could be up to 450 square metres, with an average of 100 square metres. This land was divided into as many as 12 different plots, though the mean was about three per household. Those without livestock rented out the plots informally, or allowed the grass to grow, and then cut and sold it. The second source of pasture was from agricultural land after the crop had been harvested. There was general acceptance that anybody was free to take their livestock to graze on such land, which provided additional fodder from the stubble that remained on the ground.

The third form, the feeding of livestock from the chaff of one's own crop, provided a greater contribution. More importantly, it was a source of fodder which could be stored for use when necessary, though in practice the shortages were such that many households often ran out of cattle feed. We have already seen that the barley crop was sometimes weeded for fodder. Cattle can eat the chaff from all harvests, whereas smaller livestock cannot digest the chaff from wheat and barley and were therefore fed from the remains of other crops such as lentils and beans. The husks and chaff were generally stored in two different piles from which they were fed, as required, to the different forms of livestock by both men and women. Again, households without livestock could use their chaff as a source of income.

In the cases mentioned so far, grazing tended to be a private household affair. Exactly who did the herding depended on the household's composition. If there was a young child above the age of about nine, male or female, this child was likely to be responsible at least for the sheep and/or goats. If there were several children, they would take turns or herd together. Larger livestock generally needed the supervision of an older person. During much of the year, men were likely to shoulder half the burden of looking after the livestock, husband and wife arranging to herd on alternative days. However, sometimes the burden fell more heavily on the woman and this was often a source of bitterness and quarrels. I once heard one woman remark to another: 'There are two things I hate in this world. Herding and water.' The reference to water, she explained, arose from a fear of crossing rivers because of the deadly flash floods in the rainy season, and because of the daily drudgery of collecting water. However, it was the first part of her remark that the listener picked up, and the conversation developed into a more general complaint about herding.

Often households with livestock, but lacking the necessary labour, would lease out their animals to other households in a clientage scheme known as *ribbï*. Under this system, the livestock owner and the livestock herder divided equally all offspring produced during the period, and usually half the wool shorn from the sheep. According to responses to my questionnaire, 18 per cent of the sample said that they were looking after the livestock of others and 12 per cent claimed that someone looked after their livestock under a *ribbï* system.

Finally, there was the *Gwassa* land, which constituted one of two communal pasture areas in Menz. If they so desired, all 42 peasants' associations in Menz could come and graze their livestock on *Gwassa* and *Amed Gwaya*, the pasture land more distant from Gragn. In practice, it was usually the adjacent peasants' associations which regularly used the area. The estimate by the Ministry of Agriculture for the *Gwassa* area in Menz was 30,000 hectares. The Ministry also estimated that in 1989 around 15,000 cattle, 50,000 sheep and 5000 equines were brought to graze there. The *Gwassa* was highly appreciated, as made clear by such comments as: 'the *Gwassa* is vital to our livestock, we cannot live without it.'

From October to July, cattle, pack animals, sheep and goats were taken there if possible. Some households, however, always kept their donkeys, horses and mules at home since pack animals were often needed, especially before the long rains, to carry brushwood for fuel or grass for thatching. In addition, during ploughing or threshing time oxen and other livestock would be returned to the homestead, and cows that could be milked were also kept at home.

The *Gwassa* had been a communal pasture area as long as people could remember. However, there was a legend that told of times when it was prime agricultural land.

The *Gwassa* area used to be the best *t'eff* land in the region [*t'eff (Eragrostis-teff)*, is the favoured grain in much of Ethiopia]. A monk called Ch'é Yohanis [or Abba Tséhos, depending on source] used to live in the area. He was a very good and wise person, who took his duties seriously and would give blessings, right across the land, always arriving on time and then rushing off for his next appointment. Once upon a time, a woman gave birth claiming that she bore the child from the monk, who was supposed to be celibate. She swore in front of him and others that he was the father of her child, adding; 'Let me turn to stone if I tell a lie'. Even as she was swearing, she was transformed into stone. The monk, not satisfied with this act of retribution, and angry with the populace for believing her, abandoned the area with a curse saying: 'Let this land turn cold and bleak for evermore, and the rich *t'eff* land become scrub.' As he spoke the weather changed, and the *t'eff* land became the present day *Gwassa* scrub-land.

Many years after the curse had reduced the area to poverty, the elders of the land decided to beg for mercy and forgiveness. They searched far and wide for the monk, but heard that he had long since died. It was then decided to search for his body and, in due course, some shepherds found his bones. These were unearthed and reburied in the *Gwassa*, in the hope that the monk's spirit would take pity on them. The bones were reburied near Firkuta Kïdan Mihret a long time ago, but the land has remained under the curse. It is also said that while the bones were being transported, a drop of blood fell to the ground from the skeleton. At that place, near Welde Ch'erech'er's homestead, there is now a tall fir tree. The wind picks up whenever someone touches the tree.

The story portrays the *Gwassa* land as a bleak and unwanted curse. It is a parable about poverty and its rationalization through self-blame. The more prevalent attitude to the area was that it was a valuable source of pasture. In the past, in the times of *rist* tenure rights, there used to be a stratified and rigid system of rights of access, and an annual *Gwassa* tax of 3 *birr* at a time when the land tax was 7 *birr*. Then, as now, access would sometimes be prohibited for a while to allow the grass to recover. It was suggested several times that in the past restrictions would only be imposed in times of plenty, when people had enough husks from their crops to supplement their private grass plots. At the beginning of my research, people were banned for a couple of months from sending their livestock to the area. The Ministry of Agriculture aimed to control and reduce the rate of scrub and grass depletion. This occurred because of drought and fodder shortages, resulting in increased reliance on the communal pasture, but also because of the sudden demand for new thatch as a result of the Villagization Campaign. The policy was later dropped in response to pleas from the population through the local leadership. Just before I left, there were rumours that the restriction was being reintroduced as a temporary measure, and talk about fencing off some of the area, perhaps in connection with a UNICEF sheep-breeding project.

From time immemorial, grazing had been carried out communally, under a rota system, called *Gwassa tera*. Ten to 20 people joined together and usually two people took turns to look after the joint livestock, lots being drawn once a year. The sheep and goat rota was usually separate from the cattle rota. However, sheep needed more guarding against attacks by hyenas and jackals, and many households preferred to keep sheep and goats outside the *Gwassa* area, for as long as possible. The amount of time each person spent at the *Gwassa* depended on the number of livestock they had; usually it was one night per head of large livestock or five sheep/goats. People often stayed out for two nights at a time, taking some cooked food with them. Once in their teens, boys could, and usually did, take their father's place. If someone failed to turn up they were fined bread and beer or 2 *birr*, paid to the person who had to remain for an extra night.

Households with only small amounts of stock were likely not to bother entering the *Gwassa tera*, and used family labour and grass nearer at hand. Of those questioned, around three-quarters had joined a *Gwassa tera* although there were times when part, or all, their livestock would be kept at home and needed daily attention. Only men were involved in the *Gwassa tera*, and the idea of women going there was found hilarious and preposterous. In practice, this meant that households without adult men were excluded from a free and relatively abundant form of pasture. Very often such households kept their livestock with a relative who had the required form of labour.

There were thus four different forms of pasture and fodder available to households: very small amounts of private grass land, free grazing after the harvest on agricultural land, fodder from chaff together with weeds from the bean crop and, finally, communal *Gwassa* land. The forms of pasture available led to complementary strategies. Which one was used depended on the season, the type of livestock, their condition, and the type of labour available to the household. Herding was usually a private occupation carried out by a member of the household. The exception was in the *Gwassa* case, where it was communally organized, with people taking turns and staying away for a couple of days to look after the joint herd.

Livestock were of vital importance to survival, a source of both investment and consumption. The economy was complex, with different types of animals and various requirements at specific times. The attention of all members of the household tended to be required, and nowhere was the unity or disunity of the household more clearly apparent than in the arrangements made to ensure that livestock were cared for, while at the same time other labour commitments were also fulfilled.

The wool economy

The processing of raw cotton into cloth occurred in many parts of Ethiopia, although increasing availability in the countryside of factory-made cloth decreased the reliance on hand-spun and hand-woven fabrics. In most parts of highland Ethiopia, as in Menz, hand-woven and factory-produced cloth coexisted, with some people preferring one or the other and most wearing both. Factory-produced fabric was often not liked as much as the warmer, traditional, white cloth, though the status of a modern look competed with that of the traditionally correct one. The two differed little in price; home-spun cloth was a little cheaper but the machine-made fabric often lasted longer.

In most households, cotton processing was undertaken for personal use, whereas wool processing also had exchange value. Both were based on very rudimentary technology. Spinning was undertaken by women at the same time as other domestic tasks; weaving, on the other hand, was considered a specialized job and undertaken by a small number of men. It had, however, the craft taboo attached to it.[9] The discussion here concentrates on the wool economy because it was more central to the Menz household economy, and also relatively unusual in Ethiopia.

Tradition holds that wool has long been spun in Menz. In the past, and until a generation or so ago, it was used to make *bernos*, a type of cape made from black wool, worn by the wealthier male population. These are now rarely seen, though the other predominant use as *bana*, blankets, remained a central strategy against the cold, windy and damp conditions characterizing Menz and other highland parts of the country.[10] These *bana* were worn by men and boys as a warmer alternative to the more common cotton *gabï* or *shamma* worn in much of Ethiopia. Some men despised this apparel, preferring factory blankets which were smoother in texture and more colourful. This was particularly the case for the urban population and persons of higher status in the rural communities. Women do not wear *bana*. The reasons given by both men and women were that the material was too coarse for them, and that they preferred cotton shawls. However, at nights and in the huts, the distinction was forgotten, and the whole family could be found buried under as many *bana* as were available.

Sheep were shorn twice a year, around June and November. The shearing from each sheep yielded between a half and two kilos of wool, though improved breeds produced more – up to four kilos in the best conditions. Much of the wool on the market in Menz came from Tegulet in Shewa, and from Welo, rather than from local sheep. It was bought there, shorn by local farmers or, more often, by people from Menz involved in seasonal out-migration. A Menz peasant would sometimes leave his home for about a fortnight, shear 30 or so sheep, and receive half the wool in return for his services, leaving the other half for the sheep-owner to sell, or buying his share, for about 10 *birr*. All the wool would then be sold in Menz for at least 40 *birr*. A growing market for spun wool also derived from the carpet industry, now located almost exclusively in the urban centres, notably Addis Ababa.[11]

Wool preparation was defined as women's work. The first process was picking out the dirt from the wool. The wool was then teased, and beaten to fluff it up, with a *degan*, a simple instrument consisting of two pieces looking like a bow and arrow. Made of wood and gut, the *degan* cost about 1 *birr* and lasted a lifetime. Next, spinning was carried out with a spindle, also costing about 1 *birr*, though its components sometimes need replacement. The woman used her right hand to hold the spindle, rubbing it against her thigh and letting it spin for a moment whilst she held the teased wool with her left hand. Women spent up to 15 days per month, six hours a day, on wool processing, an average of 31 hours a week. Of the fifteen days in the month, around six were for *fato*, separating out the wool, seven days for *fetil*, spinning, and two days for *aker*, winding it up.

Spinning was not carried out on the saints' days honoured by the spinner. These usually numbered about six per month, though there could be as many as thirteen.[12] In addition, Saturdays and Sundays were holy days. Most women considered only the spinning as disrespectful on holy days, and continued with the rest of the wool preparation, though a few devout women argued that all such activity was unacceptable. Spinning was also the most time-consuming activity of the whole enterprise. After it was completed, the wool was wound into large balls, the separate pieces being knotted together to form a *kub*, or ball. One ball weighed about a kilo. White wool sold at up to 4 *birr*, brown or mixed wool, up to 3 *birr*. The work yielded a profit of between a half and 1 *birr* a kilo. At this stage it was often taken to be sold at the market. When these balls of wool reached the weavers they were wound onto bobbins ready for weaving. The winding was also considered women's work.

Men's work in wool processing consisted of shearing the sheep at the beginning of the process, and then, at the other end, weaving and 'felting' the wool. Far less than half the men in the area were involved, mostly young adults occupied with felting, or shrinking and thus thickening the garment by soaking it in water and stamping on it. Near the rivers, basins were constructed with one side built up into a short wall of stone. The basins retained the water and the walls were used for support as the men trod on the material. A *bana* bought for 20 *birr* could be trodden and sold for up to 26 *birr*. Men were, therefore, likely to receive between 2 and 6 *birr* profit from their labour. It took about two days to felt one *bana*, which was then stretched out, held in place with stones and left to dry; this work ceased during the wet season.

Weavers of the *bana* were fewer than felters but more numerous than cotton weavers. Working with wool was easier and quicker than the more delicate cotton weaving. It took a man less than a day to weave the wool for one *bana*, and he was usually given up to 3 *birr* for the job. One *bana* was 2 by 3.5 metres pre-felting and about 1.5 by 3 metres once felted. It was made from 6 to 8 kilos of wool. The traditional wooden loom cost about 30 *birr*.

When questioned, many men did not admit that they wove. This was partly the consequence of the general taboo against crafts in Amhara society, and the associated beliefs that artisans worked spells and had the evil eye. It was also partly a reflection of the fact that many people only occasionally practised their skills and therefore did not think it worthy of mention. All men involved in some aspect of the wool economy complained that the amount of time they could devote to the work had fallen because of *sira zemecha*, the communal labour discussed in Chapter 3.

Women tended to sell the spun balls directly as a source of income, rather than accumulate them for processing by men into a complete blanket for home use or for sale. The spinners explained that, although the latter option gave the higher profit, households could not afford to wait, since they relied on the weekly income as a source of cash. The women of a household spun half to three kilos a week. They tended to work mixed-colour wool, as it was more readily available, although the profit that could be made from white wool was usually greater. There were various dubious and notorious strategies for stretching the profits made. For example, some women spun parts of the wool very coarsely and hence more quickly, or they increased the weight of the wool by putting it in water, and finally they sometimes hid pieces of stone or un-spun dirty wool in the centre of the woollen balls, thus increasing the weight. The woollen balls were sold at the market in the nearest town, usually at the Saturday market. Adult household members often took turns. However, the decision as to who should go also depended on other considerations, such as health, preference, and work in need of attention on the market day. In general, even when men did the selling, the income was seen as women's.

This was not the case when the *bana* was sold; even when the women had been the main producers, men had control over the larger sum of money. The price of a *bana* was determined by size and colour, and on whether it was trodden or not. A large, white, trodden one could be sold for up to 60 *birr*. The minimum cost of an untrodden mixed-colour *bana* was about 18 *birr*. A pure black one lay somewhere in between. If used on the bed a *bana* lasted about ten years; if it was worn it lasted about half as long. *Bana* were sold locally, as well as in Welo and further north. The trade in *bana* gained momentum over the last decade. In former times, people made these blankets for themselves, and left the rest of the wool to rot. Now the Menz population are much more involved in making and selling any wool it can acquire. The change appeared to be a reflection of both a gradual impoverishment resulting in the need to look beyond crop production for household survival, and an increased awareness of the market potential of wool production.

Prices of *bana* had doubled over the five years preceding fieldwork, because of an increase in the price of wool and increased payments to weavers and felters. The inflation in unspun wool, however, seemed to be less than that experienced by other goods. For example, the price of sheep in the period tripled and grain prices more than doubled. The cost of goods imported into the area rose sharply, and was associated with the increase in the urban population and a greater involvement in exchange circuits by the peasantry. The relatively low inflation in the cost of wool was probably a reflection of an increase in supply. More wool was coming onto the market as other forms of income were threatened by drought and government policy, and because of the UNICEF sheep-breeding projects. Significantly, however, the profits of the women spinners did not seem to have increased in line with the profits to male labour and the increases in the price of wool, let alone with the higher inflation rates elsewhere in the economy. Explanations are firmly rooted in the position of female labour within this society, as elsewhere, and the unspecialized nature of their skills. The profits that women reaped were declining, yet the wool economy was becoming increasingly more important in supporting a precarious existence.

To conclude, the wool economy was central to Menz, though it was largely invisible at the level of the society. It was a regular form of modest income for most, if not all, women. The work was undertaken at the same time as domestic and reproductive activities, for example while keeping an eye on an infant and on the cooking pot. The income women derived from the work was regular and relatively reliable, in comparison with the income from butter, eggs and young chicks, also considered as women's income, which required initial capital and depended on the animals' reproduction. Though men sometimes sold the wool, it was still perceived as women's money, and the women could exert control over it, especially when sold in the form of woollen balls.

The wool economy was the most flourishing manufacturing sector in the area, and the only one that embraced almost every rural household. It helped to reduce reliance on crop production not only for direct domestic consumption but also to meet exchange and cash requirements. Revenue from wool production was significant in providing money to meet the considerable weekly cost of coffee and other outlays. In general, the local market for spun wool seemed to be reliable, with possibilities for expansion. There was also room for increased sales by diversifying into carpets, and coloured or decorated *bana*. This could, in the future, complement the existing large trade in a rural basic good with a growing trade in a parallel urban luxury market.

In terms of the sexual division of labour, it was clear that men's involvement in crafts, be it wool or cotton processing, was considered a specialized activity which only a few men undertake. Women's involvement, on the other hand, was more general, and though the time spent on the activity was considerable, it was a part-time occupation integrated into the domestic economy. This reflected a general characteristic of the sexual division of labour in the household, namely that female labour covered a greater range of activities than male labour. In one day most men did a fewer number of jobs than women, which suggested that the former were placed on a more specialized terrain, and this in turn, according to economic theory, would suggest that they were able to be more productive in their tasks.

An increase in the productivity gap sometimes emerges with the introduction of modern technology.[13] Here it existed even despite the most rudimentary of technologies. The loom used by men was considerably more advanced than the spindle used by the women, the difference in the costs of the two implements being at least 20-fold. However, it took a much shorter time to learn how to operate the loom than to learn to spin using a spindle. Ironically, weaving is considered a craft and as such has a taboo associated with it, whilst spinning is not considered a craft and is therefore not viewed negatively. Nevertheless, spinning is not highly esteemed either, because of its location in the female sphere of the sexual division of labour.

The dung economy[14]

It is part of conventional wisdom to assume that vocabulary attached to a particular concept expands in proportion with its importance to its population. The example often cited is that of the Inuit Eskimos who have a large array of terms for snow. In the Amharic of Menz there were at least fourteen words for what is called dung or manure in English. These are listed in Table 5.3. The Amharic terms qualify the kind of livestock producing the dung, and the forms in which it is collected and used.[15]

Dung plays a central and complex role in the economy and society of many countries, but has been little studied.[16] No doubt this is because of its connotations, but also because of an unfamiliarity with its usage which makes it invisible, and perhaps also because dung work has a low position in the division of labour and is often seen as women's work.

In Ethiopian society there was an ambivalence in the conception of dung as a whole as well as differences in attitudes to the various kinds of dung. On the one hand it was excrement, considered dirty, and unpleasant to deal with. On the other, it was vital to the rural economy and was used as a metaphor for prosperity.

The role and uses of dung in Gragn were important. The area suffered from a shortage of wood, and dung was therefore the major source of fuel. Dung was also employed in the building of huts, furniture, and other household articles, and was also valued as a fertilizer. These uses were usually complementary to the value of dung as fuel, since ash, the by-product from the burned dung, could be re-used in building and as fertilizer. To some extent, however, dung was also applied directly in building and as fertilizer, in which case these were alternative and therefore conflicting usages. The livestock producing the dung were oxen, cows, horses, mules, donkeys, sheep and goats. Unlike Chinese and other East Asian societies,

Table 5. 3. List of dung terms

• *Azeba*	Wet ox and cow dung
• *Bet'et'*	Wet or dry sheep or goat dung
• *Dirdir*	Dried dung-cakes piled up into a circular stack
• *Fig*	Fine dung-powder of crumbly consistency from sheep and goat, horse, mule and donkey
• *Gelebuna*	Ox and cow dung collected off the ground outside the hut, not made into cakes but left to dry directly
• *Godeda*	Usually sheep and goat dung collected outside the hut in the area where livestock are kept enclosed overnight. The term is sometimes also used for donkey, mule and horse dung dug up from inside the hut
• *Gucho*	The term refers to small wigwam-like stacks of dung, and is also used for the dung itself
• *Ibet*	Similar to *Azeba*
• *K'imit'*	Similar to *Azeba*
• *Kubbet*	General term, usually referring to all dried dung
•*Sheleshel*	Similar to *Gelebuna*
• *T'ibot*	Impure dung which has earth or mud mixed with it
• *T'ift'if* or *T'ift'afo*	Dung cakes made from the dung of all livestock, those made during the rains specified as *yemeher t'ift'if*, long-rains cakes, or *yebelg t'ift'if*, short-rains cakes
• *Fando* or *fandiya*	Wet or dry donkey, horse or mule dung before it has crumbled into *fig*

Amhara society did not utilize human excrement, which was a taboo, 'dirty' topic.

Uses of dung

Fertilizer

In Gragn, dung was employed directly as fertilizer, though its value as such was summarized in the remark that: 'the *k'ollegngna* [lowlanders] practise this and it is good; but for us the need for dung as fuel is too great to be sacrificed.' In other words, survival and consumption needs placed too great a demand on the resource for it to be applied as an investment. However, some dung called *t'ibot* was applied as fertilizer if it had been too contaminated with earth or mud to be used as fuel.

Once the more important fuel needs had been met, most of the dung, in the form of ash, was scattered as fertilizer on the *dej-merét* – the small back-yard plot. This might have been sown with wheat, beans or one of the two kinds of barley, *mawgé* or *ferké* . The *dej-merét* crop was tended carefully, and its yield was estimated to be up to twice that from other land. In addition to the main crop, dung was used as fertilizer for the small quantities of cabbage, garlic and onions that some households planted at the beginning of the long rains. A few households sold some vegetables at the market, in which case the ash may also have gone towards income generation.

Regardless of the fact that in practice dung was not extensively used as fertilizer in Menz, the concept of *fig* dung was retained in the language as synonymous with prosperity[17] – the metaphor being derived from the potential of dung to fertilize the land. The association was particularly strong between *fig* dung and *dej-merét* – the former term being used sometimes to designate the latter.

Building

Huts in this area of the country were stone-walled and thatch-roofed. The walls were constructed by men, preferably using an ash-based plaster between the stones. Internal walls were usually plastered with dung or a mud-ash mixture. Inside the hut, partitions, benches and the fireplace were made and periodically replastered with dung. The floor likewise was smeared with dung.[18] All these activities were performed by women.

Much household furniture and other articles were also made of dung. These included the *akimbalo*, the lid to the *mit'ad,* the large pan used for baking. The *akimbalo* could also be made of clay, but dung ones tended to be preferred as they were lighter and less fragile. Dung combined with hay was also made into bowls, used as containers of wool and grains. Other goods made in this way included the base on which the grinding stones were constructed, *wefch'o*, and two sizes of grain stores, *dibignit* and *rik'*. The construction of most of these articles was considered women's work, the only exception being the larger grain stores, the *rik'*, which were sometimes considered too high and difficult for women to construct.

Fuel

Dung was the main source of fuel and therefore had use value in the household economy. Dung was also of exchange value when sold by households that had a surplus. The attributes of the different types of dung were taken into account in its usage. Thus, for slow and lengthy cooking, such as when making *shiro* sauce, dung cakes were preferred as they produced a low but constant heat, did not require much looking after, and were relatively economical. On the other hand *injera*, a pancake-like bread, required a stronger heat over a shorter period of time, for which the loose bits, *fig* and *godeda*, were preferred. When *dabbo*, a large, thick piece of bread, was baked, low but constant heat was required, both underneath the pan and on top of the lid, on which burning pieces of dung were placed, the heat thus being evenly distributed and forming a type of oven. Here *t'ift'afo* was a useful form of dung, while *fig* and *godeda* were not at all appropriate.

Finally, the fire was usually kept burning overnight. To ensure that the embers did not die, the ideal combination was first *fig*, then *godeda*, and finally a layer of *t'ift'if*. Should her fire burn out, a woman would light it again by going, or sending a child, to a neighbour, with two broken pieces of *t'ift'if* for scooping up and carrying the embers.

However, dung was rarely used exclusively as fuel since people had access to other sources. Expeditions went to the *Gwassa* highlands to collect brushwood (*ch'irinfé*), or to *k'olla* lowland areas where there was a greater quantity of wood, or twigs, that could be gathered and brought home. Locally, there was some *kochelé*, a type of cactus, and some people had or bought wood, leaves and seeds of the eucalyptus which could grow in the area but was in short supply.

The combination adopted by a household depended on:

- ownership or access to different types and quantities of livestock, and location, in particular whether they were brought home at night or herded in the Gwassa area;
- supply of labour, in particular whether it was male or female. Men were considered able to travel greater distances and were therefore more involved in Gwassa brush collection, while women were more involved in dung collection;
- season, the rainy seasons being difficult times for the collection of all fuel, but of dung in particular;
- ownership of wood and cacti. Any such supplies were likely to reduce dependence on dung;
- household preference. This varied, though in general households preferred to use wood rather than dung, the latter being looked down upon because it smelled and produced acrid smoke. Some people, if they could afford it, made the switch to wood and brush when guests arrived, or for special occasions, such as *mehaber*, a traditional rotating social and religious gathering discussed in Chapter 8.

In the recent past, wealthy households would have a sizeable number of livestock: two oxen, a cow and calf, a horse or mule, two donkeys and up to fifty sheep. These households would build up to three dung stores known as 'holes' (discussed later), the number of which was a sign of economic standing. Such households would often have additional labour, male and female, increasing their ability to release labour from other tasks for wood and dung collection. They were also likely to have planted eucalyptus trees as a source of fuel and timber and as an investment. When a household had a surplus of dung-cakes, the dung was not thereby released for use as fertilizer. Dung-cakes continued to be made and were often sold in June, just before the long rains, at which time those without reserves would be stocking up for the rainy months. Rich households had the luxury of a choice of fuel, yet the scarcity of fuel in the society resulted in dung being reserved for use as fuel rather than as fertilizer. The pattern was therefore one in which even those who had a choice decided against invest-ment in the soil in favour of conversion into dung-cakes, a more reliable and liquid asset.

Poorer households were most reliant on dung. This was, firstly, because they were less likely to have their own stocks of wood; secondly, because if they had to buy fuel, dung was cheaper than wood; and, thirdly, because they were less able to afford days of labour used in expeditions to *k'olla* or *Gwassa* areas in search of wood.[19] However, poor households were also less likely to have their own livestock, sometimes having none at all, more often having one large animal (ox, cow, horse, mule, or donkey) and a couple of sheep. Such households therefore had less access to dung. Some households solved this problem by looking after the livestock of others under the *ribbï* patronage arrangement discussed previously, under which the livestock-minder was usually given total rights over the dung. Others were likely to spend more time picking *sheleshel* dung in the vicinity, or collecting half-dried *kubbet* dung which they brought home and made into cakes, and all maximized the use of the dung from whatever livestock they had.

Preparation

Dung was gathered and prepared in different ways. It was picked up from the land surrounding the homestead, from a wider area of land in the vicinity, or from land further afield by girls, women, young boys and even, though rarely, by men. The dung from the larger forms of livestock was taken back to the hut and stored either directly or after drying in the sun. It was not processed in any other way. The collection of dung from the homestead or vicinity was a relatively easy and spontaneous activity, while gathering from further afield was a greater enterprise involving more planned allocation of time. Collection of dung from the *Gwassa*, the pasture area discussed earlier, was rarely undertaken by itself, though very occasion-ally young boys and men combined it with the gathering of *ch'irinfé*, brushwood. A spatial consideration thus entered into the sexual division of labour and fuel types. Dung accessible nearby was gathered by women and formed the primary source of fuel. Dung from a considerable distance was rarely collected and, if so, usually by young men. Men in turn focused more on the collection of brushwood, a more distant and secondary contribution to the provision of fuel.

Dung produced during the night from a household's livestock was taken out of the hut daily, to be patted into dung-cakes approximately 30 centimetres in diameter and 2 centimetres thick. These cakes were left to dry on each side. Women, often the young girls in the family, were involved in this task. When it was taken out of the hut, some of the sheep and goat dung, which consisted of small droppings, tended to remain embedded in the floor. Men were periodically asked to dig this up which they did with a pick or axe. Depending on its consistency, this dung was called *fig* or *godeda*, and when burnt produced particularly strong heat.

The drying of dung and making of cakes had to be interrupted during the long rains, June to September, but also to a lesser extent during the more unpredictable short rains, which tended to begin around February and finish in April. The strategy adopted at this time was to collect the dung in *gudgwad*, holes in the ground about one metre deep by one metre wide, the sides of which were reinforced by a stone wall. They were dug within, or just outside, the compound and the manure was thrown in daily.

After the end of the long rains, and usually on a Saint's Day, the hole was 'opened'. This event was important and set the scene for a traditional type of communal labour, mainly carried out by women. Groups of people started by discussing when the openings should take place and households then picked their preferred day. Several households in one neighbourhood often opened their dung-holes on the same day, although neighbours and friends arranged to take turns at their opening so that they could help each other. Well beforehand, the women began brewing beer. On the day, the woman in charge of the household, or some other woman in the family, called female relatives, neighbours and friends, and then returned to the hut to prepare some food. Meanwhile the women who were summoned would arrive, making a team of up to ten people.

Some of the women began by bringing water to the hole where the dung was trodden. The treading took place inside the hole and was carried out by a man from the household. He entered the hole and started working the dung with his feet, loosening it up. Water was added as necessary, to soften the dung's consistency, and to make it more malleable. As this was done, the dung was thrown out and piled beside the hole, whence a woman would take it to a patch of grass nearby, pat it into a cake and then repeat the process. As the cakes were made, they were spread out, left to dry for a few days on each side, and then piled up inside the house or outside it, where they were often covered with thatch.

Once the work was done the labourers partook of the feast prepared for the occasion. Eating and drinking took place amidst a lot of joking and fun, and it was not unusual for other guests to be asked to join in the merry-making. The dung-opening day was considered quite an occasion, marked by considerable comment and conversation before, during and after the event. Its importance was surprising in that all work connected with dung was considered to be of low status, and was described as 'dirty' work, which people would rather avoid doing. Even on this occasion it was the less important people who did most of the 'dung' work.[20] Importance was here defined primarily in terms of age and gender, but it was also a question of status or wealth, and some of the discussion surrounding the event focuses on who was found to be treading, and making the cakes.

The events described above were those associated with the end of the long rains. There was less ceremony attached to dung collection during the short rains. In this season, the hole was opened several times, whenever the rain stopped for a few days, and the women of the household made the cakes without the help of others. If the short rains were prolonged, people started using their stocks of dried dung. However, they were reluctant to deplete their reserves, which should be kept for the long rains. During the rains, it became difficult to collect and then dry the dung. In fact, this was the season when people were most likely to search for alternatives.

To conclude, in Gragn peasants' association as in many other parts of the country, there was a severe wood shortage. Dung was, therefore, reserved primarily for fuel. However, wood was preferred to dung because of the latter's smell, smoke and negative associations. There would be an increase in welfare if afforestation produced a sufficient amount of wood to allow people to switch to wood as their source of fuel, in accordance with consumer preference. There would also be some value in increased afforestation to the extent that the switch of fuel from dung to wood would release dung for other uses, in building and as fertilizer. The use of dung in building would result in the production of articles that were more durable and therefore of better value. Moreover, were dung to be used in greater quantities as fertilizer, this would lead to an increase in income through increased crop productivity. The prevailing situation was one in which dung was used for consumption rather than being invested or used in the improvement of capital goods.

Trade

Though the role of the bi-weekly markets in town had undoubtedly increased over the years, much of the trading that took place in Menz, whether within or between communities, occurred outside the market place. Trading exchanges were more diffuse in time and space, and for the most part invisible to the outsider. The tendency of observers to focus on the market place therefore means that they are ignoring a significant amount of formal and informal exchange that characterizes the Amhara peasant economy. The Mengistu government, however, tended to ignore even the market place, seen as a backward practice to be superseded by more 'modern' and 'rational' forms of exchange, such as the service cooperative shops.

Every household was involved in some trade and both consumption and production needs were increasingly met by an involvement in exchange circuits. Salt and *berberé*, the ubiquitous spice, and coffee had to be bought regularly. In addition, there were occasional expenses on some other foods, grains and manufactured goods such as needles, razor blades, kerosene, matches, cloth, shoes, and even the DDT with which to spray flea-infested homes. Non-monetary exchanges were transacted also within and between communities. Anything could be bartered, ranging from dung-cakes to raw wool, from an *injera* to an ox, from a few coffee beans to a bottle of *arek'i*.

These consumption needs were met by selling something or by digging into previously earned cash. Usually women were involved in the former, men in the latter source of finance. Thus men tended to sell livestock and return home with a considerable amount of cash. The household would then gradually use up the money on weekly expenses, either the wife or the husband actually going to market. Women tended to be more involved in small-scale exchanges, the selling of home-spun wool, eggs, or a small quantity of grain, in order to meet regular household needs. Various payments to the state – taxes, levies, and membership fees – were all paid in cash and were thus met through involvement in trade. Production needs were also increasingly met through the market. These included buying or repairing tools and agricultural implements.

The trade mentioned above entailed ongoing expenses which were considerable for the individuals involved, though they appear marginal when compared with a peasantry involved in cash-crop production. At this point I should like to return to comments made in Chapter 2, when it was suggested that an uneasy relationship between subsistence and exchange might be an underlying cause of poverty. I argued there that the term subsistence had two meanings which were related, the first implying a lack of involvement in exchange, and thus self-sufficiency, the second implying an existence on the margin, or having just enough to survive. The Menz peasantry has been experiencing a long-term impoverishment, jeopardizing their self-sufficiency. As mentioned above, the daily needs of the peasantry in terms of consumption (the word being used in its economic context – spending for immediate use rather than savings or investment) necessitated an involvement in trade. This involvement was increasing in magnitude and the costs seemed to be rising along with a decrease in the relative terms of trade between manufactured and some agricultural produce, such as coffee, and the locally produced agricultural goods. More fundamentally, the population was facing growing difficulties in producing enough to consume, let alone enough to find something to sell, hence the important role of women, described earlier in this chapter, in processing exchange value. However, the very inability to produce enough to feed one's own household meant that, with increasing frequency, something had to be sold in order to buy the basic foods – barley and beans.

As a way of coping with the agricultural shortfall in their own production, or, less dramatically, as a way of supplementing their resources, some households became more actively involved in trade circuits. Thus some took part in the retail marketing of sheep, buying them in Gishe, the northernmost part of Menz, and selling them in Mehal Meda or even as far away as Addis Ababa for a higher price. The 'socialist' government of Mengistu attempted to control these entrepreneurial activities by demanding that those involved should take out trading licences. In practice, many peasants continued in the trade, operating without licences. Those with less capital but an equal enthusiasm for such ventures tended to trade in grain and vegetables. They took some of their own crops or bought highland crops, transporting them down to the lowlands where they fetched a better price. They then returned with goods which were comparatively more expensive in the highlands. These were then sold or stored for future use. Examples included exchanges of beans, barley or lentils from the highlands for onions or sorghum from the lowlands.

In Gragn, as elsewhere, there was a category of women who earned money by selling alcoholic drinks. Some women were known as brewers of *arek'i*, a barley spirit, or *t'ella*, local beer. They either sold the drink locally, retail (a glass at a time) or wholesale (a bottle at a time), or took it to sell in town. Another group of women, usually those without the capital and/or distillation equipment, bought the *arek'i* from others, sometimes even from town, and sold it from their homes which became drinking houses. Female heads of households and married women alike were involved in this trade.

Poverty and the increasing precariousness of conditions is a constant theme in this chapter, reference to the deteriorating situation being necessary in each section, and each component of the household economy. Nevertheless, indebtedness was not as common as before the revolution. In my sample, only 28 per cent of households were in debt at the time of the interview.[21] Explanations for the reduction in indebtedness lay partly in reduced stratification as a result of the land reform. However, as we have already seen, households were far from being equal. The relatively low figures of indebtedness was a reflection of absolute poverty, of the economic difficulties of even the comparatively well-off, rather than the absence of social stratification.

To recapitulate, the household economy in Gragn at first sight looked as if it stood alone, reliant on its own production for its consumption. In practice, this was far from being the case. Undoubtedly, some households were more self-sufficient than others, but because domestic production and trading relations were so intricately interlinked, it was not always clear when or why some categories of people were trading in a particular good. To give but one example, people both at the poorer and at the richer end of the wealth spectrum might be seen trading more than those of average means. At the richer end, the ability to trade was a reflection of the ability to make choices about different forms of consumption or production; at the poorer end, the greater involvement in trade was a reflection of the inability to provide for subsistence, in both meanings of the term.

Before concluding, a comparison can be made between the extent of state penetration and the penetration of the market. This may be done in the context of the debates about the African peasantry in the literature.

Hyden's[22] presentation of a peasantry independent of the state and capitalist forces because it operates through cultural patterns of obligation within the community, through what he calls the economy of affection, fails to portray the situation in Menz. As we have seen, people attempted to minimize the costs of state actions whilst also taking advantage of any beneficial policies. There is thus an element of reciprocity in the relationship. The inhabitants were also minimally involved in some, but not all, forms of trade, primarily because they had little to sell. The key to understanding the subordination, and the extent and kind of actions in which the peasantry were involved, lies in the relationship between them and both the state and the market.[23]

With regard to crop cultivation, neither state nor market exerted a major influence, though the state attempted, generally unsuccessfully, to improve production through the provision of extension services. The peasantry in Menz was nevertheless involved in cash-raising activities, predominantly through the livestock economy, in order to meet consumption needs and pay state duties. The influence of market and state alike was significant both negatively, as an added burden in meeting consumption needs, and positively, as safety nets, providing a way out when subsistence production failed (the state distributing aid, trade providing a way through which capital goods could be sold to buy grain). In addition, some individuals within the society were linked into a long-distance trading circuit, while some were more centrally involved in the state apparatus. However, those involved in the long-distance trading circuits were on the whole unofficial players, since government policy in the period under review was to discourage or at least tax entrepreneurial activities. The parallel between the extent of state and market penetration and conflicts between involvement in these two spheres is useful in describing a peasantry essentially going its own way, yet, sometimes to its detriment and sometimes to its advantage, inescapably bound to external forces.

Conclusion

In this chapter attention was given both to the sexual division of labour, and to the material conditions under which the community strove to survive. The core of the argument is that there is more to production than the crop cultivation which most observers tend to focus on. Thus the importance of livestock, with the associated fuel and wool economies, and the involvement of the household in trade were documented at length. Dung was seen as the dominant source of fuel; the spinning of wool as a regular income; and, for some wealthier households, butter and eggs as a more occasional revenue. Concomitantly, women's economic contribution was shown to be in numerous 'other' spheres, beyond the agricultural work symbolized by plough and ox.

A woman's life was once described to me by a woman as *'yedoro nuro'*, 'a chicken's life'. The analogy operates at a number of levels. In contrast with men's involvement in the wider world, the life of most women unfolds in the homestead, like that of chickens. Unlike all other forms of livestock taken to pasture lands or given fodder, chickens have to scrounge around for food and look after themselves. Similarly, women fetch their own water, and make their own meals, whilst the menfolk are fed and given drink. At the symbolic level, chickens are ritually slaughtered to celebrate childbirth; women's blood discharged during delivery and the chickens' blood jointly result in the taboo against most people entering the hut for the first three days after delivery. Chickens, like women, are considered as smaller and of lower value, once again unlike the larger forms of livestock, and their contribution to the household economy is not acknowledged by men and external agents who laugh at the suggestion that they should be.[24]

The role of women in the domestic economy helps to explain their position in the household and society. On the one hand, there is a tendency, by both men and women, to dismiss and belittle women's work. The menial tasks they are allocated in the sexual division of labour, for example their involvement in dung work, reinforces the social devaluation of their labour. On the other hand, this social attitude is belied by the consciousness of women's economic contribution and their paramount importance to the running of the household on a day-to-day basis.

This chapter has examined the work that people do, and the valuation of this work both from within the society and by policy makers working from outside. Underlying the ethnographic details was the theme that activities which are central to the economy are not necessarily perceived as such. In the case of the livestock and wool economies, devaluation was essentially an external phenomenon and despite their importance to the household economy, the state had not directly participated in them. In the case of the dung work, as in many other activities in the female sphere of the sexual division of labour, devaluation started within the community. The need to distinguish between social and real or economic valuation, and the need to take heed of activities beyond cultivation, has theoretical, methodological and substantive relevance beyond this particular case study.

Notes

1 These figures and other quantitative data are from my questionnaires; see Appendix C for the raw data.
2 The total number of *t'ind* plots were added up and the *belg* was taken as a percentage of the total. The calculations were made for the 1988 crop (a bad year), and a good year's crop separately, the figure in the text being an average of these two figures.
3 Examples of the same trend could also be given for trees. The flat pan used in making bread and *injera* was greased using oil extracted from the seeds of a tree which used to grow wild. Several respondents in the area commented that these no longer grew naturally, and that they were obliged to purchase these, or other seeds used for the same purpose, in town.
4 Lentils, however, cannot be relied upon. People say of this pulse, *libs yelewim,* 'it does not have clothes', meaning that the pod is very thin and can therefore easily be damaged by excessive water and frost.
5 Harris, 1844; Parkyns, 1868.
6 E.g., Fassil Gebre Kiros, 1980.

7 The difference in plots sown was between 722 and 619, whereas the yield difference was between 2821 and 560.

8 In the past the pattern in much of northern Shewa was one in which cultivation plots were redistributed, whilst pasture lands were maintained in common within the descent lineage, McCann, 1984: 23. This pattern of private use of cultivation plots and communal use of pasture lands was not altered by the land reform.

9 I return to this point in the section on *buda* and spirit beliefs in Chapter 8.

10 Harris, a traveller in the mid-nineteenth century, noted: 'This fabric ... furnishes a costume indispensable in so rigorous a climate, where the bleak unsheltered hills, swept by a cutting easterly wind, rank among the coldest portions of Abyssinia', Harris, 1844, II: 348.

11 There is also a small urban market for white wool *bana* that are then embroidered, for example, with a lion motif and a geometrical design on the borders.

12 Lideta, Abbo, Hanna, Mikaél, Egziéram, Kidane Miret, Gebriél, Maryam, Giorgïs, Tekle Haymanot, Medhané Alem, Ammanuél, Bale Weld. See Chapter 8 for further discussion of the religious influence on work.

13 For example, Boserup, 1970: 213.

14 An earlier and longer version of this section has been published under the same title, see Bibliography.

15 I translated parts of this section, which I had written up for a conference, to a couple of my women friends in the village. Both laughed, and, when I had finished, one commented: 'That is right, you have written well, it is only chicken droppings that you have left out.'

16 My thanks to Patricia Jeffery for alerting me to the issue early on in my research. See Jeffery, *et al*, 1989.

17 Several years after the great rinderpest epidemic of 1888–9, which resulted in large-scale cattle mortality, Emperor Menilek arranged for the re-introduction of livestock in some of the worst affected areas. People came from afar in search of animals which were, however, in very short supply. Some of the famine victims, unable to obtain any cattle, are said to have picked up dung, and taken it back to their homesteads. It seemed, according to chronicler Gebre Selassie, the 'sweetest of scents'. See R. Pankhurst, 1966 (b).

18 In some areas of Menz, though not in Gragn, the threshing floor outside the compound was smoothed out with a layer of dung. This is again women's work.

19 The assumption here is that poor households are often poor in labour as well as in land and capital. This is usually most visible in the case of young or elderly small units, i.e., households at the beginning and at the end of the demographic cycle.

20 The sexual division of labour within dung processing accords the few men that are involved a degree of ceremony and reward since they are the ones primarily involved in the opening of the hole. Also, there is perhaps a distinction between their work in treading, which they do primarily using their feet, and women's work using their hands.

21 Sample size, 90, of whom 66 were not indebted to an average of 40 *birr*, see Appendix C for questions asked. Writing just before the revolution about a community in Tigray, Bauer, 1973, gave a figure of 57 per cent of households indebted to the richest 8 per cent.

22 Hyden, 1980, 1983.

23 See Kasfir, 1986, for a critique of Hyden which develops this argument.

24 The equivalence has also been noted in other societies, thus O'Laughlin's study, 1974, suggests that the food taboos prohibiting Mbum women from eating chicken arise from a similar equivalence of women and chicken which functions to ensure male privilege.

6

Careering
Through Marriage

Because women are one-sidedly viewed as the objects of marriage, their contributions, strategies, risks and rewards as makers and breakers of marriages
are unexamined. Until we begin to consider women as individuals with their
own economic interests and strategies, our theories will remain deficient.[1]

This chapter is concerned with marriage, divorce, remarriage and single
households. Why do women and men seek certain kinds of marriages?
Why divorce? Why so many remarriages? What is the position of single
and female-headed households? What are the trends and changes? What
do we learn about the question of power and rights across generations and
between spouses in the past and the present? The data lead to questions
about the rationale behind people's decisions.

The marital histories of friends in Gragn are puzzling because they
portray a situation which is a far cry from the primacy accorded to questions
of kinship and lineage in the anthropological literature on African
marriages.[2] These histories are also intriguing in their complexity, and
neither the trends nor the practices are easily unravelled at any point in
time. The wide choice of behaviour in, for example, the kinds of marriage
seems surprising. It is not immediately evident whether the overall
complexity is a function of a wide choice of situations experienced at
different stages by individuals, or whether the variations arise from the
aggregation of people with different experiences, or both.

Underlying the empirical detail of this chapter is an attempt to provide
explanations of the ethnographic data in terms of gender relations and
trends since the revolution. Given the complexity of the scene, it is only in
the last section that I concentrate on so doing. First the data show the
variety of considerations pertinent to marital histories.

Types of marriage

Marriages in Menz, and other parts of Ethiopia, can be divided into the
following six types:

- *Serg*, ceremonial marriage
- *K'urban*, religious marriage
- *Semanya*, civil marriage
- *K'ot'assir*, marriage preceded by provision of labour

- *Gered* or *demoz,* paid labour marriage
- *T'ilf,* marriage by abduction

The categories are far from rigid and conceptually not very satisfactory, as will become clear. They obscure distinctions between, differences within, and similarities across categories. In the course of interviews it quickly became apparent that, even with in-depth life histories, many marriages could not easily be fitted into one or other type, hence the absence of statistics on the prevalence of the different kinds of marriage. The categories, however, provide a useful starting point.

Of all the marriages, *serg,* the ceremonial marriage, involves the most prestations and rituals. Wesené described hers, as follows:

> I was first married at the age of 15; after two months my period started, but I only gave birth after about six years. My marriage happened like this; my uncle [her father's brother's son] went from here and married and stayed there, where I come from. My uncle returned here for a visit and found Tesfayé making coffee for himself. He said that Tesfayé should get married and that he would look for someone himself. I was living with my father's mother at the time. She said she would give me as a bride. My uncle returned and told them there, and I came.
>
> It was a real marriage ceremony. First his party came on a Sunday, about ten of them, with a lot of noise and singing. At our place there was a feast with food and drink. One ox which had been slaughtered, 20 *gan* [large pots] of beer. He dropped [gave] a scarf, a dress, a mirror, and a glass. People from my side picked up the gifts and gave them to me on another day, after the two parties had mixed. Also when they came they contributed 20 dollars but it was returned during the *millash* [return feast given by the family of the bride's party to the wedding]. That took place after eight days. My own mother and father gave me the name Alem; here everybody calls me Wesené, it is my *mirat sim,* the name that my mother-in-law gave me during the wedding.

Serg is sometimes preceded by an engagement lasting a month to a few years, at the onset of which some of the gifts from the groom might be offered. It is almost exclusively a phenomenon of the bride's first marriage; a divorced woman will not have a *serg* (though a divorced man may, in exceptional circumstances). The term *serg* focuses attention on the form of wedding rather than on the characteristics of the rights within the union. The rituals associated with the *serg* include considerable feasting and dancing at each homestead in turn, the offering of gifts, a spoken and/or written contract, display of defloration and the giving of a new name by the groom's mother to the bride who enters her homestead. The *serg* is a match orchestrated by the parents or other kin and comes closest to the pattern of African marriages described in the literature. Another description is given by Yirgu:

> My first marriage was to Gétachew. I was aged about 14. He was a neighbour a bit older than me, around 25. It was arranged by the parents on both sides; I was not told. Beer and food were prepared at my parents' place, I thought

it was for a *mehaber* [socio-religious gathering] or something, I did not ask, I was ashamed to do anything when I found out. There was a big feast, five days in our place. Then five days in his household. I stayed on and the others – my kin who had come with me – returned. I was given a dress, shawl, scarf, cotton belt, glass, mirror, necklace and a ring. I still have some of these things. Then it came to speaking the words, to seal the marriage, they asked me to say 'Gétachew is my husband'. I said nothing, it was a friend who said it for me. He [the groom] also spoke and said I was his wife. The first day I slept in our home, the second in the one in which he was put. At first I cried, said I would not sleep with him, but there was nowhere to run to.

After six months, both our families gave between them one calf, five sheep and two goats. This was celebrated with one *gan* [large pot] of beer at his place, and some of my relatives came for the occasion. The signature was at the beginning, I saw them write, but it was my parents who signed, and kept the paper. I was still a child. I lived there in his parents' hut for two years.

K'urban or *aklil,* literally the 'Eucharist' or 'crown', is a religious marriage. It is the first and only type of marriage sanctioned for priests and their spouses. In this case, the event is usually orchestrated by parents of the spouses, the fathers themselves often having a religious background. The same terms are also used for the second step after an earlier form of marriage, a deeper level of commitment that lay couples, in particular the elderly, may decide to make. This marriage is theoretically indissoluble and *k'urban,* perhaps for that reason, is the rarest form of marriage. However, even priests and their spouses are known to remarry, retracting their vows. Given the highly religious nature of the society, it is a curious fact (to which I return) that religion and the Church play such a small role in most marriages.

The *semanya* is a civil contract, commonly known as a contract of equals. The marriage, especially if it occurs early in an individual's life, tends to be organized by kin or friends of both parties. A couple might decide on a marriage informally and subsequently refer to it as a contract marriage. Particularly in this case, the term is often used by women in conjunction with expressions such as *dolegn* or *amet'agn*, 'he brought me in'. However, when the marriage is formally instituted, it involves a witness and usually the signing of the contract on two pieces of paper, one for each party, either at the time of the marriage or at a later date, once the union shows signs of being successful. Thus, in Dessita's case:

Yilfu's father asked my mother, she was agreeable, and so was I. I did not know him, but he was my age and it was said he was a good man. The feast was in my parents' house. We did not prepare much, then I went with bread to his place. After two to three months we did the writing up. Everything for both, in an equal *semanya* contract. The scribe was a student; there were also two people on both sides. We had acquired some wealth, four or five sheep and one cow from my parents and his. I stayed with him for four years, then I left. We tore up the contracts.

If the term *semanya* is used loosely, it implies little more than a union, and applies to all marriages with the possible exception of the *demoz* marriage (see below). When used strictly, the *semanya* marriage is less common than more informal contracts, though it still overlaps with the formal arrangements in the other categories, including *serg*, *k'urban* and *k'ot'assir*. In urban centres, and to a lesser extent in some rural communities (though not the one discussed here), there has been an attempt to set up a registry for equal contract marriages.

K'ot'assir is a form of marriage in which a young boy comes to work and lives in the household of the girl who will eventually becomes his wife. The *k'ot'assir* marriage defines little more than the existence of groom service and, in all likelihood, the young age of the bride.

Zenebech told of her marriage as follows:

> First I was living with my parents, I must have been about twelve. He was much older, more like my father, when he came to work in our household. At that time, we slaughtered a white sheep and a red chicken, we ate bread and drank beer and coffee.
>
> After three years and six months he said *darugn* [give her to me in marriage], so then there was a *serg*. My parents wanted him to continue working for them so they agreed. For the marriage, the ceremony was in our house, for the main event at my family's home there was a bigger feast than when he first came, we slaughtered one ox, and had beer. Then after two months came the *millash* [the return]. We stayed one month with them. There was also meat and a feast there.

The *k'ot'assir* marriage is usually an arrangement between the families and speeds up the time at which the kinship can be created and, perhaps more importantly, labour and capital are exchanged. The arrangement was common in the area, in particular among the wealthier households with a daughter and a shortage of male labour.

The *gered* (servant) or *demoz* (salary) marriage involves payment by the husband to the wife of a monthly or annual salary, usually in cash or grain. What is often a temporary event may be transformed into a permanent marriage, with the question of payment forgotten, at least until divorce brings it up again. This marriage is associated with urban populations and the contracts of traders and warriors far from home. Nevertheless, it has long been considered a form of marriage amongst the sedentary peasant population of Menz and is more common in the area than the religious, *k'urban* marriage.

The *t'ilf*, or abduction form of marriage, is the overall term used for a variety of non-arranged marriages. Asnak'ech's account is clearly one of abduction:

> The third marriage lasted three months. Isheté came and took me. I cried, I was forced. My mother had previously also said no to him. He got some of his friends together and they carried me. I was kept there by force for three months. He had children and wanted me to look after the house. I eventually left him, walked home, about two hours distance, and stayed once more with my mother.

Three of Sindé's marriages might be described differently:

I was first married at the age of about 15, he was aged about 18. It was a
t'ilf marriage. Well, what happened was a *t'ilf* because I had problems. You
see, he lived in Gragn also, but my parents had died. He took me because I
could not arrange anything, so there was a bit of feasting at his place, nothing
much, no signing or words spoken. His parents had liked the choice, the
union had been decided on even before my parents died. I had accepted it,
we grew up together, we were from the same river. I lived with him for five
years and six months. We got on well. The divorce happened because we
were young, seeing other people we both wanted others. I left, and went
back to my sister. We had not quarrelled. I went with another man initially.
He left me after one week.

My next husband was somebody brought by someone we know who
recommended him; I agreed. Meanwhile someone else was going to take me
so we plotted and I ended up with him. I stayed with him until he died of
some stomach illness.

When he died I took food to the church. On my way back, Bogale, who
did not have any children, saw me with Taddelech on my back and took me.
I did not know him well, only by name. I said I would not go, closing my
hut. He said, 'Do not worry I will look after you'. I stayed with him for nine
months. Then came the revolution. Since they had started counting the huts,
I decided to come back to my hut rather than lose it. He accepted the decision.
I was stupid, it was good with him, no problems with food and he looked
after me – I should have stayed.

As the above quotations show, the *t'ilf* marriage can be either pre-
meditated or impulsive and can include various degrees of cooperation on
the part of either parents and/or the bride. Thus the term, which implies
the taking of the bride without her consent, might well be used to describe
an elopement. In the case of a real abduction, or when the ritual is enacted
despite consent, the bride is captured by the groom and his friends, often
on her way to or from the market, from collecting water or from school.
When carried off, the woman will often scream and fight her 'attackers',
even when the match is to her liking.

The abduction might be a prelude to a *semanya* or even a *serg* marriage,
with negotiations subsequently taking place between the two parties. The
term *t'ilf* is widely used, as is *semanya* in its looser meaning, for a union
in which the bride was brought into the groom's household without much
ceremony. Abduction is therefore a form of marriage associated with the
impatient, the desperate or the impoverished. My respondents suggested
that it was increasingly common.

It should be clear from the above summaries that the categories of
marriages, given the confusion between and within them, are far from
satisfactory concepts with which to work. What they do suggest is that a
number of considerations are taken into account in the form of marriage
chosen. These include differences in the parties involved in the selection
of spouses; varying degrees of formality, ceremony and expenditure;

different expectations about the direction of labour exchange; and, in general, different reasons for marriage.

Polygyny and extra-marital affairs

To this already complex scene must be added the existence of polygyny and extra-marital relations. Though monogamous relationships are the rule, there is also a considerable amount of polygamy. This is sometimes openly acknowledged, both wives living together; or it is kept quiet, the women living apart. Where the two wives are separated, they might not know of each other's existence, in particular in the case of a town wife unknown to the rural one and *vice versa*. Where the two wives cohabit, the arrangements are more often than not because the first union was thought to be barren, in which case the two women are distinguished as the barren one, *mehan,* and the fertile one, *wellad.* Polygyny might also occur where a previous union is patched up, despite the fact that a new one has theoretically replaced it. Alem, Yematawerk' and Yetimwerk' told me their stories as follows:

Alem

I went to my mother's place; there Assefa saw me almost immediately. He had another wife and children. Assefa took me having asked my mother and my uncle Cheré. I said we should sign first. We both signed. There were six people who signed and two pieces of paper, one Assefa kept, one stayed with my uncle. I went to live in Assefa's peasants' association, about one hour from here. Now he had another wife, Gét'énesh, from before. We all lived together for nine years. It was fine. Then Gét'énesh left and after that he had a daughter from someone else. In the end I left too. First I went without anything, then came back and took my clothes. He married another woman who gave him a child.

Yematawerk'

My third husband was Isheté. I went to his house. We discussed it first, then he got rid of his old wife and brought me. The old wife went to her father's place and soon after gave birth. I did not give birth then, but she did! He counted her and the child as his, and wanted to bring them back. There was some arguments with *ch'ewa* [elders], and then I pretended to agree and said, 'I do not mind, why doesn't she come back.' He went to get her and meanwhile I disappeared to my mother's house only to find out that I was pregnant too! Then I returned to him. We got on all right. She had given birth to a son. She was the one together with his mother who looked after me during the *aras* [the convalescence period after delivery]. After I had given birth, after ten days, I took Bizunesh [her daughter] with me and left. I did not like the arrangement, but she was a good woman. In total I stayed about two years with him.

Yetimwerk'

I had seen Mulaté at the market, he came to the house, then I went to his, following him. He had another wife and had told her he was looking for a woman to bear him children. As we returned to his house we met his wife on the way, she told him to send me back, he said no. In the end she stayed, she and I lived together for a long time, then I got rid of her. When I became pregnant like this, he suggested she come back to help, I said no, that I would go back to my relatives. When I had gone he called her back. Now I do not want to go back there. [Soon after this discussion she returned to her husband who continued to live with both wives.]

Even where there is no polygamy, a man is likely to retain an economic and social tie with one or more previous wives. Assets, in particular land, which continue to be held in common and the existence of children provide a rationale for maintaining the link. Alem told me:

Arega, the husband I had at the time of the revolution, the one with whom I have land, he is 'my brother'. The three I have been married to and divorced since then, I do not know any more, we do not stay in touch; but Arega, 'my brother', now ploughs for me, pays the tax, and gives me my share of the crop.

Extra-marital unions are also frequent. Below are two examples from my diary:

Fight over the latest affair. Atsede is caught in between. Beyene has become Bek'elech's lover, he is officially living with her since his gun is kept in her hut [he is one of the local police]. Beyene's wife, Nigist was particularly close to Atsede, in fact one of Nigist's children is Atsede's god-daughter. In the past Bek'elech was also a friend of Atsede's. It ended in insults only, but talk about Atsede and Nigist having planned to attack Bek'elech who guessed a trap and kept away. [Nigist went to her parents not long after this. Beyene is now 'married' to Bek'elech, they use both huts.]

Mekonnen [prominent official in Gragn] is rumoured to have had an affair with a relative of Asfaw. The woman already has two sons out of wedlock. The story is now in the air because it is time for the christening of her latest son. The christening was delayed apparently because of ambiguity over whether Mekonnen would declare himself the father. On Friday Mekonnen's parents told Mulu, his wife, that they wanted to contribute to the payment of the ceremony, thus recognizing the child. Mulu says she wants out of the marriage. [Another note in the diary continues the story]. Mekonnen claims he is not the father after all, another man has been named. Mulu was reconciled with him after he bought her a dress. [Mekonnen and Mulu only have daughters. Mulu's younger brother seems to have joined the household, providing male labour.]

Most extra-marital relationships that are mentioned seem to be temporary; however, some turn into 'marriages'. Neither these nor the polygamous relationships are admitted to in the questionnaires, though they are the subjects of numerous jokes and poems. Below is one such poem in which a duped husband bemoans his fate.

እይድረስባችሁ፡	Let it not happen to you;
ደርሶብኛል፡በኒ ፤	It has happened to me;

በገንቦት፡እገብቺ፡
ወለጸች፡በሰኔ።

I married her in May,
And she gave birth in June.

Such relationships were also mentioned in interviews, and I, like most other people in the community, followed the rumours about current goings on with interest. There were four polygamous households among the 80 allocated a hut in the new village, and extra-marital affairs abounded. In the past, these were associated with particularly wealthy individuals;[3] in keeping with this tradition, the peasants' association leadership was linked with such affairs. One individual in particular was rumoured to 'use' whatever woman appealed to him and to have 29 women of his own.

Endowments and transactions

Traditionally, the literature on marriage has been presented with an anthropological angle which focused on the exchanges that occur and the implications these have on social formation and control over the younger generation. The literature has tended to be much less conscious of the gender dimension of these marriages and has thereby failed to elucidate a whole area of power relations.

The data here are not presented within a paradigm constructed to fit a single theory of equality or hierarchy between men and women within and between generations. This is partly because the population did not explain their behaviour in such a way, but also because of the very flexibility of interactions alluded to earlier. Even when we focus on endowments and exchanges, and avoid falling into the anthropologists' habit of treating women as objects,[4] the picture is complex. Transactions appear to be constructed to facilitate divorce and the redivision of wealth between husband and wife. Theoretically, they are in an equal position, though in practice women can more easily be marginalized. It is the wife and husband themselves, rather than their kin, who, after the initial wedding, are given restitution for the labour invested in the marriage. To consider the issues of endowments and exchanges, this section will examine in turn feasts, presents, exchanges of livestock and land, and questions of labour and reproduction.

The wedding feast

As mentioned in the previous section, in Menz, the wedding feast in *serg* and in other formal marriages is usually celebrated first at the bride's home. This is then followed by a feast at the groom's. The cost of the groom's feast should equal, or be less than, that of the bride's initial celebrations. In the case below, Asselefech's marriage is 'wrong' and unsatisfactory because the rule is broken.

My first marriage was arranged by my father's sister with my mother. At the time I had gone to a christening. I returned to find it all arranged. . . . The feast was supposed to be mainly at my place: bread and beer were prepared and chickens slaughtered. The groom came in the day; in the evening we went to his place with my brother; a goat was slaughtered there. The next day my brother returned. It was his mother that did not want much of a celebration in our place. We were angry: *Igna keswa inansallen indé, iswa tillik' igna tinnish*, 'Are we then going to be less than her, her great and us small?' We slaughtered only a chicken, they a goat. He had come with three relatives and there were not many of my relatives either. When we reached her place there were lots of her relatives [the groom's mother's] and only two of us.

The marriage did not last long. I did not quarrel with him, but with his mother. It started because of the feast, as I told you, it was wrong. I liked him. Now we sometimes meet, but are very shy of each other. I was aged about 16, I got up and left, it was less than a year since the start of the marriage. There was no attempt to get us together again. She [husband's mother] did not give me anything, no *demoz,* no salary for the work I did whilst I was with them.

The groom's party is expected to contribute to the cost of the animals slaughtered for the first occasion, and vice-versa.[5] Some kind of food and drink is likely to be prepared, regardless of how many marriages have preceded the present one, and however informal or impromptu the event. This might be no more than a simple meal and the carrying of a loaf of bread from one household to the other.

Prestations

For *serg* marriages, it is customary for the groom to offer some trinkets to the bride. Sometimes the groom also gives money to the bride's mother, usually specifically for a scarf or some other article of clothing. As we have seen, the presents to the bride may include a mirror, items of clothing such as a scarf or sometimes even a dress, and rings to be hung round her neck. The groom's parents may be involved in meeting the costs. The fact that this tradition is only for the first marriage and would not apply to a *fetté,* a divorced woman, would suggest an association with the consummation of the marriage and the 'gift' of virginity. The presents are given to the wife, who keeps them regardless of what happens to the marriage.[6]

No payment is expected from the bride's family to the groom. The only exception is the fine paid if a wife abandons a priest-husband after a *k'urban* marriage, since this behaviour is liable to compromise the priest's future. A priest, like any other man in Ethiopian rural society, needs a wife; if he has to remarry, he can no longer officiate.

Livestock and land

When livestock is brought into a marriage, a contract is likely to be drawn up ensuring that, in case of divorce, the person who brought in the animal retains rights over it. Theoretically and almost regardless of the form of marriage, any livestock reproduced during the duration of the union is divided equally.

In terms of land, as we saw in Chapter 3, the tradition in northern

Ethiopia was that women did not receive land rights at marriage. Instead they were granted usufructuary rights through an ambilineal inheritance system. In theory these rights were equal to those of men. In practice, the virilocal form of marriage and a whole social structure, which placed men before women, ensured that by and large it was men who activated their rights to land, and were thus the major resource owners. The situation in post-revolutionary society no longer relied on inheritance rights but rather on membership in a peasants' association. Once again, in theory women were equal, although, as we saw in Chapter 3, their membership in the peasants' association was indirect, *via* their husbands. One of the results of the land reform was friction between spouses over the issue of rights to land. Conflicts over land within marriage were beginning to emerge, though these were bounded by the notion of rights based on residence, a system not dissimilar to that of inheritance within a community. I shall return to the question of changes and trends in the final part of this chapter.

Labour

The labour expended by the party who leaves a homestead is, theoretically, repaid in the event of divorce. The recompense is to the individual, not the family, and operates regardless of whether it is the man or the woman who has contributed. Labour can be translated into grain, livestock or money, and the exact amount to be paid can be negotiated by representatives of the two parties. The tradition implies that after the first marriage parents of both parties cease to have ultimate control over compensation. They will, however, have a hand in the selection of new spouses and provide a base for people, particularly women, between marriages.

As has already been hinted, the theory of equality is not universally upheld in reality, since the ability of women to ensure that they are repaid is considerably lower than that of men. The case of Lak'ech is not unusual.

> I have had four marriages including this one. The first was with Dammena. We lived in the same area, in a neighbouring peasants' association to this one. His father had come looking for a wife for him. The marriage was a *serg*. ... Altogether we stayed together more than two years. He was a *kés temari*, an apprentice priest, I am the one that made him 'chuck it' (*iné negn yast'alkut*). I do not know why I divorced, it was a childish thing (*yelijint neger*). He would get drunk, I was very young. I returned to my father, but quarrelled with him and went to my mother. My father said, 'return to him', but I refused. In the end he [the husband] was given 100 *birr* by my parents and relatives because I left him – they [husband's family] were rich people.
>
> Of the four only the first had been signed. I always made the decision to leave. Only in one case was I given grain or anything when I left; that time I got two sacks of grain, that is about 40 birrs' worth. From the others I was supposed to get grain, but never did. What woman has not been 'eaten' [cheated]! ... I do not have land with anyone, I abandoned it when I left the husband who then went to resettlement.

The custody of children varies according to circumstances, though some generalizations are nevertheless possible. Until the child is past weaning, the infant will almost always remain with the mother. After this stage, the pattern of expectation is sometimes along gender lines as mothers are more likely to keep daughters, and fathers, sons. However the needs of the father tend to be considered first, and both boys and girls generally stay with the father if he desires to have them as labourers, in particular to help with cattle minding, an activity that even a seven-year-old can be expected to perform. Fatherhood is usually claimed and some support provided, openly or in private, regardless of what happens to the marriage.

Overall, the position of endowments in the marital scene is determined in a way that allows mobility. Feasts are, in general, of an almost equal nature, although the parents of a bride can spend more on the first *serg* ceremony; wedding gifts are on a small scale and are made by the groom; land is not exchanged, livestock rights are clearly defined for ease of separation, and labour expended on a homestead can theoretically be translated into grain or money, and can thus be repaid.

The picture that is beginning to emerge is one in which there is considerable flexibility, not only in the type of marriage a person undertakes, but also in the sequence of arrangements within an individual life history. The marital possibilities seem to point to adaptability and to a lack of great formality; options are chosen and rejected as and when necessary. This point becomes clear when the spatial and temporal nature of unions is considered.

The spatial dimension

The overall pattern is one of virilocality, husbands bringing in a bride first to their parents', and then to their own homestead. The locality has implications in terms of whose labour is being transferred, but also where shelter and the establishment of a home is undertaken. Both *t'ilf* and, in the rural setting, *demoz* marriages are, by definition, virilocal.

In the case of a minor argument, the wife in a virilocal marriage seeks refuge among the relatives of her husband, whose households are nearer than those of her natal relatives. If the quarrel is more serious she is likely to return immediately to her parents' home. Meanwhile her husband, who lives near his own relatives, will join them; or he will find a sister or mother to take over the household chores until the quarrel is resolved, or a new wife arrives.

Uxorilocal marriages in which the husband's labour is brought into the homestead can also occur. *K'ot'asir* marriages are, by definition, uxorilocal, at least in the first few years of the union. The assumption, both within the society and in the wider literature on Amhara populations, is that uxorilocal marriages are the minority. Although my data confirm this, they appear to be a significant minority; 32 per cent of the marriages on which I collected data had an uxorilocal period, and 22 per cent were completely uxorilocal.[7]

Where the marriage was uxorilocal, reasons were given in terms of the wealth of the bride's family, or their greater need for a male labourer. A man who marries into his wife's community has a lower status. From this, the implication is sometimes drawn that women in uxorilocal marriages are better off, that they have more power within the household, since they can call on their own relatives for support. If the wife is an adult with independent means such a marriage is generally to the woman's advantage. However, I was alerted to the fact that young women in uxorilocal marriages were sometimes particularly vulnerable: they had nowhere to escape to if their parents wanted the marriage to continue in order to keep their son-in-law's labour. Yetimwerk', for example, had difficulty obtaining a divorce:

> I used to refuse to sleep with Arega. After five years, *kobliyyé hédku*, I got up and left, escaped to Mehal Meda and went to some relatives there. He had not hit me or anything, I just did not like him. When I had gone Arega left the house and I returned home. Before then, I had asked my father to get rid of him, but my father needed him for the work so he refused. When Arega eventually left, he had to be paid for the work he had done; I do not know how much, it was in grain.

Bride and groom are preferably sought from neighbouring communities rather than from great distances. Traditionally for a *serg* marriage, the number of neck-rings that were included in the trinkets that a groom had to offer his bride increased in proportion to the rivers that had to be crossed between the two homesteads. The custom points to distance as an unfavourable factor for the woman, since if recompense is required, it is proportional to distance. On the other hand, a man is said to be more likely to lose his wife if her own family lives nearby; he has more control over her if she is far from her natal home. For him, proximity of wife's kin tends to be looked on unfavourably. There are, nevertheless, some benefits, in particular during his wife's pregnancy, when additional female labour and support is necessary.

There is a rule against the marriage of kin within seven generations which encourages the searching beyond immediate surroundings. The rule is based on biblical stricture and is common to other cognatic systems in the world. Asnak'ech, for example, told me:

> I returned to my parents after eleven years with Alemayehu. The next one [husband] was Molla; it did not last long because they said he was a husband of a relative by four 'houses' [generations]. They had given me by mistake before they knew. He lived far away, at Amed Washa, about four hours walk. He came with bread and one relative and took me. Then, we returned for the *millash,* taking bread with us. Mother and father slaughtered a sheep. He and I got on well, but, after all this, it was discovered that we were related. He had two children. The children did not want me to leave. I did not either, but had to.

In Menz, the rule preventing marriage within seven generations is also applied to socially created kinship, for example, women in the same socio-religious gathering, the *mehaber,* are not supposed to marry a man previously married to any of the members. In both socially created and biological kinship, the rules are not always kept, especially at the more distant levels of kinship. The conflict between the desire for geographically close marriage ties and the dangers of breaking the kinship rule means that compromises are inevitably negotiated.

The temporal dimension

We can now look at the different steps that can be taken in the marriage process. This need not start with a wedding, a contract, or any other single occasion. In fact, a series of different events which should not be conflated are associated with a single union. They can be listed as follows:

- An optional engagement period, sometimes associated with an exchange of gifts and/or labour.
- The wedding feasts, usually first in the bride's homestead, then in the groom's and then sometimes once again in the bride's. The interval between first and second feasts is usually one week, though it can be considerably longer. Sometimes a third feast is organized by the party who hosted the first event. In this case the interval between the second and the third feast can be several months.
- The setting up of an independent household, *gojo mawt'at*. This can be a separate event or might be established from the beginning.
- Sanctifying the wedding as a religious *k'urban* one: from the beginning, in the case of priests; years later, for lay couples in old age.
- Signing a contract, at any stage in the course of the marriage, sometimes several years after the wedding. If wealth is brought into the union from either or both sides of the marriage, this is more likely to involve a signed contract, as Wesené's rationalization of the negative case makes explicit.

Troubles came my way; this is how we are now, without anything. Earlier on in the marriage when we had livestock we had planned to be signed, but then this happened, we lost everything and decided that since we did not have any wealth there was no point, so we have not signed.

Marriages might contain any combination of the above events. In general, though not necessarily, the wealthier the household, the more likely will be a greater formality, and the larger the endowments. There is also a correlation between duration of marriage and investment in it – the longer it lasts, the more likely that, over time, economic investments and greater ritual will be attached. Conversely, marriages which do not involve significant outlays are more easily dissolved. However, this does not mean that all or even most ceremonial marriages are stable. Even in the case of the most lavish *serg* marriage, the expectation is still that divorce will ensue.

Divorce and remarriage

For an outsider, probably the most remarkable feature of Amhara households is the frequency of divorce and its correlation, the high incidence of serial marriages in what is a strongly Christian community. The ease with which men can dispose of and replace their wives is vividly portrayed in the following rhyming stanza:

ትመፁ_ ፡ እንደሆን ፡ ነይ ፡
እኔ ፡ እልግለድኽም ፤
በሌት ፡ ሌት ፡ ይተካስ ፡
እናት ፡ እይደለኽም ።

If you want to come, come;
I will not entreat you [to return]
One woman [wife] can be replaced by another;
You are not [my] mother.

My data, based on 95 questionnaires administered to heads of households, gave a range for the number of marriages per adult from nought to twelve, and an average of 3.3 marriages per adult head of household.[8] Table 6.1 shows the distribution of marriages, and thus the frequency of remarriage. These can be taken as an underestimate, since respondents tend to take pity on me and simplify their often complex marital histories.[9]

Table 6.1. Frequency of remarriage

No	0	1	2	3	4	5	6	7	8	9	10	11	12
Frequency	1	24	22	10	14	10	5	5	1	0	0	0	3

Taking all marriages for which duration was given (260 cases), the range was from eight days to 50 years, with 49 per cent of marriages lasting under five years.[10] The discussion that follows attempts to elucidate the factors that lie behind this marital situation and the frequency of divorce.

In an article entitled 'Amhara marriage: the stability of divorce',[11] Weissleder argued that if a rational, material basis was suggested as an explanation of marriage, the motives for divorce should not be sought elsewhere. If marriage is based on economic considerations, rather than emotional ones, divorce is likely to have the same motives. The argument seems sound, but the evidence from my life histories points to the futility of advancing a strictly materialist reduction of complicated marital decisions. The discussion about whether divorce is an economic or an emotional/social decision, or even the attempt to decide which of these motives is the more important, runs counter to the mix of factors behind an individual's action, not to mention the varied considerations relevant in a multitude of cases. Perhaps the only generalization that can be made runs counter to the Weissleder thesis: in Amhara culture, marriage is most often perceived in economic terms, and emotions are not taken into consideration since the individuals usually do not know each other. Divorce, on the other hand, tends to be explained in more complex terms of incompatibility – emotional and economic.

Two types of reason are almost always given for divorce: the precipitating factors and systematic ones, the latter usually being a number of complaints over time which come to a head and lead to divorce after a precipitating event. Men complained of such factors as wives' adultery; barrenness; not keeping house properly; disobeying them and challenging their authority.

Women had a greater number of grievances against husbands, who beat and ill-treated them, especially after drinking bouts at the Saturday market; wasted money; committed adultery; gave them too much work, including obliging them to mind cattle; restricted their activity and mobility; and forced them to have intercourse more often than they desired – with attendant fears of pregnancy. Other reasons women gave included bad relations with mother-in-laws, escaping from a barren union and, especially in the case of first marriages, homesickness and a great difference in age.

Men and women alike suggested that women were the prime initiators of divorce, though this was not a universal pattern. Three friends explained:

Yirgu

I became homesick, that is why I left. I just got up and went. They, his parents, came to try and get us together, but each time I would flee; this happened several times. There was no particular reason, I did not want a marriage, it was a childhood thing. He was the hitting type. I left after two years, asked for a divorce. I think there was a settlement with elders, but my parents went on my behalf, I did not go. Our cattle were divided, we kept our own and shared the sheep that had been born over the period.

Bek'elech

Tidar, marriage, did not suit us. There was the stick. He would hit me and there was forced intercourse, is that not what makes for dislike? (*yemi-yast'ella yaw aydelle?*) I lived approximately three years with him. He said, 'Go, this is my house', so I left. Relatives tried to get us together, but I went to my mother's place. It was not a long marriage, so I was not given much. Words were spoken by elders to end the marriage.

Almaz

We got on well, but he used to get drunk and was jealous. I do not really know why, I started disliking him (*k'effefegn*). Also I did not get on with his mother. There was lots of work and I was tired of it all. Once he came back and was abusive and I decided to go. I left without telling him, he would have hit me, had I told him. My parents lived about twenty minutes away.... There is always disagreement, it would have been best to be with one man, if you get on, if God wills it.... It is the person who has grievances, who has been damaged/hurt (*bedel yalew, yetegodda*) who leaves.

So much for the push that results in divorce, but why do people remarry, and keep on remarrying? The first answer is that the position of a single person, particularly a man, is more precarious than that of a married one. In peasant economies, the household is the centre of production and consumption, and the division of labour within the household is sexual. Men's contribution to the household is of a more episodic nature, women's contribution more continual. Thus a man cannot easily survive without the labour of a woman, who, among other things, will process the harvest into his daily meals. He is also socially stigmatized, and made fun of, if seen to be fending for himself. An adult woman is also in difficulty without a male protector and labourer. Social and economic vulnerability apply, particularly if there is no substitute male figure in the form of an adult son.

Thus one reason for remarriage is to escape from being single. Another is the search for an ideal union. Almaz's comment is often made, namely that if a marriage is good, there is no reason to look elsewhere, but that otherwise the search must continue. The nearest I got to a general discussion about divorce was with a group of three women, Abeba, Dessita and Felfilé, who offered the following statements.

Felfilé
In general, divorce is about anger, about other people or about not having offspring. It is usually the woman who leaves, but if it is the woman's place, he goes. She says *botahin fellig*, 'Go find your own place'. It is best to stay with one man if you get on, it is a lot less hassle that way – *géta talew*, 'if the Lord says it can be so'.

Dessita
Divorce . . . it happens sometimes when they see someone else, sometimes because of growing poverty and a feeling that the spouse is not good with money. More often it is the woman asking for divorce, but it is best to live with one [husband] if it works, otherwise, to try all over again!

Abeba
Men cannot live without women, women cannot do without men. . . well, they can, but if there is nobody to help it is useless, *mewdek' new*, 'it is to fall' – you cannot call it a life without a man.

Usually, it is the women who ask for divorce, but this is not always the case. Moreover, that the petitioner or the one who walks away from the home is usually the woman, does not necessarily mean that she is the one initiating the break-up.[12] In a virilocal society, the husband's effective control over the home is greater than that of the wife, and she in turn can find more support by returning to her natal community.

But what do these patterns tell us about gender relations and the position of women? Should divorce be interpreted as a reflection of female power or the lack of it? Support for the former comes from studies of the position of women in Cuba and China,[13] where increases in the divorce rates were registered when women's emancipation became a political issue, and women were released from some elements of traditional subservience by new socialist structures. In the case of Cuba, Bengelsdorf and Hageman pointed to the ten-fold increase in divorce rates between 1958 and 1970, adding 'this gives a succinct indication of one enormous change: women are no longer locked into the prison of an oppressive marriage by economic necessity.'[14]

There is a difference between these cases in the comparative literature, which focus on a rise in divorce rate, and the situation in northern Ethiopia, and Menz in particular, which is clearly an area of ongoing high divorce rates. Nevertheless, the long history of rights to divorce in Ethiopia has been similarly attributed to the power of women within the household, even before any talk of socialism. For Poluha, this is the tradition of women's 'economic independence and respected right to leave partner and area'.[15]

Reminick,[16] writing before the revolution, relates high divorce rates to the instability of an egalitarian institution of marriage in a society which in all other aspects is hierarchical. Neither of these explanations is very convincing, if only because the so-called equality in marriage is partial and debatable; indeed, the very ambiguity of the position of women is part of the dilemma.

Furthermore, what about the association of high divorce rates with economic difficulties? In *The Story of an African Famine*, Vaughan[17] suggests that famine leads to an increase in the divorce rate and a fall in the marriage and birth rates. Brown,[18] writing about the Dominican Republic in an article entitled 'Love unites them and hunger separates them', suggests that the number of serial marriages increases as economic conditions deteriorate. Given harsh economic conditions, and a context in which women fear that men will squander resources on luxuries, serial marriages give women greater flexibility, freedom and control over their own money. In the society, the ideal remains one of a single partner. Similarly, Stack,[19] in the article 'Sex roles and survival strategies in an urban black community', argues that household mobility is regarded as a strategy for dealing with poverty, and that under such circumstances household boundaries become 'elastic'.

The literature on divorce seems paradoxical. It is seen negatively as a reflection of economic and social considerations which produce dissatisfaction and tension rather than cohesion. At the same time, it seems that divorce is a positive tool used by women, who thus express their economic independence and improve their livelihood. To put the argument differently, mobility is often the last option for those in distress, as the history of refugees and famine victims has shown. Perhaps the fact that so many women in Menz so often abandon the homes that they have toiled to create is similarly a sign of hardship.

The literature and the data suggest that high divorce rates reflect both women's power and their dissatisfaction: the power to exit from a relationship in search of a better one, and dissatisfaction resulting from stress, poverty and oppression. This is likely to be so particularly in the cases instigated by a husband against the wishes of his wife. The ideal remains one of a stable union.

In the attempt to portray the amount of marital instability – people careering through marriages – I have directed no more than a cursory glance at dispute settlement. Yet marriages are sometimes put right if the offended party, usually the woman, is recompensed. Thus, in the section on extra-marital affairs, I mentioned the case of a marriage being repaired by the gift of a dress from the husband to his wife. Reparation usually takes this form, though, for a lesser offence or a more impoverished household, payment is in other luxury goods associated with women such as coffee or honey. The record of marital dispute settlements confirms the story presented here of the woman as the plaintiff, and the husband as the one making amends.

Church and state

The Church

We have seen that the Church is involved in the *k'urban* marriages, and, more generally, in both the rule against marriage within seven degrees of kinship and the injunction against polygamy. It is surprising, however, that in a society in which religion is so visible and all-encompassing, the Church plays such a minor role in marital unions. In Chapter 8 I shall return to the way that Christianity affects the daily actions of individuals, provides the scene for social interaction, and in many ways defines the community. In the next chapter, it will be shown that most life-cycle events, including birth and death, refer to Christian belief and that a priest presides over the events. Why, then, is the Church's role in marriage so minor? Why are church marriages not the rule? Why is there no tradition of parish registries?

It might be argued that it is not the Church itself that forms the focus of the religion, but rather its priests. Though the church building traditionally defined the parish and the community, the latter rarely came together under the auspices of the Church. Regular communal attendance of services is not as central to the religion as in many other societies. Yet people go to church for christenings and funerals, so why not for marriages? And if priests are mobile enough to attend and officiate in other events, why do they not do so for most marriages?[20]

The absence of a parish registry of marriages is easier to explain as part of the absence of a tradition of recording life-cycle events: births, marriages or deaths. Yet it remains surprising that when a marriage contract is written out, and a priest is sometimes sought to prepare the two copies, his services are called upon as scribe, not as priest.

The only credible explanation is that marriages are too unstable for the Church to wish to be involved, or for the population to wish to sanctify unions. Where the Church has tried to regulate practices, it has had little success. It has attempted to prohibit polygamy, yet the practice is far from abandoned. It has imposed its own form of indissoluble marriage for priests, yet many are those who fail, and there are numerous accounts of trainee priests giving up a future in the Church because their marriage, avowed until death, breaks up well before.

The state

Assuming, then, that the Church is impotent in the face of the forces that lead to high divorce rates, what about the state? Both in the past, and in post-revolutionary Ethiopia, the state attempted some action to modify the forms of marriage. For exampl, child marriages were declared illegal. Thus *k'ot'assir* was an illegal form of marriage, and if the couple came to court on some other grounds, their parents might have been fined for having organized such a union. However, the law was not enforced and the practice has not ceased.

As mentioned above, polygamy is prohibited by the Orthodox Church which was the state religion under the imperial *régime*. With the revolution came the lowering of the status of Christianity, and equality with Islam which allows polygamy. The draft revolutionary constitution, Article 38, Clause 1 stated:

> Marriage is based on the consent of a man and a woman who have attained majority. Bigamy is prohibited. Spouses have equal rights in their family relations. Marriage shall enjoy the protection of the state.

Significantly, the sentence 'bigamy is prohibited' was dropped in the final version, in deference to Islamic pressure. Whatever the exact reason for its inclusion and then its exclusion, the rationale for the prohibition lay at least in part in a view that equality in marital relations should be encouraged and it was quickly abandoned when found to be antagonistic to Islamic customs.

In unions involving a contract marriage most oaths in the past were sworn in the name of the reigning Emperor. This was replaced by specific reference to the *Derg*, the name given to the Provisional Military Government, to Chairman Mengistu, or by not calling on any individual or body, and referring rather to the law, *be-hig*. Thus in contract marriages an oath was made in which legitimation was achieved through mention of the state. However, the oath did not carry any implication of 'till death do us part'. It was made as an acknowledgment that a union had occurred and to record the wealth that each individual brought into the partnership.

In the past, most divorces in Gragn would be settled locally through elders. However, the state was involved in setting up organizations to hear divorce cases. When a case came to court, the law referred plaintiffs to a local committee of elders who gave their decision to the court. During the period of research, the peasants' association leadership was involved in the informal settlement of disputes. The concern of each of these bodies was always to dissuade the couple from divorcing, if at all possible.[21] Within the formal dispute settlement organizations, delays were instituted in the hope that tempers would cool and reconciliation ensue.

It remained the case that the state, both in the past and during the research, had little direct effect on marriage and divorce. It attempted to limit some forms of union, such as child marriages, and made its most significant contribution in the realm of divorce proceedings. Registration of civil marriage remained unheard of in an area in which, ironically enough, written divorce records were kept in files.

Single women and female-headed households

So far I have made little mention of women without husbands; in the following chapter we will see that women are expected to marry, and that spinsters are an anomaly. Widows who do not remarry are more common, though remarriage is still the rule. For analytical purposes, the population can be divided into two categories of single women. The majority comprise a transitory group of divorcees or widows between marriage; the minority are those disillusioned with marriage and seeking an alternative career. The division is artificial if applied to an individual over time, since a woman who seems to have settled down alone might well enter a union in later years, and *vice versa*. However, for discussion of the general position of single women the division is helpful.

In the permanent category there were those with few resources who were most likely to abandon their community and migrate into urban centres. There they would attempt to earn a living by working in bars, hotels and restaurants, work which almost invariably involved prostitution. They might also become water porters or petty traders, or make and sell alcoholic beverages. Many worked their way up to a relatively comfortable urban life. Even those women whose lives seemed insecure and marked by endless toil rarely regretted the move away from rural married life.

There also existed a category of female-headed households with means. Thus there were women with direct rights to land, a hut and some livestock, who might well decide to avoid marriage. In Gragn, households that fitted this category were a significant proportion, 23 per cent, of the total. However, the figure is deceptive since some of these had retained their own wealth and an image of independence, despite remarrying. At any point in time, the figure of single women who were registered as heads of households was nearer 15 per cent. The transitory group resided alone, if they had the means to do so, or otherwise with relatives.

The picture for single women and female-headed households was thus confused by the conflation of two factors. In local terms, *sét adarï* was the woman who lived (literally, slept) alone, and *sét abal*, literally woman member [of the peasants' association], the woman who was the head of her household. The two did not necessarily go together. The single status, the absence of a man in the household, was not desired since it resulted in vulnerability and the likelihood of a greater burden associated with house-hold maintenance and marginalized social status. However, the economic position of the single woman was highly dependent on whether or not she was a head of household. In general, those women with independent incomes but in a stable marriage were considered to be in the best position. Marriage provided an element of security whilst independent wealth provided security against the husband. In addition to this distinction, there was a difference between female-headed households that contained an adult male, usually a son or a husband figure, and those that did not. The first had more secure access to necessary male labour.

Most single women were thus those between marriages. Their status and economic position tended to be unfavourable since they had the stigma of not being in a union and were dependent, usually on kin. There was also a permanent group, and amongst these there were women who, without kin or resources to rely on, tended to migrate in search of an urban career.

Female-headed households, *sét abal*, were not necessarily single. Those that were not (8 per cent) were in the most favoured position since they had the security both of an independent position in the community and of husbands protecting them from stigma and providing labour. Women heads of households with another source of male labour, in particular that of adult sons, were also in a comparatively favourable position.

When looked at in the broader context of women's status in society, the position of single women without independent resources were at the least favoured, most vulnerable, end of the spectrum. Married women were in the centre with different degrees of worry according to the character and means of their husbands. At the most favoured extreme were a few women with independent rights, *sét abal*, and with secure access to male labour, preferably in the form of a satisfactory husband.

Explanations and trends

Having begun with six categories of marriage, we have seen that there was considerable flexibility in the type of marriage that could be contracted. The various forms allowed for the different conditions and rationales underlying a marriage. The differences can now be briefly summarized. A distinction can be drawn between first marriages, which tended to involve greater outlay and ceremony, and subsequent ones, which were simpler affairs. The special significance of the first marriage reflected the economic value put on virginity and the greater likelihood that the marriage involved a bond between households, rather than a personal arrangement by bride and groom.

Another distinction can be drawn along the lines of wealth and status: the wealthier the households, the greater the event, be it formal or informal. A difference was also made between the clergy, who can marry only once, and the lay population. The more informal and contractual forms of marriage reflected the desire for, and the necessity of, female labour within a household. Finally, the *t'ilf* abduction marriage provided a socially sanctified means of circumventing parental or bridal aversion to a match. Thus one explanation for the variety of forms of marriage lay in the various settings within which marriages occurred, all of which provided a demonstration of stratification and individuality.

With regard to women's position, we have seen that the *semanya* marriage was the form assumed to be the norm. Here the theory of equality, and individual rather than parental rights, was clear. However, a number of structural conditions existed which meant that women's position was not equal to men's. These included such factors as the age difference between wife and husband, especially for a first marriage where this could be as much as 25 years. A number of asymmetric customs also operated, such as the one dictating that a woman should stand up when her husband enters the hut, that a wife should wash her husband's feet, be humble and, in general, servile in front of husband and master. Male adultery and polygamy were considered far more acceptable than their female equivalents. At the symbolic level, the *serg* marriage presented women in a particularly subordinate position. It included such factors as the display of defloration, and other traditions such as fasting by the bride and feeding of the groom.

Yet, despite all this, we have seen that women were not powerless, a point that also emerges from poems such as the following one in which a husband who is being ordered to do 'women's' work attempts to do so, but fails abysmally. In the poem he admits to being made fun of by his wife; implicit is the valuing of work which men, without the training, are unable to perform:[22]

መቀጪ፡እንድወቅጥ፡አዛኝ፡	Having ordered me to grind,
መቀጪ፡ስወቅጥ፡ትስቅብላች፡	When I do, she laughs at me;
በእጅህ፡እሳት፡እምጣ፡ብላ፡ታዘዛኛች፡	She orders me to bring her fire in my hand,
ረጀኝ፡ብዬ፡ስላት፡ትስቅብላች።	When I tell her it burns me, she laughs at me.

Theoretical equality found some practical support both in the day-to-day organization of the household and, notably, in the rights that many women had in divorce. Women could take action: they exited from a marriage more frequently than men purposefully ejected them. I have already emphasized that this does not mean that, in all cases, women were the prime initiators of separation, and, even when they were, their actions were often in response to male power – sometimes to the physical expression of patriarchy, as when they were beaten. For many, however, women's power to act by leaving was the right to choose the least damaging option, within a context of dissatisfaction and marginalization.

The society was one in which men were more important than women, and this was expressed in a number of different but integrated ways. Nevertheless, women were an indispensable component of the household; their needs had to be considered and, where they were not, a pattern emerged in which women expressed their dissatisfaction and their constant search for better opportunities. The marital scene was therefore one of negotiation between men's greater and women's lesser powers of action.

We can now bring together a picture of the marital situation in the context of the changes stressed by informants. The most noticeable of these was the decrease in *serg* marriages; as Asselefech and Bek'elech told me:

There is no more *serg* here. It is different in the towns, there is more ceremony there.

In the past the *serg* was a big thing, many people came and feasted and danced. Now there is no more of this, it has stopped; all that happens is the woman coming into the homestead. Today with the revolution the whole thing has been left, the 'ho ho' [noise associated with the arrival of the celebrating parties] has been abandoned.

There has been a reduction of ritual and expenditure for all marriages, combined with a shift towards informality. This may, in part, be explained by a reduction in stratification brought about by the policies of the state, in particular the land reform, as well as by the ongoing impoverishment of the region. Yet we saw in Chapter 3 that, increasingly, the leadership was considerably better off than most of the population, and that a new hierarchy had thus emerged. However, display of wealth in the traditional way, through feasts and celebrations, was not common. Even where the degree of stratification would allow for differences, the absolute poverty in the region, together with the socialist image, ensured that these were not displayed. As Asselefech and Bek'elech record, *serg* marriages, the most formal and costly of them all, have almost totally ceased.

In parallel with the disappearance of *serg* marriages that embody rituals of women's subordination, there seems to have been an increase in women's say in marriage. Where the marriage was a *t'ilf* one, it was usually of the elopement rather than the abduction kind, and the bride was in league with the groom. *T'ilf* and informal *semanya* were becoming the standard forms of marriage.

The increase in the power of women to make decisions over their choice of partner was illustrated with exaggeration in the following poem, in which the poet argues that it is no longer the man who does the wooing.

የዛሬውስ፡ፍቅር፡	As for the love of today
እደስ፡ሱሪ፡ታጥቋል፤	it has put on new trousers;
እባክሽ፡ቀርቷ፡	'Please' to a woman has gone,
እባክህ፡ተለቋል።	'Please' to a man has taken its place.

The verse is meant to amuse, but it is also picking up on a trend in which women are seen to be more active partners within marriage. This occurred partly because first marriages took place later in the life-cycle. As Wessené put it: 'In the past, here, the woman was about Bizunesh's age [16] when she got married, but now she is older.'

There was also a delay in the setting up of a separate household. These changes were a result of the new rigidity in land allocation, labour mobility and hut construction. Given chronic land shortages, a growing population, and increasing corruption, most aspiring young households had to wait a long time before being allocated their own plot of land. Livestock could not in themselves provide a means of livelihood and were, in any case, being depleted by the worsening economic conditions. The sale of labour within the community and seasonal migration in search of work were not supposed to take place. Finally, after villagization, even building a new hut had become problematic. Thus, in Menz, delayed marriages were occurring both as a consequence of impoverishment and as the indirect effect of state policies. They were not happening as a response to conscious government intervention, as had been the case in China, for example, where exhortations and incentives for late marriages were applied.

The implications of these changes in terms of power between generations are unclear. On the one hand, the importance of elder kin was declining in this and other spheres of life. As we have seen, in the case of marriage this gave the individual a greater say. On the other hand, there was an increased dependency on parents and on the peasants' association in the context of decreasing resources in the community as a whole.

Despite the earlier argument about a relationship between economic hardship and divorce, the continuing impoverishment seemed to coincide with a decrease, or rather the expectation of a decrease, in divorce rates. As Asselefech tentatively put it:

> Now it is all more difficult. I think there is going to be less divorcing than in the past, now we try and stick together. . . .

The problems of land allocation since the land reform seemed to be one of the main factors putting a brake on divorces and serial marriages. A married woman who was allocated land with a husband, and wanted to retain access and rights to the produce from this land, had the choice between staying with him, and attempting to separate her land from his, or, as we saw earlier, retaining socially created 'kinship' ties with him.

A clearer pattern was the reduction in the distance from which a bride or groom was sought. As we saw earlier, the proximity of natal kin tended to be favoured by women and disliked by men in virilocal marriages. Given the practical problems of transferring land rights between peasants' associations, marriages across even neighbouring communities had become more difficult where both parties had the possibility of acquiring rights to land. Marriages within peasants' associations had therefore become particularly attractive. However, marriages across communities continued to take place. This can best be explained as the creation of two categories of men, and even more distinctly, two categories of women. One category had some degree of rights to land. They retained these in the locality in which they remained, or left the land in the hands of a relative or (in the case of a woman) with an ex-husband, returning to it between marriages. The other category consisted of people who had lost their rights or were too young to acquire them. These, predominantly women, tended to be more mobile than the former category.

The side effects of some forms of state intervention, as well as impoverishment resulting from climatic and environmental stress, seemed to be operating in the same direction, namely towards less ceremony, a more narrow choice of marriage format, partners from geographically closer communities, and later unions. Poverty and hardship notwithstanding, divorce rates might also have been falling as an indirect consequence of state policies in general, and land reform in particular. A local adaptation to restricting conditions had resulted in a reduction in both the flexibility and complexity of marital arrangements. The changes were unintended repercussions of the state's policies rather than a planned intervention in marital relations.

As for the relationship between age groups, the younger generation seemed likely to be dependent for longer on the older one, but to have more control over the choice of partners. With regard to gender relations, the trend was ambiguous. On the one hand, equality in marriage had increased, as seen for example in the reduced expectation of a wife's symbolic subservience to her husband. On the other hand, if serial marriages became an uneconomic option because of the indivisibility of resources, this meant that a form of action hitherto regularly chosen by women was being eroded. More research on these trends is necessary before confident statements can be made. Doubtless, the patterns could be picked up and explained more easily by disaggregating the category of women and focusing more on women in different situations, particularly *vis-à-vis* access to resources.

Notes

1 Bossen, 1988: 142.
2 'In Africa a marriage is not simply a union of a man and a woman; it is an alliance between two families or bodies of kin. We must consider the marriage payments in this connection.' Radcliffe-Brown, (1950) 1986: 51.
3 R. Pankhurst, 1990 (c): 69–71; 264–7.
4 'Most of the literature on marriage negotiations and transactions takes a social or androcentric perspective in which marriageable women are portrayed as passive objects rather than active participants whose livelihoods are at stake.' Bossen, 1988: 127.
5 *Lekebtu waga yit't'alal*, 'Money is thrown [given] for the cost of the livestock [slaughtered]'.
6 'There is also in Africa nothing exactly corresponding to the English "morning-gift" regarded as a payment for accepting sexual embraces, though it is usual for the bridegroom to give gifts to his bride.' Radcliffe-Brown, (1950), 1986: 46. I would argue that the presents here *are* 'morning-gifts' given in exchange for the consummation of the bride's first marriage.
7 From the in-depth interviews, out of a total of 71 marriages described by 23 women.
8 The literature provides a similar picture: in a study of Menz, Reminick, 1973, arrives at a figure of up to fifteen divorces per individual. Bauer, 1973, gives an average duration of 2.7 years for all existing marriages in a community in Tigray.
9 In the in-depth interviews, there was a significant difference between the number of marriages about which people initially told me, and those that emerged in the course of the life histories.
10 The data also give a mean of 6.7 years. First marriages lasted a mean of 3.9 years, ranging form 20 days to 45 years. Last marriage lasted 11 years on average, ranging from 2 months to 40 years. The duration of single marriages was a mean of 16.1 years, ranging from 2 to 50 years. Total sample under 5 years = 128, i.e., 49 per cent of sample.

Duration of marriage

Duration	< 1 month	<1 year	1–2 years	2–3 years	3–4 years	4–5 years
No	5	45	31	23	17	7

11 Weissleder, 1974.
12 'Petitioners in divorce cases are usually women, regardless of where the fault lies or who actually wants the divorce. The man customarily ejects the woman from the household and keeps all the property, forcing the woman to initiate action if she wishes her share.' Messing, 1957: 301.
13 Cuba: Bengelsdorf, 1985; China: Stacey, 1983.
14 Bengelsdorf and Hageman, in Eisenstein, 1979: 291.
15 Poluha, 1989: 63.
16 Reminick, 1973: 316.
17 Vaughan, 1987: 34.
18 Brown, 1975.
19 Stack, 1974: 120–2.
20 This is also in contrast with Islam, in which the marriage has to be sanctified by a religious leader.
21 Divorce committees were set up in resettlement areas, A. Pankhurst, 1992: 242.
22 But note that the second poem in this chapter points to the greater value placed on a mother as compared to a wife. Divisions and distinctions between the experiences of women is an important area of research which it has not been possible to cover in depth.

7

Blood and Tears:
Matters of Life and Death

There is little of more importance to individuals, households and society than life and death. In issues of birth and reproduction, the absence of the Ethiopian state was telling, given the precedents of the involvement of other socialist governments, for example in population policies and the provision of nursery facilities. Curiously perhaps, no socialist government, to my knowledge, has been involved in the opposite end of the life-cycle, in providing funeral arrangements – except when heroes and leaders are given state funerals. This is despite the religious character that funerals take and the ubiquitous existence of traditional systems of social and economic support for such eventualities.

In Menz, as in much of northern Ethiopia, there are few symbolic markers of the stages of life. A number of ceremonies take place in the first few months of the child's life, and these will be discussed first. The next stage of importance is marriage, or rather the series of marriages and household formations, which involve unions between individuals rather than events focused on a single individual, and these have already been considered. Finally we come to death, in which most of the discussion will focus on mourning and *iddir*, burial associations.

The aim in this chapter is to draw attention to the links: the social, economic and political contexts within which activities related to reproduction and the life-cycle are situated. In the section on life and reproduction, I will look at biological events and stage markers, at what women experience and how their role in reproduction is interpreted. To quote de Beauvoir:

These biological considerations are extremely important. In the history of woman they play a part of the first rank and constitute an essential element in her situation. . . . For, the body being the instrument of our grasp upon the world, the world is bound to seem a very different thing when apprehended in one manner or another.[1]

The life-cycle: biology and culture

Women's blood

In the section on *serg* marriages in Chapter 6, we saw that what distinguishes this first form from subsequent marriages is that the bride is considered a virgin. Defloration is exhibited to neighbours and kin with chants and the display of a bloodstained cloth, counterfeited with chicken's blood if necessary.[2] Moreover, unlike brides in subsequent marriages, the virgin bride is given presents that remain her property regardless of subsequent events. These gifts from the groom are a form of payment or reward, an acknowledgement of the uniqueness of the event in the woman's life.

In Amharic, the menstrual period is called *yewer abeba*, literally the monthly flower, an association of fertility with flowers that is common to many cultures, as in the English term to 'deflower' or the French *'prendre la fleur'*. Such terms denote a positive attitude to women's blood or, more precisely, the symbolic appreciation of the male capture of women's 'flower'. The taking of women, symbolized by the discharge of hymen blood, is what is desired; for this the woman is repaid. In this case the blood is not only a fertility marker,[3] but is also seen as a proof of 'purity'.

Hymen blood and the onset of menstruation are not clearly distinguished in Menz culture. Both are associated with penetration. A first degree of explanation of menarche is thus linked to the coupling with a man rather than being explained in terms of the biological development of the girl/woman. Events sometimes disprove the cultural explanation, since unmarried 'innocent' girls experience menstruation. However, this eventuality is generally overlooked and, wherever possible, action is taken to ensure that it does not happen by arranging early marriages.

Menstruation can start when a girl is 13 years old; however, most of the women in Gragn give an age of between 14 and 18 as the date of menarche, and none of the girls I knew who were born after the revolution, 14 years previously, had started their periods.[4] The age at which most women begin to menstruate seems comparatively late, both by national and international standards, no doubt a reflection of poor nutrition and high altitude.[5] Sindé, for example, told me:

My period comes monthly, often on the same day. It lasts about seven days with most of the flow in the first few days. I think I first had it soon after my marriage to Hagmasu [when she was about 18]. . . . I would not have had it if I had not had intercourse. It always comes with marriage and then it stops by itself when you become old.

Most of the pain is in my stomach when it starts and just before. I cannot eat grain and find it difficult even to drink. Once the blood flows properly there is no problem . . . no, there is, what I mean is that it does not hurt but spills instead! We do not use anything to prevent it spilling. If we go out we try and put on proper clothes but otherwise there is nothing, no cloth or anything. . . . The person that is not a woman has an easy time of it!

Sindé focuses on the pragmatic reactions to the monthly flows, to the pain and inconvenience. Alem, in the extract below, is not unusual in seeking divine help:

I first got married when I was about 15. My period had not started then, it came when I was about 18 in '79 [1987]. It comes about monthly, but not always, it starts and stops. When it flows it is really too much during the first four days, that is because of the 'evil eye'. I used to have a *gedem tsifét* (an amulet) to reduce this. Now I put on trousers under my dress but I have no other protection. I just let it run.

As with women worldwide, the period lasts about seven days. It is often irregular and women expressed complaints of all kinds, including pre-menstrual pain and heavy flows. The difficulty encountered in dealing with the menstrual cycle is common to almost all women in the society. It is a regular problem and one that they deal with efficiently. However, it is not much discussed and remains invisible to outsiders. This is not the same kind of constraint as childbearing or other obvious and dramatic 'female burdens', yet it is in such seemingly insignificant ways that the economic poverty and the conditions of life are particularly wearying.

Some women keep an old piece of cloth which they tie between waist and legs; a few have trousers and even fewer possess underwear of some kind. Most have no protection. As mentioned in the above quotations, women lie down when the flow is heavy, or just let the blood drip to the ground. Cleaning up and keeping the blood out of sight is not easy, given the need to fetch water from the spring or the newly installed water pipes.

To discomfort should be added embarrassment. In the case of the few girls or young women attending school, there is the fear that their period may begin while they are in class. Given the lack of sanitation facilities the problems of menstruation are particularly acute. Many do not even attempt to come to school during this time, and may thus miss up to one week in every four. Even if this happens only a few times every year, it can amount to significant absenteeism.

Women's blood is associated with pollution in this society, as elsewhere: menstrual blood soils. The association is particularly developed in the religious sphere. The Church sees menstruating women as unclean,[6] hence the prohibition on their entering the church and on drinking from the *tsiwwa,* the symbolic pot which passes round members of *mehaber,* socio-religious associations discussed in the following chapter. Parallel with this, in the spirit beliefs discussed in the following chapter, a woman will not honour her *ch'ellé* spirit during menstruation.

Pregnancy and delivery

A sixth-grade student summarized the local explanation of reproduction by saying: 'When she has intercourse with a man, the period ceases and the blood sets inside and becomes a child.' Thus a pregnant woman has an accumulation of blood in her stomach, a condition 'camouflaged' for as long as possible. Pregnant women do not tell people of their condition, sometimes not even their mothers, and nobody talks about it openly.

Alemïtu
I was thirteen when Abeba was born. After I became pregnant I began to eat a lot and when I became ill my mother-in-law knew. I tried to keep the knowledge of my pregnancy secret and they did not mention it, but people knew, they would say 'get out of the sun', 'be careful', and so on. I was embarrassed, I was still a child. The child became big inside me, but I said

nothing, I was too embarrassed, nor did anybody else say anything.

People learn for themselves by observation or from veiled oblique references by others. To act more obviously would be inviting trouble from the spirits. Concern for the pregnant woman can be expressed by all with such comments as, 'do not do this work, it is too hard for you', 'rest', and the continuous refrain 'keep out of the sun'. The pregnant woman will also often be given a protective charm, *shotelai*, by her husband, usually around the seventh month of pregnancy.[7]

The themes of camouflage and protection are repeated in sundry ways throughout the pregnancy and continue even after delivery. They include the construction by the new father of a partition for the mother and child. This is made soon after delivery using fragrant plants – in the past, *weyra,* the wild olive tree [*Olea Africana*], and now eucalyptus branches and leaves. During the convalescence period, incense is burned twice a day after delivery, to keep evil spirits away. Protection is also the logic behind the careful burial of the placenta, called *ingida lij*, literally the guest of the child, by the father of the new infant. It is buried inside for a boy and outside for a girl, probably as a symbolic expression of the virilocal tradition in which boys marry in, and girls out of the homestead.

A metal knife is put on the bed after delivery and the mother often wears a metal chain when she begins to move around.[8] Both during the delivery and at circumcision, the new father is supposed to stand guard with a spear in his hand. These different forms of metal are aimed at warding off evil and safeguarding women and their offspring. Prayers are also offered at this time, almost always to the Virgin Mary. After delivery, the greeting from anyone who comes to visit is *Inkwan Maryam marechihu,* 'It is good that Mary spared you,' to which all those in the hut answer: *Maryam tanurachihu.* 'Let Mary make you live/feed you'. When a pregnancy ends in miscarriage or death soon after delivery, precautions are found to have been wanting or an explanation is given in metaphysical terms: *Géta t'eltogn new,* 'It is because God took a dislike to me'.

Food taboos also operate during pregnancy and these are described by women as a form of protection for mother and child alike. Wesené and Yematawerk' explained:

> When we are pregnant we cannot eat milk, nettles and cabbage. These foods would change the colour of the child, they would be on the child (*liju lay yihonal*). Most other things women can eat, except after birth we do not eat roasted grains, *k'ollo*, since it breaks your teeth at this time.
>
> I could not eat *shiro* [a spicy sauce], or coffee unless it was cooled first. They say it is bad to eat hot things; also milk and castor seed are bad, these stay on the head of the child and will not come off, they will not wash off. *K'iraré* [diluted beer] is good.

The birth of a child is also celebrated by the consumption of certain kinds of food. *Genfo,* a dish of boiled wheat or barley, is prepared for all who attended the birth. It is eaten soon after delivery. *Intiktik,* a drink made from wheat or barley, is prepared for the mother during convalescence, especially if she is having problems breast-feeding the infant. After delivery, one or two chickens are slaughtered. They are often of a particular colour and sex, almost invariably a red hen and a cock which is *gebsemma*, the name given to describe a mixture of black and white. The chickens are made into *wet'*, stew, expressly for the mother, although in practice other members of the family also partake of the meal.

The slaughtering of chickens is carried out in the hut, rather than outside, as it would be ordinarily. Unless present during the delivery, well-wishers should not come until after the third day, because of the blood in the hut, both from the delivery and from the slaughtered chickens. Slaughtering occurs even during a Christian fasting period.[9] If the fast is a short one, the meat is consumed when the fast is broken, otherwise it is given to children under seven years of age, who do not have to fast, or thrown away. The symbolism behind the slaughtering of chicken was never explicitly explained, though it is clearly a way of greeting the propitious event. There is also a parallel between the ritual blood of the chicken and that discharged by the woman during delivery, and the association between women and chicken is one which occurs repeatedly. The event of a birth is surrounded with symbolic rituals which, given cultural differences across different societies, can also act as ethnic markers. Births provide a sphere of tradition which defines the community and provides group identity.

Perhaps the clearest indication of society's concern for the mother can be seen in the tradition of *aras*, up to 80 days of convalescence for the new mother. During this time the new mother will be looked after by her mother in either her natal or her current homestead. Nowadays, the convalescence period is far from assured and usually lasts only ten to 20 days. During this time the new mother is not expected to help in the running of the household. The grandmother or another female relative has to be released from her own household's duties to take on those of the convalescing mother, and this other woman also has to be fed. The marked decrease in the convalescence time that most mothers could expect was the result of gradual impoverishment, and a shrinking sense of responsibility between generations.

Most of the examples given above show how a pregnant woman is carried through her delivery period by a set of culturally created protections. The fear seems to be less one of woman's fertility *per se,* and a need to control it, than a dreading of the dangers that she and her child might encounter. The fears are founded on the real dangers of mortality, for which accurate figures are among the hardest to obtain, since women do not like to remember their losses. For the thirteen women that I knew best and on whom I gathered a full pregnancy record, eight had lost a child before it reached the age of three. Three of the women had had two miscarriages, one had had one miscarriage. An additional three women had lost a child under one year of age and two more of the women's children had died before they reached their third year. Maternal deaths were also a real danger, though I only knew of one case in the immediate neighbourhood.

The attitude towards women's blood in the context of pregnancy and delivery is most clearly associated with fertility and reproduction. The fundamental importance of birth is culturally hidden, introducing a negative connotation to a development, which, if successfully carried through, is positively valued. As in the case of menstrual blood, an unfavourable stance is struck, and compounded by the religious association of all women's blood with pollution. People who have been near a newly delivered mother are unclean in the eyes of the Church, and both they and the child will need to be ritually cleansed.

Reproduction and contraception

Childbirth is a cause for celebration, especially if it is a couple's first child. Women who have not given birth successfully are often openly worried about it, and spend time and money on priests and soothsayers. Barrenness is seen as the woman's fault, until proved otherwise.

The birth of twins is considered unfortunate, since the infants are less likely to survive and the mother's ordeal is considerable. A woman is considered to have problems enough ensuring that one child at a time has enough milk, without having to cope with two. In Ethiopia, abortion is illegal and culturally taboo. As elsewhere in the world, this does not, however, prevent the practice. Women use mixtures made from plants such as kosso (Hagenia abyssinica), and indod (Phytolacca dodecandra), which they make into a drink. Sindedo, a long thin type of grass, or any other sharp long instrument, is also poked through the vagina. Finally, some women are known to use contraceptive pills available from the clinic in town, taking a large quantity of them in one go.

The issue of controlling fertility is rarely broached directly. When questioned, the first reaction of both men and women is always that 'God decides such matters', and 'the more He gives the better'; that they 'would be happy with as many children as possible'; and that 'it is none of their business to think or plan conception in any way'. However, this reaction masks the knowledge that most households do regularly practise birth control, the most common form being extended breast-feeding and the decision to sleep separately. Disagreements over sexual intercourse because of women's greater fears of pregnancy were often mentioned to me as a cause of marital tensions and break-ups.

Tat'ere
What I have is enough. I have two boys and one girl. Men are the ones who want more, they would be angry at the thought of stopping the numbers.

Some men and women commented that these were hard times, and that it was therefore better to have fewer children.

Asnak'ech
I have never used any kind of contraception, I have heard about such things but I do not think they are good. 'It is drying up a fertile area' (limat madrek' new), one gets everything by giving birth and being replaced. Besides, they

say that you become ill if you do it, if you take the medicines. If I were rich and well, then there would be no problem about giving birth, the older children would help in the household. But I am poor, what am I to feed them with?

The Family Guidance Association, working through the Ministry of Health, provided contraception facilities on two days a week. The contraception clinics were appended to the health clinics in the area, most of which were in the towns. Initially, the facilities were available only to married women whose husbands were willing to let them use the facilities. In 1982, these two conditions were relaxed when Ethiopia, together with 87 other countries, signed a United Nations Convention which aimed to give women greater control over their own lives.[10] The forms of contraception available included the loop and condoms, but the use of pills was the most common. Sterilization was not available.

Since 1983, 809 women have registered in the Mehal Meda clinic, and there were, at the time of the research, some 397 who regularly came for more pills. By far the majority of patients were urban dwellers. None of them came from Gragn peasants' association. Out of 149, the average age of women attending the clinic was 24, and the estimated age range 16–45.[11] The women who made use of the contraception clinics were considerably better educated than the average rural or even urban woman, with just under half the sample having been to school, and, of those, the average having attended for six years.

Returning to the data on Gragn, for those willing to give a figure for the kind of children preferred, the questionnaires indicated that the difference between desired boys and girls was at the aggregate level, a 12.5 per cent greater interest in male children.[12] Dessita explained the situation to me in the following way:

We can give birth to up to 12 children, but what do you do with them? They die. We only want about five, that is if we are rich; these would be let us say three boys and two girls. A poor person is happy with three: two boys and one girl. Boys are better, they are more important in terms of making a strong relationship outside. The girl will marry and leave, though until then, she is the one that will help her mother.

In answers to the questionnaire, the preference for boys was also reflected, in real terms, by the gender composition of offspring. When we look at the aggregate of children said to have been born to the households, there were 5 per cent fewer girls. This distinction was likewise reflected in the data on the region, women being 46 per cent of the population, and this despite the constant recruitments of boys and men for military service.[13] It is difficult to explain the reasons for a lower proportion of female births without relying on an explanation in terms of reduced social value. Girls and women have a lower profile *vis-à-vis* the community and thus might not be recorded in the statistics. The low female figure among the adult population can also be explained by proportionally fewer girls surviving because of the preferential care given to boys, women's greater vulnerability, in particular during childbirth, and women's greater out-migration.

Nevertheless, it should be pointed out that, in Gragn, the kind and amount of ululating with which a successful childbirth is greeted is the same for boys and girls. This is in marked contrast to the reported widespread custom elsewhere in Ethiopia of ululating more for boys than for girls. For example, Parkyns[14] gives a figure of twelve ululations for boys and three for girls. In Menz, even after the event, one of the first questions is never, 'Is it a boy or a girl?', and neither relatives nor neighbours automatically know the answer even when the question is put to them. Given the importance of gender divisions in society, and the tradition of a different degree of celebration between the genders in other areas, the lack of interest in the sex of the child is surprising. An explanation might be sought in the considerable amount of infant mortality in the area. Until the child survives, it is perhaps irrelevant whether it is a girl or a boy. The tradition of not specifying the sex might also be part of the wider fear that asking about, looking at, or talking to the child might somehow cause harm.

The discussion so far makes it clear that the state had had little impact on the ideological or material conditions in which reproduction occurred, despite its importance to the society, and the conditions of and attitudes towards women that it engendered. The issue of family planning and population control, however, provided an example of how factors that affect women in particular were broached in the light of the socialist government's own priorities. The question can perhaps be asked why the *Derg* did not attempt a grand population control policy. Clapham's suggestion is that of fear of opposition:

> There has been no sustained government attempt to control the rate of population increase . . . the government is increasingly aware . . . any attempt to reduce the birth rate would require a large-scale campaign which would tax its resources and possibly bring it into headlong confrontation with peasant attitudes and religious convictions.[15]

I would argue that the answer lies not in an inability to do so, but in the location of birth in the private domain in general and 'women's business' in particular. This is not to say that had the government woken up to the issue and acted, peasant attitudes and religious convictions would not have opposed the new policies. However, the history of Mengistu's régime was one of massive campaigns (villagization, resettlement, military service), most of which were unpopular and yet were implemented regardless of 'current opinion'. As for the issue of 'taxing [economic] resources', money could have been gathered by forced national contributions, as was the case for the war effort and the famine.

In terms of future developments, a population control policy or a contraception campaign might well be introduced as part of developmental objectives, in which case political and economic backing is likely to be given to it. However, such polices are more likely to arise from a Malthusian association of poverty with population increase rather than in response to an understanding of women's position. Furthermore, where a population policy has been introduced as a strategy of the state, the record has often been one of oppression, not liberation. Thus the evidence on the one-child policy in China[16] suggests that it resulted in ill-treatment of women and female infanticide, given a social context in which boys and men were more valuable to a household than girls and women, in particular because of virilocality. More generally, the policy created increased social pressure on individual women and their households, because kin and state priorities conflicted and economic incentives and disincentives were in force.

Circumcision

Unlike blood discussed earlier, which is rooted in developments within the female anatomy, circumcision is a culturally created event, and one which in Menz affects both infant boys and girls. The circumcision of boys and girls remains located firmly in the female sphere of expertise, since it is a woman who performs the operation. Furthermore, as we will see, the operation is deemed to be more important for the female sex.

In the case of boys, the operation involves the removal of the foreskin. The circumcision of Amhara girls is a mild operation when compared with that performed in many other societies.[17] It involves no infibulation, no sewing up or joining together of amputated edges of the genital organs. However, both clitoridectomy, the removal of parts of the clitoris, and labiadectomy, the excision of the *labia minora* and *labia majora*, can occur. Although infibulation does not take place during circumcision, it is reportedly quite common that during childbirth, the skin will be cut to 'ease' the child's passage. Even where this does not occur the skin sometimes tears and is then left to heal on its own.

In Amhara society circumcision of boys should occur when they are eight days old[18] or on any even day thereafter. Girls should be circumcised when they are seven days old or on any odd days thereafter; both operations are carried out on infants much earlier than in many other societies. The basis for the distinction between boys and girls is a representation of the belief that girls are placed on the left, the odd, side of Jesus, boys on the right, even, side. This is a symbolic division which unequivocally values boys more than girls. Also connecting circumcision with Christianity is the tradition that sometimes, though rarely, the operation is found to be unnecessary because the child is said to have a *'ye-Maryam girizat'*, 'circumcision by Mary', meaning to be born already circumcised. Despite the above links, circumcision in the area seems to be pre-Christian and pre-Islamic. Herodotus, among others, suggested that in many areas, including Ethiopia, female circumcision was known 500 years before Christ.[19]

The custom is sanctified on religious grounds and on the basis – a negative rationale – of difficulties which would arise if it was not observed. Stopping the practice, it is argued, would bring problems of premarital sex, dishonour and trouble in marriage, since uncircumcised women are said to be more selfish and demanding. Men are therefore less likely to marry uncircumcised women and a husband might even sue the parents if the union took place without his knowing that the bride had not been circumcised. In pregnancy, uncircumcised mothers are said to have difficulties, making a successful birth impossible or at least more difficult. More generally, it is considered unclean, immodest and polluting not to be circumcised, for a boy and a girl, but in particular for a girl. The difference seems to be that for a boy it is shameful to him only, whereas an uncircumcised girl shames her whole family. Uncircumcised boys are more common than uncircumcised girls. To my queries, Dessita answered:

> You ask 'why does it happen?' – what a question! . . . It is because of our tradition, our belief. It is done to ensure that when the girl grows up she can give birth, that is why. Also it is an insult for boys and girls, and to the boy it brings disease, *yibelawal,* it eats him [causes itching]. It brings them more pain when they are corrected [circumcised] later, in particular for a boy who feels it for about a month, the cut for the girls is less painful. Everybody is circumcised. . . .
>
> . . . This one [a son, aged about two] I have not had circumcised. The one who died was, so I have not yet had it done to him.

There is no public ceremony attached to the circumcision act. Nor is it perceived as an initiation, or a rite of passage, since it is carried out in infancy, almost before the child is given an identity.[20] In Menz, as in Amhara culture more generally, it is seen as a private event, which takes place when an individual infant has reached the right age rather than *en masse;* within the household and not in the wider community. This is not to say that there is no symbolism or ceremony attached to the event. On the appointed day, food is prepared, and as the child is operated on, the father or some other man stands by the entrance to the hut with a dagger or other metal tool, a repeat of the performance enacted at the time of delivery.

As we have seen, there are specific days on which circumcision is supposed to take place in the first few weeks of the child's life. However, it is not always easy for a family to find a woman to circumcise their child on the right day, since women with the skill are scarce. It might also be an inconvenient time for the household. Other reasons for delay might be that the infant seems unwell, or that the mother has lost infants in the past. There is then a reluctance to expose the child to circumcision quite so early. Especially in the case of boys, where the shame of being uncircumcised is less of a condemnation than in the case of a girl, the operation is sometimes postponed. My data from 97 interviews suggest that 22 boys between the age of 1 month and 22 years were not circumcised. The corresponding figure for girls was 12, and the age range was smaller; I did not obtain any examples of uncircumcised girls above the age of 14. The rule that boys are circumcised on even days and girls on odd days is also not always followed.[21] This can probably be explained by practical considerations which do not always fit the rigid distinctions that the culture enjoins. There are time constraints on both the household and the 'circumciser', and there is the need to find some cash and/or food with which to pay the woman. It could also reflect the fear of performing too much by the letter, yet another way of deceiving the spirits intent on doing harm to the child.

As we have seen, circumcision occurs because people believe that to do otherwise would have dangerous repercussions. Nonetheless, the operations are feared. The side-effects associated with female circumcision are numerous. They can include haemorrhage, which is particularly dangerous given the anaemia prevalent in the area, infection, and complications including swelling, incontinence, the possibility of dysmenorrhoea (painful menstruation), blockage of the vagina and hence partial or total amenorrhoea (the absence of menstruation), painful sexual intercourse, infertility; complications during pregnancy and childbirth and anxiety if any of the above occur. In the case of male circumcision, the dangers are fewer, though haemorrhage and infection can also result in the child's death. In terms of local explanations, circumcision is feared because it might be the cause of, or more precisely, the vehicle through which evil forces can weaken and kill the child and, in the case of the mother, lead to complications during delivery. Beyond these feelings of fear and negative associations (both if the operation is undertaken and if it is delayed) is the practical attitude of 'getting it over with'. Mothers cover their ears and turn away from a sight that causes pain and holds danger, but which they believe to be necessary.

Aspersion and christening

Aspersion, or purification with holy water, usually takes place in the hut where mother and infant are living. It is a ceremony undertaken by a priest, usually the father confessor of the household.[22] The 20th day is said to be the most important for the event, though many households also call their father confessor on the tenth day, and in practice the exact dates are not always strictly kept. One such aspersion is described in my diary as follows:

> Ayele called me at seven in the morning for the aspersion of his infant brother aged 20 days. The whole thing lasted about half an hour. The people present consisted of the hut members: Mammit, the mother, Zegene, the father, Ayele and Alemayehu the sons, and a daughter. Then there was the *nefs abbat*, the father confessor, the new mother's brother, and various neighbours who were invited to receive the holy water if they wanted to. The ceremony consisted of simultaneous, but not synchronized recitals in Geez, by the father confessor and Zegene, himself a priest.
>
> After about a quarter of an hour of this, the father confessor started spraying us with water, each person mumbling *yeftugn*, 'release me', as the spray hit their foreheads. The water was taken from the household's domestic water jug. The father confessor started the spraying with Ayele, the oldest son, a child that was known to be afflicted with a type of madness, then the rest of us. Mammit and her new child undressed in a corner and received most of the water, being drenched rather than sprinkled with it, a gasp escaping Mammit since the water was very cold.
>
> That was it, the priest was invited to stay to lunch but refused, he also tried half-heartedly to refuse 1 *birr* that Zegene was giving him but then accepted. The brother of Mammit then gave her 1 *birr* for 'coffee money'.

Sindé was called but didn't come, perhaps because she was going to be working on opening the dung-hole of Dimmim, another neighbour. Abeba came, got sprayed and left. Asnak'ech, also a neighbour, turned up late with her young son Babush after Zegene and the father confessor had left. She wanted to be sprayed with the holy water, and after some discussion, Alemayehu, the twelve-year-old son who is studying to be a priest, was persuaded to do the job; his initial reluctance turning to enjoyment at the fun of splashing people.

Much more central to the life-cycle, in Amhara society, is the christening or baptism. This occurs for boys on the fortieth day and girls on the eightieth day after birth.[23] On the appointed day, kin, friends and neighbours are invited to church and then to the household's homestead. Considerable preparations revolving around food and drink are organized in advance, and the guests usually contribute gifts of money, from 50 cents to about 2 *birr*, or presents of cloth or beads.

At church a christening name is given to the child. This name is kept relatively secret, and is rarely used, since once known, those with evil intentions can do harm to the individual by using the christening name. It is not unheard of for a boy's christening to be delayed until the eightieth day, the date for a girl's christening, in cases where the 'proper' fortieth day is inconvenient. A godmother or godfather is selected, usually along gender lines. Once again, the rules are sometimes ignored, with godmothers chosen for boys and godfathers for girls.

Yeshewagét' is among the women known in the village as good midwives. She is also a friend of Nigist, a recently widowed woman. When Yeshewagét' gave birth to her son, Nigist was the one who helped her with the delivery. Yeshewagét' told me that she had given her son to her friend as a godchild to thank her.

Thus, although gender distinctions exist, with different rules for boys and girls, when it comes to the dates of circumcision and christening as well as the choice of godparent, the distinctions are not always found to be practical or desired, and are sometimes circumvented.

We have seen that both men and women see the connection between women and blood as the women's source of power and value, but also as a fearful, dangerous and polluting involvement. Yet women are not secluded at the time of menstruation, and midwives – the women whose acknowledged sphere of specialization is by definition the reproductive – are not marginalized in society. Water, purified ritually by a male priest, cancels the negative associations. There is also an extent to which symbolic valuation is forgotten in the way men and women cope with the blood at the more pragmatic day-to-day level.

But where in all of this, if anywhere, did the state make an appearance? In practice, none of the various organs of state have influenced the ideology or the practices discussed. The clinics under the Ministry of Health have not been given the kind of funding and resources to organize systematic and ongoing education and services. There has been no question of setting up tampon or sanitary towel factories, for example. Pregnant women sometimes attended the clinic in order to receive a tetanus injection, and if there were complications the woman would be carried on her bed to the nearest clinic. In addition, nurses visited peasants' associations so that infants could be inoculated.[24] However, the support was so inadequate that even the casual mention here is liable to exaggerate the extent of health provision.

In the case of circumcision, I was informed that in the early days of the revolution, people were given a lecture against circumcising their daughters. They were told the practice was dangerous and 'backward' and that they should bring their sons to be circumcised under more hygienic conditions in clinics. These instructions did not carry much weight in the face of traditions and were never followed up. The dangers of infection, complications and death from the operation were acknowledged locally, but the fear of repercussions from not having children circumcised was even stronger, fears that a few words by an official could do little to assuage.

Expertise and kinship

The life-cycle is an important component of the individual's position in any society, including that of Menz. This is particularly so for women, since their role in reproduction is emphasized culturally. The heterogeneity of women's experience lies not only in wealth and status, but also in whether or not they have given birth, and the number and gender of their offspring.

The situation is complicated by other conditions. For example, I argued in Chapter 7 that there is a difference between the position of married, single and female-headed households. In addition to these differences, there are those introduced by the involvement of some women in events surrounding reproduction. I shall now examine these spheres of knowledge briefly before considering the opportunity for social kinship creation that such events afford. A number of women in the society have acknowledged skills. Some women are known as midwives; others perform circumcision; still others are healers, fortune tellers, women who interpret dreams and witch doctors of various kinds. The first two of these activities will be examined here, while the role of some women in fortune telling and mediation with spirits will be considered in the following chapter.

When contractions start, a midwife is called and female neighbours and relatives come to show support. The midwife's role is to keep an eye on developments, offer advice and take charge of the practical aspects of the delivery. When the time comes, she holds the baby, ensuring it is protected on entry into the world. She cuts and ties the umbilical cord, and often smears a bit of the liquid from the umbilical wound on the child's lips. A mixture of egg and dung is then, sometimes, rubbed on the umbilical wound. Finally, the midwife cleans the baby and puts a small pat of butter in its mouth. Other women, such as a younger sister or, if there is nobody in a lower social position, the new grandmother, wipe up the blood.

Unlike their counterparts in India, for example,[25] midwives in Menz tend not to be despised. There is little degradation associated with mid-wifery, or rather, the negative views about blood and pollution are countered by a value set on ability and knowledge. Thus midwives, *awwalaj*, are often also called *awak'ï*, those who know. They are not a separate category or class of people: any woman who is thought to be knowledgeable can be called upon.

Usually on the day before households plan to have their child circumcised, the father goes in search of a circumciser. In Gragn, most men headed for a neighbouring peasants' association looking for one particular woman. Some men asked a woman from Mehal Meda to come and help. Many more women had a reputation as midwives than were known to perform the circumcision. This latter occupation seemed the most feared because of the dangers of causing the infant harm or being blamed for any subsequent illness. If this is so, circumcision would seem to be a more dangerous event in an infant's life than entry into the world. Circumcisers seemed to be given a lower status in society than midwives or other skilled women, for which reason outsiders to the community were sought.

After the operation, the circumciser helps to heal the wound by putting something on it. According to the preference of the woman who does the operation this can consist of egg and dung, oil, alcohol or juice from medicinal leaves. In exchange for doing the job, the woman is given a meal after the event, processed food to take home, such as a *ch'ibbit't'o'* (a ball of *injera* with *berberé*), and/or unprocessed food, such as grain and eggs. Increasingly, a cash payment was also expected, of up to 2 *birr* for one operation. These rewards were in contrast to the midwife's, which were less formalized, probably because she was chosen from within the com-munity and could be thanked at some later date, for example by choosing the midwife as the godmother, particularly in the case of a baby girl.

Respondents suggested that it was experience that made a woman knowledgeable, that you were not born a midwife or a circumciser, but made yourself one by reputation. In practice, women also branched out from one particular skill until they became known for a number of different ones, for example, as circumcisers, healers, interpreters of dreams and fortune tellers, as midwives and beer brewers. In Gragn, skilled women were often, though not exclusively, in female-only or female-headed households. This was explained to me pragmatically: such women, it was said, could go to the people who call for them without having to make lunch and supper for their husbands first. Such women were also more likely to look out for means of supplementing their livelihood.

The focus on the individual is in many ways contrary to the way in which women perceive the life-cycle. In particular, in the first few years a child's life is intimately linked to that of its mother. Thus the study of conditions and attitudes surrounding infancy easily develops into a study of motherhood. Furthermore, as seen earlier in this chapter, women's kin become important during the *aras* period, the time in late pregnancy and after delivery when women turn to their mothers for help and support.

In addition, the importance of reproduction is such that the time is used not only to activate biological kin but also as a way of creating social kinship in the form of 'eye mothers' and 'godparents'.[26] In Menz, the woman who holds the infant as s/he is being cut during circumcision becomes known as the *yeayn innat*, 'the eye mother', a very loose bond between the woman and the child which is rarely officially activated. The woman chosen is usually a close friend of the mother who can be trusted to hold the child. The mother herself tends to be unable to bear the sight and sounds of the child being operated on; she looks away and blocks her ears in order not to see and hear what is going on.

A godmother or father is selected by the parents before the christening:

Alemïtu
The godmother I chose for my child was my stepmother. I liked her, and gave her my child; it was a way of making sure the friendship would last even if she left and divorced my father. She had told me I should give it to the woman who was the midwife, but I gave the child to her instead.

The kinship thereby created is sometimes kept active through friendship and the gift of presents from the godparent. Sometimes it ceases to operate altogether and it is also possible for parents to offer the child to the Church rather than to a living individual. A godparent is initially chosen in order to create a kinship between the godparent and the child's parents, and only if this relationship endures is it likely to develop into a relationship between godparent and child.

It is not obvious who benefits more from the tie, since the kinship can be between equals or unequals. Generally, in the former cases it represents an expression of friendship, often between neighbours. In the latter case, the tie can also be made by a poor person to establish patronage from a rich or powerful one, as a form of homage and with the hope that it will be beneficial to the parent. The kinship is hardly ever created by a richer household to link it to a poorer one. The choice of godparent also tends to run along gender lines, women being more important in the choice of a godmother for their daughters and men for their sons.

Death

In Menz, as in Amhara communities more generally, birthdays are not usually recalled and are never celebrated. This is in marked contrast to death, which is commemorated several days, months and sometimes years afterwards. The most important of the commemorations usually occurs on the fortieth day, the *tezkar*, though it can also take place nearer the time of death or several months later.[27] The Church and its priests play a central role in all events associated with death. These range from the last rites to burial on consecrated land. The Church provides the ritual, and local burial associations the material and social support. In contrast to the role of the Church, the state has had no involvement in events associated with death, except to discourage certain traditions seen as unhealthy or dangerous. The absence of active participation resulted in the irony of party officials being buried on Church land, under the jurisdiction of priests. It also meant that the state was cut off from an event that is central to individuals, their households and the wider community.

In the funerals of the past there was an attempt to de-beautify clothes and express grief through lack of ornaments. The oldest clothes were worn, sometimes smeared with soot. This tradition is being replaced by one encouraging clean attire and the wearing of 'best' clothes. Increasingly, women's mourning is indicated by turning up the border of the scarf. The physical expressions of grief can be extreme, including tearing one's face and beating oneself. The death is announced by wailing, but also by shots being fired into the air, especially in the case of the death of an important person. These traditions are ones that the state tried to abolish.[28]

Rather than go through all the ceremonial and ritual elements of a funeral, I will focus here on the *iddir* – also known as *k'iré* – the burial associations, and then comment on mourning.

Burial associations

In the past, very strong informal support systems existed at times when households faced personal distress, and where custom required expenditures which were so high that they could not be shouldered easily by the individual household. In Gragn these help-lines have only recently been replaced by *iddir,* geographically defined burial associations, which, through urban influence, are becoming formalized. Several of my informants observed that *iddir* did not exist in their parents' day and one added, *yezaré lij new gud yawet't'aw,* 'it is today's child that has come up with amazing things'. But in the case of the burial association she added *k'il aydellem,* 'it is not stupid'. Several of these associations had come into being recently, though during the time of my research many people in the peasants' association had not yet joined.

The model for the new forms of burial associations in the rural communities could be seen in the town of Mehal Meda. The town had two *iddir* with around five hundred members each. Most people, including Party members and government employees, belonged to one or other of these. Each association had a card membership system with an entry fee and monthly dues, and hence a capital fund. Tents and equipment could also be borrowed or rented for other occasions. When a member or a close relative of a member had died, the burial association summoned its members with a trumpet. A sum of 100 *birr* and some grain was provided to the family so that a feast could be prepared for people to eat on their return from the church and burial, as they paid their respects to the relatives. There were fines if people did not attend.

Returning to the discussion on Gragn, in 1989 there were two functioning burial associations. The most active was in one of the eight zones of the peasants' association, which had gathered together everybody from that zone. This burial group started soon after the revolution, as a result of locally generated interest in formalizing the existing system. There were about 60 people in the association, with an executive of 14 men. Meetings were held at weekly intervals but after the advent of villagization ten of the 60 members had moved away. Meetings thinned out and became irregular. Belonging to the burial association entailed passing on information regarding the death of someone when you were advised of it, and giving a quantity measured out as three *birch'ik'k'o* [glasses] each of barley and beans. It also involved going to church for the burial and performing a number of gendered tasks such as, for men, carrying the body, digging the grave and burying the corpse, and, for women, helping with such tasks as taking food and drink to the church.

In Gragn the association worked in other ways beyond help for relatives of the deceased. When a person incurred the condemnation of the burial association members – if they stole, or their cattle ate the grain of others – the association could impose a fine, usually of 2 to 5 *birr*, according to the severity of the fault and the warnings previously given. These fines could be applied not only to the burial association members but also to those outside the community. If someone committed an offence and was not a member, he or she was still perceived to be liable under burial association law. This legal system worked in parallel with the officially state-sanctioned *fird shengo*, the law courts mentioned in Chapter 3.

More recently, there were attempts to start a burial association in the villagized community of Gragn. This association had come into being just before I left, and had a membership of about 20. It was based on monthly payments of 10 cents. In addition, when someone died, members contributed one tin full of barley, and two dung-cakes. The association from Gragn, unlike the main one in town, did not observe strict definitions of the relatives for whom the support could be activated. This matter would no doubt have been defined later, since, as we have seen, the process of change towards formalization of the system was already under way.

Some people felt that they had been bullied into joining the burial *iddir* in Gragn. Social and economic pressure could be put on those who did not want to join. For example, we saw in Chapter 5 that herding could be done in *Gwassa tera*, groups of up to 20 people involved in a system of communal herding. Those who initially refused to join the burial *iddir* were told that if they did not do so, the *Gwassa tera* would disintegrate, an event which could lead to considerable trouble and hardship until a new one was organized. This should be taken as a warning against seeing the state as the only coercive institution in modern rural Menz. Nevertheless, there is a difference. In the case of the local change towards more formalized burial associations there was a reciprocal and actively negotiated relationship, in contrast to the patronage relationship which, I argued, explains the limited acceptance of state policies by the peasantry. Furthermore, in the case of *iddir*, there was debate and discussion and a resulting involvement in the new policies, brought about through community pressure.

Ironically, however, the formalization of burial association rules in town proved wanting, at least according to some women who introduced what was known as a *sét iddir'*, women's *iddir'*. It was a comparatively small association of about 30 individuals who could be called upon when *any* relative died, not only a close relative as was the case with the 'dominant' burial association. In this *sét iddir*, the women each brought 25 cents and some wood on the day of the death. They all mourned the dead and were supportive of the bereaved. The formation of *sét iddir* suggests that some women felt the need for less formalized structures. Left to their own devices, they reinstituted these in parallel with the formal burial associations.

Mourning

The task of mourners is to make the funeral a success, to have tears and sorrow expressed loudly and lengthily and thus honour the departed. The first two poems below were delivered by people who are known as *alk'ash*, literally 'one who cries', or professional mourners. Both men and women were called upon, usually if they had experienced considerable losses themselves. They are repaid in kind or cash for their services during funerals. Women *alk'ash* predominate and are vocal not just in the home but in the public domain of the neighbourhood and the church. Men, women and children are all mourned; however, a man's death tends to be surrounded with greater ceremony and expense.

The purpose of the mourning is not just to honour the passing of a particular person, but also to express the sorrow felt by those left behind.

እናት ፡ ትሙት ፡ አሉ ፡	They said 'let the mother die',
እናት ፡ እንዴት ፡ ትሞት ፤	How can a mother die?
ሳትጠይቅ ፡ አታድርም ፡	She will not stay away without asking
የልጇን ፡ እድራሻ ።	For the whereabouts of her child.

እናት ፡ የሌላችሁ ፡	Those that do not have a mother,
እንሂድ ፡ እንግዛ ፤	Let us go, let us buy [one];
አባት ፡ የሞተባችሁ ፡	Those of you whose fathers have died,
እንሂድ ፡ እንግዛ ፤	Let us go, let us buy [one];
እህት ፡ የሌላችሁ ፡	Those who do not have a sister,
እንሂድ ፡ እንግዛ ፤	Let us go, let us buy [one];
ባል ፡ የሞተባችሁ ፡	And those of you whose husbands have died,
እንሂድ ፡ እንግዛ ፤	Let us go, let us buy [one];
ልጅ ፡ የሞተባችሁ ፡	Those of you whose children have died,
እንሂድ ፡ እንግዛ ፤	Let us go, let us buy [one];
እኔ ፡ አልመልስም ፡	I will not return them,
ዋጋም ፡ ቢበዛ ።	Even if the [asking] price is too high.

The dirges are often at the general level, addressed to 'those who have lost a father, mother. . .'. Mourning is thus a time for communal remembrance; a time during which all participants together recall their own previous losses. Sometimes, however, the departed are remembered explicitly by name, people joining in by adding their own laments. The following two dirges are examples of verses that people recited when they felt the need to add their own accounts of woe and want, using the occasion of another funeral for remembering their dead.

እለቃኝ፡እጸሞጥኩኝ፡	Mourner, I listened to you
እዚህ፡ቆም፡ብዬ ፤	Standing over here;
ጥላሁን፡በየነ፡	T'elahun Beyene [name of deceased]
ተስፋዬ፡መስፍን፡	Tesfaye Mesfin [name of deceased]
ትይለኝ፡ብዬ ፡፡	Hoping you would say.
	[Hoping you would add the above names to the list of those being mourned]

እለቃኝ፡እለቅሺና፡	Mourner, mourn and then
መልሺልኝ፡ለእኔ ፤	Reply to me;
በረዶ፡የመታው፡	As if hit by hail
ሆነዋል፡ወገኔ ፡፡	Have my relatives become.
	[I have lost all my kin and need to mourn them now]

The end of a person's life is an important event, its cultural importance underscored by considerable economic outlays. As we have seen, the funeral itself is organized with the aid of an *iddir*, a social organization instituted with this need in mind, although its importance is such that it transcends the specific to incorporate additional functions. The whole event stresses the sense of community and duties to kin and friends alike, each funeral reminding people of the death of others and the scene creating mass catharsis. The importance of these events hardly seems to square with the view held by some outsiders of a peasantry that is so individualistic that households cannot cooperate without suspicion and ill-will.[29]

Conclusion

The first part of this chapter considered issues of reproduction and attitudes towards women's blood. I argued that reproduction, nurturing and child-bearing are realms in which women see themselves as, and are acknowledged to be, important and pivotal. At the same time, there is a tradition of camouflaging, fearing and suspecting any disclosure or representation of reproduction and fertility. Such attitudes have their source in the fear for mother and child, and suspicion of spiritual and human evil-wishers. There is also a negative association expressed through Christian values in which women are polluters, contact with their blood needing to be countered by the blessings of water and the prayers of a priest. There is, in addition, a conflict between these forces encouraging seclusion and the way in which the culture requires the heralding and celebration of life, with the ritualization of births, circumcision and baptism. Moreover, it is often these very events, located firmly in the female sphere of action, which define the community and its roots.

The overall effect is an ambivalence towards women, by women themselves as well as by men, a sense that women grow up valuing and devaluing themselves because of their role in reproduction, their sexuality, and in the events associated with birth. Finally, there is also a realm in which symbolic valuation or devaluation is interfered with by prosaic practical inconveniences and problems of dealing with such matters as menstruation. This results in a down-to-earth unashamed attitude towards the body and bodily functions, an attitude that sends warning signals against giving too rigid a picture of women's power or oppression based on an interpretation of symbolic rituals.

The second major component of the chapter considered death, the way that it was observed and commemorated. It was noted that death involved the community as a whole, not just the household which suffered the bereavement. Life and death were socially constructed and economically enacted without the state's direct involvement. In contrast, the Church was seen as playing a central role. Trends developing during the period of research included reduced expenditures as a result of scarcity and impoverishment. Nevertheless, internal structures of support continued to evolve, as we saw in the trend towards an increasing formalization of burial associations.

The gender construction of death was less categorical and rigid than that of birth. Men, being of higher status in the society, were likely to be mourned more fully than women and they presided over the religious element of the event. Membership of a burial association was predominantly in their name, as heads of household; however, women tended to participate more in attendance of associations. Women were the more vocal mourners, vocal even in a public domain; they perceived themselves, and were perceived, as the main bearers of sorrow.[30]

Notes

1 De Beauvoir, (1949) 1972: 60.

2 Similar traditions exist in many other countries. For example in France, see de Beauvoir, (1949) 1972.

3 In this book I do not look at menopause and the position of women once they have ceased being involved in reproduction. This is partly because I was never made aware of menopause as a clearly defined stage, or post-menopausal women as a distinct category in society. This is not to say that attitudes of, and to, women might not change at this stage in the life-cycle.

4 From 149 cases of women using contraception facilities in Mehal Meda, the average age of menarche (for a predominantly urban population) in the area was 15 years; it ranged from 11 to 18.

5 In many ways, however, it was the beneficial side-effects of the late menarche that struck me. The earlier menarche occurs, the more restrained a girl's life, the sooner she is married off and the greater the likelihood of numerous pregnancies. For the link between high altitude and late menarche see Malik and Hauspie, 1986.

6 See Young and Albert, 1965, for a study and interpretation of the menstrual taboo as a social separator and abasement. For a positive valuation of menstruation, see

Powers, 1980.

7 Similar to other societies. See, for example, Cesara: 1982: 140. Given the degree of silence which prevails over the matter, it is curious that men and women identify the giving of a *shotelai* with a particular month of pregnancy. The tradition of a gift in the seventh month is far from rigidly held; nevertheless, its existence assumes a general knowledge of the stage of pregnancy reached.

8 For parallels with other parts of the world, see Maloney, 1976. Jeffery *et al*, 1990: 90.

9 The fast includes the prohibition against eating meat products on Wednesdays and Fridays, and during other longer fasting periods. See Chapter 8 for details on the rules of fasting.

10 Cook and Maine, 1987.

11 Data were also collected on how many children the women had had before registering for contraception. From a sample of 149 cases, this ranged from none to ten, the average being 2.4. The age of first pregnancy was available in 64 cases, and ranged from 11 to 31, the average being 19.4.

12 The total number was 198 male and 154 female children. It should be noted that this figure, on its own and out of context, is meaningless. But it can be used amongst a number of indicators which reveal a significantly greater value attached to men than to women.

13 In 1989, the total Menz population was estimated by the Party office in Menz to be 303,277, of which women accounted for 138,482.

14 Parkyns, 1868: 252.

15 Clapham, 1988: 188.

16 Davin, 1971, Croll 1981, 1983, 1985.

17 Following Harris and Bond's classification, into clitoridectomy, labiodectomy and infibulation; used in Passmore-Sanderson, 1981: 18.

18 'He that is eight days old shall be circumcised among you', Genesis 17,12.

19 Passmore-Sanderson, 1981: 27, although this might refer to other parts of the country, or a wider undefined area referred to as Ethiopia.

20 This occurs at christening, more than a month later. Unlike some communities in which circumcision is a more communal ritual, as it is for example, among the Sandé, MacCormack, 1977.

21 Ten cases of circumcision on an uneven day for boys and eight on even days for girls were recorded.

22 The father confessor is a priest chosen, usually by the household head, to carry out the religious offices for the household. He is the priest most likely to be present at life-cycle ceremonies and to visit during Christian holidays.

23 The date of infant baptism is not set in the Bible, but the date is related to Saint Thomas's statements about the soul entering the body after 40 days for a boy and 80 days for a girl. For parallels, see de Beauvoir, (1949) 1972.

24 Vaccination of BCG, Polio, DPT and measles. Mothers are vaccinated against tetanus.

25 Jeffery, *et al*, 1987.

26 People are involved in other forms of kinship. As we have already seen, households also have *nefs abbat*, father confessors. In the past, and to a lesser extent today, full ritualized adoption took the form of 'breast' father or mother, *yet'ut' abbat* or *innat*, or the weaker tie of a stepfather or stepmother, *injera abbat* or *innat*. Thus relationships of varying importance are constructed beyond consanguineal and affinal ties.

27 Messing,1957:485, observes that even the peasant in 'modest circumstances' slaughters 'about five sheep and two old oxen'. As in the case of marriages, even the richest peasant would not celebrate as extensively today. Similarly Bauer, 1973: 118, writing about Tigray, notes that attendance at a funeral is more important than at a marriage.

28 Previously, Emperor Haile Selassie also tried to reduce the amount of self-mutilation which resulted from expressions of grief.

29 The ubiquitous image of the peasantry. In the Ethiopian context see, *inter alia*, Levine, 1965.

30 An exception to the relative voicelessness of women, discussed in the following chapter.

8

Other Worlds in Other Words: Juggling with Gender

In Gragn, it was on the ideological front that the state had the least influence. Religious beliefs remained fundamental to the population, both as explanations of natural and social phenomena and as an arena within which gender relations were negotiated. In this chapter I discuss the forms of belief that had an influence on individuals and played a large part in moulding community values and identities. Indeed, the traditions associated with these beliefs impinged upon many events that have featured in earlier chapters. Beyond a description of the supernatural, these beliefs provide explanations for a whole host of phenomena, from personal fortune or tragedy, to communal boon or disaster.

The Ethiopian Orthodox Church practises an ancient form of Christianity imbued with significant Judaic influences. Communication with God is mediated through a multitude of saints, as well as through Jesus and the Virgin Mary. Belief is expressed in numerous ways, including, for those who can manage it, membership of *mehaber*, a form of rotating socio-religious gathering. Alongside this official Christianity a disparate range of spirit beliefs are maintained. Using the literature as theoretical backing, I argue that this peripheral and non-legitimate[1] religion exists in opposition to the dominant Church-based ideology. Spirit beliefs were subject to attack by the state and were considered with suspicion even within the society. The demands of these spirits were increasingly perceived in a negative light by women practitioners, as well as by others. Though formal Christianity and the religion of spirit beliefs are described as separate and in opposition, there was a syncretism between them, and the two were sometimes interwoven and difficult to untangle.

In the final part of this chapter, the discussion shifts to a more tentative consideration of linguistic features. After providing the setting which shows that, in general, language portrays and perpetuates a gender hierarchy, we move on to a study of a phenomenon which cuts across this division. It is pointed out that, at times, gender reversals in language were heard. Such situations could, perhaps, be explained in terms of a laxity in the way people expressed themselves, yet such a rationalization seems dubious enough to require further thought.

Religion

Christianity

Under the Imperial régime, Orthodox Christianity was the state religion, the culture supporting and legitimating the power of the ruler. In socialist Ethiopia, Christianity was officially downgraded at the national level and given a status equal to Islam. In the early years of the revolution there were attempts to discourage fasting and the honouring of saints' days through work prohibitions. *Sira zemecha,* communal work, often occurred on Sundays, much to the chagrin of the devout, who perceived such activity as the cause of many evils and disasters. However, at least in Menz, the attempt to reduce the role of Christianity in society had little success. Indeed, even at the national level the socialist government accepted elements of Christian culture. Five of the thirteen official holidays were Christian in nature. Furthermore, in Menz, a church tax was established which was enforced by the new administrative structure, legitimating and perhaps even strengthening the role of Christianity in the community. Also, at least at the peasants' association level, the leadership remained closely in touch with the Church and was in the forefront at all religious ceremonies. At the local level, much more so than at the national level, state and Church were far from disassociated, a reflection of the endurance of the religious ideology in the face of change. This is not to say that the state had no hand in altering some religious practices. The case of limiting work restrictions has already been mentioned, and changes in the male *mehaber* will be described in greater detail below. In general, however, it can be concluded that, though uncomfortable about it, the Ethiopian Marxist power structures had to defer to Christianity, sometimes even operating symbiotically with it, especially at the level of local government.

The actions of individuals conforming to the Christian culture include fasting and abiding by the restrictions against certain types of work on saints' days[2] and other holy days. Fasting involves abstaining from all animal products, and, in theory, neither eating nor drinking until the afternoon. Although abstaining from animal products is strictly upheld in Menz, the delay is a token one of a few hours; most people no longer wait until after midday for their first meal. Women, in particular, excuse themselves for breaking the fast because of their addiction to coffee. Work restrictions include a total of 150 to 250 days in which some activities may not be undertaken. These operate in both male and female spheres of the sexual division of labour: men do not plough or harvest; women do not spin or grind.

In addition, Ethiopian Christianity is expressed through food taboos, with vows, pilgrimages, offerings of various kinds to churches and belief in faith healing. As we have already seen, most life-cycle events are also predominantly expressed and celebrated through religious rituals. Some young boys from within the community were, and still are, trained to become deacons and priests. The training is largely concerned with the learning of Geez, the ancient ecclesiastical language. Women's only official role in the Church is as 'servers' helping with food preparation, a role that can be taken up by 'nuns' – elderly women who have vowed celibacy and thereby their commitment to the Church. Women are excluded from the hierarchy of patriarch, bishops, priests, *debtera* and deacons, and, likewise, can only enter the outer part of the church.

Many households in the area practise their faith through actions that might not be visible to the outsider, but which have an important bearing on household behaviour and action. The fact that saints' days are honoured partly by refraining from certain types of work means that households are involved in complex calculations of time allocation. There are further restrictions and rules which some individuals follow. Thus, in addition to the saints' days, some women do not collect water on *senbet*, Saturday, and Sunday, collecting enough on Friday to last the weekend. A smaller number of women also do not grind grain, pound coffee, or take out dung from the hut on these days.

The argument that Orthodox Christianity is more the domain of men than of women might seem an odd statement to make since women constitute more than half the devotees. However, the claim is based on the power vested in men, their dominance, and the subordination of women that the Church encourages. Nevertheless, as mentioned earlier, Christianity plays an influential part in the beliefs and actions of women, who find support and explanations of their world in Christian terms. They are more likely than men to make vows, and regularly present offerings to the Church.

Within Christianity the figure of Mary stands out as one to whom women can turn. As will be seen below, their *mehaber* are almost exclusively in her name. *Filseta*, the Fast of the Assumption, celebrated in August, has its origin in the death of Mary and her assumption to heaven with the aid of Jesus.[3] Mary is also central to cultural traditions associated with childbirth, as we saw in the previous chapter.

Mehaber

Mehaber are socio-religious associations composed of ten to 30 people, who meet approximately once a month on the day of the saint that they have chosen to honour. Members take turns at hosting the event in their homes, providing food and drink for the guests who usually come on the late afternoon of the appointed day, stay the night, and depart after a morning meal. In 1989, out of a sample of 97 households from Gragn, 46 men and 39 women were *mehaber* members. At least a further eight men and 14 women had belonged to one in the recent past. The figures suggest that almost half the principal men and women of households are members, and that the numbers are marginally greater in the case of male membership. The gender difference is accounted for partly by a recent reduction of women members unable to sustain the cost. Most members tend to be above 20 years old, though occasionally a younger person might join.

The *mehaber* are overseen by a priest who is a member, and comes to give his benediction to the event. If he is unable to attend, another priest will do the office, as without a priest's blessing the ceremony would be considered invalid. In particular, a blessing over a large round loaf of bread is required. Most of the loaf is then cut up into chunks which are distributed for consumption among all the members at the very beginning of the celebrations. Once the necessary prayers are delivered, the priest may depart without jeopardizing the meeting. If he stays on, he is likely to offer a few prayers at different stages of the celebrations. Men with church schooling recite prayers in Geez together with the priest, other members standing up for the prayers and repeating incantations when told to do so. In general, friends, kin and important people in the area in which the *mehaber* is being held will be invited to make an appearance and join in the consumption.

Considerable religious significance is attached to this event. As previously mentioned, it occurs on a saint's day and is known by the name of that saint, for example, the Saint George or Saint Michael *mehaber* for men, or the Virgin Mary *mehaber* for women. The event might also be linked to the church of the region. Most men in Gragn attend a *mehaber* of 'the Saviour of the World', Jesus, since that is the name of the church which was associated with the peasants' association. In Menz, practically all women who belong to a *mehaber*, are associated with Saint Mary, the men having a greater number of saints from which to choose.

Sometimes the group also meets on another saint's day. This tradition, *ch'immir* (literally, addition), is often a consequence of a member having made a vow to a different saint, and having asked that that day be incorporated into the ritual. Thus in the Virgin Mary *mehaber* I attended, a Saint Michael's day in January was added as a regular feature as one such additional celebration.

Mehaber are constructed around religious symbolism. Associated with each *mehaber* is an earthenware pot and, often, a picture. The pot, called *ts'iwwa*, is dressed in numerous layers of bright cloth, of a type associated with the Church, and made to fit round the pot's neck. Members from the *mehaber* take the *ts'iwwa* in turn, and at the end of each event, the next person to host the celebration takes the pot home, together with the central chunk of the bread which the priest had blessed at the beginning of the event and which is reserved for this purpose. The picture kept with the *ts'iwwa* is usually that of the saint being celebrated, though a Saint George's *mehaber* might, for example, acquire a picture of the Virgin Mary instead.

Many members fast on the day of the *mehaber*, their first morsel of the day being the bread that has been blessed for the occasion, consumed in the late afternoon, or early evening. The religious taboo over menstruation results in a dilemma for women whose period coincides with the 21st of the month, the Virgin Mary's day. Until menopause, some women abandon the *mehaber* if this occurs, others still continue to attend, though refraining from eating the blessed bread and drinking from the symbolic pot.

Men and women tend to have separate *mehaber*; but it is quite common to have at least one man at any gathering of a women's *mehaber* and *vice* versa. There are several reasons for this. One is that a widow or a widower might take over their spouse's *mehaber* membership. This is said to be done as a way of honouring the dead and as an activity that brings favour to the deceased in the next world. Men, in particular sons or husbands, can also substitute for women if, for some reason, the latter cannot attend; the substitution never takes place the other way round.

Substitution in the case of women's *mehaber* is not necessary, but attendance is a sign of commitment to the saint and to the *mehaber*. If a woman cannot attend, it is therefore better for her to send someone in her place. There is the added factor that the financial outlay for each individual does not depend on the number of attendances. The costs of hosting the event can add up to about 125 *birr*, or 165 *birr* if a sheep is slaughtered. For about 20 members and 15 guests/family, the costs can be broken down as follows:

> Barley for making *injera*, 30 *birr*, and for brewing *t'ella*, 20 *birr*; wheat for making bread, 10 *birr*; coffee, 6 *birr*; *gésho* (Rhamnus prinoides), a plant used for fermenting *t'ella*, 5 *birr*; butter, 4 *birr*; lentils, 3 *birr*; onions, 2 *birr*; spices, 2 *birr*; salt, 2 *birr*, sugar, 1 *birr*.

Of the total sum, about 60 *birr* is the cost of grain that will be taken from the domestic granary. Increasingly, expenses have had to be much reduced, households economizing especially on meat, butter, lentils and sugar. Having paid for these monthly feasts (through hosting one themselves), it would be a waste if someone in the family did not benefit from the occasion. Although the associations are gender specific, at each gathering a *mehaber* will include the host's guests and relatives of the opposite gender. Women's *mehaber* will also necessarily include a priest, as well as the male substitute members mentioned earlier. In the case of men's *mehaber*, the wife's presence is particularly necessary in the preparation and dispensing of food and drink.

People of the same *mehaber* tend to live within walking distance of each other, sometimes in the same peasants' association. For women's *mehaber*, the area from which members come together is usually wider than for men's. Female respondents commented that it was the spread-out origins of the 'sisters' that they thus acquired which they valued. Women often kept to the same *mehaber* even when they changed homes through different marriages and visits to their natal home between marriages. The contrast between men's and women's *mehaber* groups can be explained, above all, as a reflection of the predominance of virilocality and serial marriages within a limited geographical area.

The whole event serves a combination of spiritual and lay purposes. The spiritual ones underlie much of the symbolism of the event as already described. When asked why they attended, the answer was often that it was '*lenefsé*', 'for my soul', part of the deeds of a good Christian. It is also an action that might be taken as a vow to a particular saint or as a way of giving thanks. Barren women join to beg the saint to make them fertile. In the case of a female member who dies childless, the members have a tradition of taking food and drink to the church on the 40th day after the woman's death as a symbol of remembrance on earth, and a reminder in heaven of the woman's good intentions.

The lay benefits derived are mainly expressed in terms of friendship and kinship. Fellow members of a *mehaber* are referred to as sisters or brothers. In the case of women, the reason for joining a particular *mehaber* is often associated with the attempt to retain ties of kinship or relationships which might otherwise break up because of marriage and divorce-related mobility. Consanguineal kin can thus be met regularly, and in-laws or friends from a certain period and earlier locality need not be lost. Alemïtu, Asnak'ech and Taferaw explained their membership as follows.

Alemïtu

I belong to a *Maryam mehaber* [Virgin Mary's *mehaber*], I grew up with this *ts'iwwa*, with *Maryam*. She makes me happy; when I ask her to make me well she does so; she gives me friends, my *mehaber* sisters. If I stop attending regularly she tells me in a dream that I must go. I started this one on my own, . . . My god-daughter asked me to join.

Asnak'ech

I used to go to another one, some friends had said, 'let us drink', so we did. But I stopped when, having become pregnant, I then lost the boy. Seven month's ago I joined this *Maryam mehaber*; I did so because my only other child was ill. I made a vow and entered. I like the *mehaber*, to drink together is a good thing; also I know that she, *Maryam,* will lighten my troubles and that it is good for my soul. In this one also it was friends who said, 'come with us that we may drink'.

Taferaw

I have been in a *Maryam*. There were ten of us, it started just over two years ago. I joined because Alemu [her son] was ill, he had trouble with his eyes. I called Mary asking her to make him better. I did this on a Thursday, the same day he got better, so I joined. Before that I had joined the same group and paid once, then I stopped. I had joined that first time because of the mother of my old husband. He died and I entered, so that I would still see his mother when I left the country [area]. I think that the *mehaber* was started by her mother. I stopped that time because I had an argument with someone in it.

This socially constructed kinship is stressed by women rather than men, or rather the women are more involved in a system of support through the *mehaber*. Thus, *mehaber* sisters are expected to visit each other when they give birth, at christenings, if there is a funeral or any other major event. Respondents, however, were quick to point out that the support system had limitations. Asnak'ech, a respondent quoted above, added:

I count other *mehabertegngna* as sisters. When a close relative dies, we give money, about 50 cents each; they come also for a birth, or a christening, or if I am ill. Sometimes if I have a problem, I might share it with them, but I am more likely to tell a close friend outside the *mehaber*, . . . I do not have serious discussions there.

Dessita likewise commented:

One of the values of the *mehaber* should be to discuss problems, but if it is deep, I keep it to myself; there is no real idea of helping those of us in the grips of some difficulty, but they come and visit if a husband dies or a child is born; they come and help with the work. We have not done anything together, but there is a code of conduct, women in the same *mehaber* are not supposed to steal each other's husbands for example, though I have known it happen!

Mehaber may have shortcomings, yet they are gatherings when a group of women can discuss events together, often in smaller, closer circles within the larger group. In the *mehaber* I belonged to, there was only one point on each occasion in which all the *mehaber* women, and only they, acted in unison. The following extract is from my diary:

Towards the end of the evening the *mehabertegngna* trooped out to perform the only really integrating act of the occasion: to crap in union in the starlight outside the compound, whilst talking to each other. This time there was a lot of joking when the female host shone too near us a torch she had acquired. After performing, the group got together in a small circle, a pot of water being passed round for each woman, in turn, to wash her private parts with. More ribald and personal comments, the closest the evening got to creating a sense of togetherness. Tonight the cold broke it all up and not too soon, as we were all perishing.

Mehaber provide an event to which women can look forward, an occasion to think about, to dress up for, and one which is socially approved. It is often an opportunity for regular visits to a different community, an important consideration given the restricted mobility of women. It is also an opportunity to sit without working, to eat, talk and relax, an opportunity which is rare for some women – in particular those with a large household to look after, or, at the other extreme, those without any children or domestic help.

The reasons for not joining a *mehaber* include cost (by far the most important), age, disillusionment and pain at the loss of a loved one and, as already mentioned, the timing of the menstrual cycle. The reasons given by Yirgu, Yematawerk' and Yeshewagét' are representative.

Yirgu
I have never been in a *mehaber,* the cost of two *mehaber* in a household under present conditions is too much, so it is only he [her husband] who has one.

Yematawerk'
It is simple, I cannot go to mine any longer, my monthly flower is at that time.

Yeshewagét'
I had joined a *Maryam mehaber,* but my daughter died when I was hosting it three years ago. She was 15, I gave it up. How can I forget?

There have been changes in the celebration of *mehaber.* In the 1960s my *mehaber* comprised some forty people, but it had dwindled to about eighteen active members by 1989. The cost of belonging, namely the feast that had to be prepared, was found to be too heavy a burden, not just because of the larger membership, but also because expectations at that time were greater. Each member was expected to prepare more and better food. For example in the morning members were served hunks of bread and not strips of *annebaberro,* a cheaper form of bread/pancake sandwich. As membership dropped, the priest of the *mehaber* began to talk about making the affair a more humble one, in keeping with the difficult times. During the 1985 famine a number of such gatherings in the region disintegrated, but a few have since regrouped.

In Menz, a different form of *mehaber* also came into existence. According to my informants the government edicts, passed on to peasants' associations and Church leaders, encouraged the men to form *senbeté mehaber* which took place in the church rather than in people's homes. The form of the *mehaber* remained the same to the extent that the groups met monthly and rotated the costs of hosting. However, the food and drink were taken to the church, and the event no longer lasted overnight. The rationale for the change given to me by the peasants' association leadership lay in the more open nature of the resulting event, one which any passer-by could be invited to share. It could, on the other hand, be interpreted as the state's attempted appropriation of the religious sphere. If so, the change suggests that the state was having to incorporate, rather than destroy, the local foundations of the Christian religion. The priests, for their part, explained the change as transforming the organization into one which was more in keeping with religion, arguing that the *mehaber* which took place in people's homes strayed towards developing into a social and political rather than a religious gathering. Church authorities, not surprisingly, welcomed the change which brought the whole event more closely into their fold.

Whatever the rationale, it was seen as applying only to male organizations: There was no question of moving the locality of the women's *mehaber.* One could speculate about the reasons for this. Perhaps the distinction was a recognition that the church, a male preserve, was an unsuitable place for a gathering of women; or perhaps it was a recognition that women would not accept the move for these very reasons. It could also be that the state acted because the male *mehaber* formed nuclei of social discussion, some of which was undoubtedly subversive. The male get-togethers might have been considered more of a threat than the female ones. Whatever the reason, the change seemed to have occurred relatively smoothly. Some men abandoned their *mehaber* because of the edict, some continued domestic *mehaber* in defiance, but they belonged to a *senbeté mehaber,* and seemed content to do so. The women's groups remain unaltered.

Spirit beliefs

Mention was made earlier of another religious component to rules and traditions in Menz culture. This one was never legitimated by the state, was discouraged as backward, and was subjected to attack by both the Emperor's and the *Derg*'s régimes. In the early nineteenth century, *zar* cults were forbidden[4] whilst in post-revolutionary Ethiopia there were campaigns to encourage people to throw away the trappings of such beliefs.

Despite such actions, these spirits continued to play a central role in the society, not only on the ideological plane, which was not shaken by a socialist ideology, but even on the material level. This was because the distinction between the material and the ideological was not rigidly upheld, or rather, the ideological impinged upon the material. Thus most events – the accumulation or loss of wealth; health and illness; birth and death – were all first and foremost given a supernatural interpretation. It would be impossible to consider the position of women in the society, or the relationship between the peasantry and the state, without reference to this area of culture and society.

The importance of these spirit beliefs was sometimes shrouded from view because they were known to be frowned upon, almost forbidden by the priests of the legitimate Christian religion, despite the fact that belief in these spirits was almost universal. It was also in some ways made invisible by the very nature of the beliefs, which deal with the uncertain relationship between humans and spirits. Spirit beliefs were also under attack by forces of modernization, and scientific explanations of phenomena. Though many of these changes also undermined the Christian component in the culture, the various spirit beliefs were more vulnerable because their religious prescriptions operated to a greater extent in terms of secrecy and individual rather than group identity, and because they have never been constructed into a doctrine, let alone used as a force legitimating state authority. They also operated in a sphere of culture in which women predominated, and perhaps, therefore, function as an alternative, a culture in opposition rather than in power. Women were more involved than men in this spirit culture – not just as worshippers, for in this role they also predominated in the Christian scene, but in the more interactive role as communicators with, and 'embodiments' of the spirits. This was in contrast with the menial role women were allotted in the Church.[5]

The spirits that visit women in Menz have in common their initial manifestation as an illness, which can be relieved through participation. However, as we shall see, there is much more at stake than the placating of a mental or physical malaise, as Lewis in his seminal work *Ecstatic Religion* pointed out:[6]

> For all their concern with disease and its treatment, such women's possession cults are also, I argue, thinly disguised protest movements directed against the dominant sex. They thus play a significant part in the sex-war in traditional societies and cultures, where women lack more obvious and direct means for forwarding their aims. To a considerable extent they protect

women from the exactions of men, and offer an effective vehicle for manipulating husbands and male relatives.

The spirit beliefs represent a sphere of culture in which women can express themselves, but also one which they can use to receive material and socio-political benefits.[7] The political rewards involve the opportunity for expression and a sphere of power. The material benefits include coffee, butter, honey, meat, perfume, beads and clothes. My respondents in Gragn estimated that up to four *birr* a week might be spent on such ceremonies. For most women it was usually much less, but it could include occasional large expenditures, such as the money for an *angel libs*,[8] a special piece of cloth worn as a scarf, preferably edged with red and black, costing about seven *birr*.

The value to women of the spirit beliefs should not be romanticized. The picture that emerges from Menz is also one in which believers and observers alike express negative attitudes to the religion, which is not legitimate in the same way as Christianity. Spirit beliefs are perceived as binding devotees to expenditures, to fear, and to a traditional behaviour pattern to which some no longer subscribe.

Like many other examples of such religious systems, one of the characteristics of spirit beliefs in Menz is that they are peripheral not only in being composed of women and low-status men, and in the amoral position of the beliefs,[9] but also because they seem to have their source outside the society in which they are located. The spirit beliefs are seen as pre-dating Christianity, yet, to the extent that this is the case, the distinction being made is between two beliefs established in the country more than one and a half millennia ago. The concept of spirits as a marginal belief surviving the introduction of Christianity draws attention away from the common past. In fact, both Christianity and spirit beliefs have links with Oromo culture and Islam, for instance in the role assigned to coffee and incense; the holy nature of Fridays, linguistic borrowings for such terms as *kutab,* amulets, from Arabic. A number of other loan words are specific to a particular kind of spirit.

It is very difficult in practice to distinguish clearly between the different spirit beliefs operating in the area. This is partly because talking openly about such matters can be courting the displeasure of the spirits, but also because not all women necessarily differentiate between the various spirits. The classification and separation adopted below is thus invalid for some respondents. To give an example, *ch'ellé, wik'abï* and *zar* could be classified as one, two, or three separate types of belief. I found that the explanation for these differences lay in the extent of involvement of the devotee. The more committed the person was to the beliefs, the more detailed their knowledge of the spirits and distinctions between them. This generalization notwithstanding, some women had a considerable involvement in, and knowledge about, one particular spirit, and very little about any other.

Confusion is increased by considerable variation among individuals in the way the spirits are described and honoured. Problems also sometimes arise because there are no routine methods of operating, even for one individual. But side by side there is sometimes a rigidity and a sense that there is only one way of doing things. For example, ceremonial slaughtering of sheep or chickens is one of the ways in which the spirits are placated. Sometimes the colour and sex of the animals are specified, and any deviation from the rule is frowned upon. On another occasion, however, the same individual, sacrificing to the same spirit, might argue that the specifications do not matter, adding: *yetegegnew*, 'whatever is found'.

The supportive and yet marginalized nature of the spirit beliefs in Menz can be illustrated by abandoning the abstract terms in which they have been discussed so far, and describing instead the manifestation in the society of beliefs in some of the main spirits, including *adbar, wik'abï, zar, ch'ellé, aganint,* and *buda*. These belief systems are not always expressed dramatically by trance or possession. Most of the time, in the majority of cases, the beliefs are ongoing conditions requiring that the spirit in question be placated periodically. Possession itself is but a rare event, though it remains central to the belief in the *zar* and *buda* spirits in particular.

Adbar

The *adbar* is a female spirit associated with a specific area, often a communal one referring to a place (*bota*) or country (*ager*), and is sometimes located by a tree or an open space. Actions are regularly taken by some women in order to appease the spirit. These include spilling the coffee dregs daily at a certain spot outside the hut, and burning tobacco leaves outside the hut on Wednesdays and Fridays. Occasional celebrations involve burning incense or sprigs of the wild olive tree (*weyra*), spreading freshly cut grass in the hut, making a dish of wheat or barley (*k'inch'é*), or a type of bread (*t'iresho*), brewing some beer (*t'ella*) or drinking a *ch'at*-based tea. Annual events, usually in May, include the ritual slaughtering and consumption of livestock. Particular types of livestock are slaughtered inside the hut, white chickens and black sheep being preferred.

When the spirit is called up, it is sometimes addressed simply with a blessing for the day, such as *megen senyo, maksenyo* ('Blessed Monday, blessed Tuesday') Otherwise it is addressed with the following prayer in which the *adbar* is given the name Awgé and addressed in the feminine:

እድባር፡እውን፡	Adbar Awgé
እንቺነሽ፡እድባሬ፡	You are my *adbar*,
ደህና፡ዋይ፡	Fare well,
ካመት፡እመት፡እድርቸኝ፡	Help me from year to year,
ልጅ፡ለሌለው፡ልጅ፡ስጪልኝ፡	Give a child to the childless for
ለታመመው፡እድኒልኝ፡	my, sake
ክፉን፡እሽሺልኝ፡	Heal the sick for my sake,
ደጉን፡እቅርቢልኝ፨	Drive the evil away for my sake,
	Bring the good near to me for
	my sake.

In neighbouring places, including the town of Mehal Meda, the *adbar* was addressed by the name of Rahélo and celebrated in other ways. Once a year, bread baked specially in the fire rather than in a pan (*rimït'o*) and some boiled grains (*nifro*) are cooked in preparation. The devotees then go outside with their fists clenched full of the grains. In unison, they clap their hands, scattering the food and saying, 'Rahélo, *hid tolo tolo*', 'Rahélo, go quickly quickly'. The individuals then return quickly to their separate huts. This ceremony can be carried out by a single household, or by a whole neighbourhood of women together. The symbolism behind the ritual clearly seems to emphasize a desire to placate and then be rid of the spirit.

Wik'abï and zar

Wik'abï and *zar* are different but similar spirits. Both are internalized – part of the individual rather than a separate external being – and they are always expressed in terms of an illness inside the devotee. This is unlike the *adbar* which has a separate identity from the person. The *zar* spirit is known in a number of other areas, including Djibouti, Somalia, Sudan, Egypt, Saudi Arabia and Iran. It is thought to have originated in Ethiopia, where it might have been part of the dominant belief as the sky god of the Agaw before being marginalized by the coming of Christianity.[10] Records of *zar* cults have been found that date back at least to the sixteenth century.[11]

The *zar* spirit takes possession of people in a dramatic way. Possession is often vocalized by speaking in tongues. Predictions can be made and the possession sometimes develops into a cult, with followers as well as 'servants' of the possessed who are there to provide offerings. The argot spoken by the possessed can be completely understood only by those involved in the spirit beliefs, though linguistic gender reversals are common and recognizable. In addition, cross-sexual imagery is common, whilst the possession itself is enacted primarily in terms borrowed from the *serg* marriage ritual.

The belief seems to be associated with older women and is seen as a hereditary one, with particular families prone to possession. Pacifying the *zar* involves more ceremony than is required by the other spirits. The woman who is in a trance tends to call for her 'daughter' Awgered while grunting for ceremonial levies in a spirit *argot*. During the event, the *masïnk'o*, a single-string guitar will be played, often by a male relative, whilst honey, *ch'at* and coffee are consumed and incense is burnt. If an animal is to be slaughtered, this is often a white sheep.

Wik'abï can be seen as a milder form of *zar* and affects a majority of women.[12] The *wik'abï* spirit threatens ill-health and discomfort and needs to be pampered, usually with coffee and a particular piece of clothing, the distinctive neck-scarf or *angel libs*. The spirit of some women can be more demanding, asking for such luxury items as a complete dress, honey, and the slaughtering of livestock.

In Gragn *wik'abï* was the most pervasive form of spirit. There seemed to be a vast number of different kinds of *wik'abï*, though many people no longer developed the belief to a degree that required naming and differentiation. Some older people talked about being possessed by up to twelve *wik'abï* at any one time. Some of these, such as Bir-Alenga and T'ek'wor, were seen to have Amhara Christian origins, whilst others, such as Sheh Abash and Abjulalé, were perceived to be Oromo Muslim.[13] I was told that if one of these Muslim spirits was particularly strong in a woman, there was the possibility that it could oblige her to change her religion and migrate. Normally, however, they did not conflict with the dominant Christian belief – Menz Christians could have Oromo Muslim *wik'abï* spirits within them without jeopardizing their Christianity – a view that would undoubtedly be challenged vigorously by the priests.

The same woman could have all the four *wik'abï* mentioned by name, though one of them was usually declared the overall leader, the *t'ek'lay*. The T'ek'wor tended to be celebrated at Epiphany, with roasted grain, *k'ollo*, coffee and the slaughtering of a black sheep with a white head. Bir-Alenga was celebrated at different times of the year. It was seen as a powerful spirit that did not let go easily. Sheh Abash was celebrated on Fridays with coffee with two types of incense, *aden* and *kerbé*. Abjulalé was celebrated on Wednesdays with coffee and, often, a simple unleavened bread, *t'iresho*.

Ch'ellé

Ch'ellé was similar to *wik'abï* and *zar* in that offerings were made to an internalized spirit. Once again, the offerings were consumed by the individuals themselves. The *ch'ellé* spirit was more rarely honoured and homage was paid at particular times, often in July or September, though minor additional celebrations, *gurcha*,[14] could also be made at other times, especially during Christian feasts such as Easter, Epiphany or Christmas.

There seemed to be two types of *ch'ellé*, called the Gurage and the Galla.[15] The latter one was said to desire white beads, barley and butter; the former preferred multi-coloured beads, wheat and honey. In both cases the *ch'ellé* disliked spices of any kind, including salt and *berberé*, and although beer was prepared this was not to be fermented with *gésho* as was the norm.[16] Usually the celebration was in July, at the time 'when the water became murky' *wiha sïdeferris*. Those who could afford it wore special decoratively embroidered cotton tops called *yech'ellé libs* (*ch'ellé* clothes). Beads were brought out from their baskets in which they had been kept together with *t'ejj sar* and *arrïtï* (*Cymbopogon citratus* and *Artemisia Afra*), two grasses which have a pleasant smell.

The following details are from the ceremony lasting three days as performed by an elderly woman then living in Molale town, who said that she followed closely the traditions of her mother. In many other cases the degree of ritual and festivities involved was much less extensive, and the decline was commonly explained by the impoverishment of the rural areas.

First the hut is made beautiful with freshly cut grass strewn on the floor. Then I put a bowl on top of a large sieve turned upside down in front of me.

I sit on the skin of a sheep which had been slaughtered for the spirit on a previous occasion. To start the celebrations I hold a few strands of special long grass, *serdo,* in each hand, and dip the grass in melted butter saying 'Sifa, sifa, sifa,' and ululating. At the same time I bring the strands of grass round my neck and down my chest while smearing the butter on my neck, and repeat the gesture three times. I then dip the white *ch'ellé* in the butter and round my neck. The barley dish, *gebs k'inch'é,* is then put in a container on a sieve, then I taste it three times, putting both hands in the bowl and ululating. It is said that the barley lord, the *gebs géta,* has tasted of the meal. Also *gebs k'eribo,* unfermented barley beer, and *k'ollo* are consumed. It is then the turn of the wheat lord, the *sindé géta.* The same process is repeated with the multi-coloured beads, honey instead of butter and wheat instead of barley.

After this food is prepared, guests and family partake of the meal from another dish to which seasoning may be added. Non-household members are sometimes invited, the reason for the feast always explained. If another person believes in the spirit, however, she will make sure she has feasted her spirit in her own home before she accepts such food in the house of another.

During the whole period, I sleep on the floor rather than on my usual bed [probably because of a taboo against sexual activity, the woman being expected to be 'clean' and devoted to the spirit that she is honouring].[17] At some stage, *k'eshir,* coffee beans in the husk, will be roasted, dipped in melted butter and eaten whole. Also if *ch'at* is available, this will be boiled and drunk early in the morning, if possible with honey, in a tea-form called *awza.*

On the third day, the ritual ends. First the grass is brushed to one side. The bits of flour that did not pass through the sieve have earlier been collected and made into three to seven little balls of dough, *rimit'o,* which are baked in the fire, amid the ash, rather than in a pan. At the same time coffee 'for the seeing off' is prepared and some food is cooked with butter and with honey separately and tasted while ululating. When everything is ready, samples of all the food, including the *rimit'o,* are put on the grass in the hut. It is said that this is done because these offerings take the illnesses with them when they are taken outside. When everything is ready, I take it all out, saying:

የጎደለም ፡ ካለ ፡ ወደፊት ፡ እምዋላሰሻለሁ ፡
ዘሙድ ፡ እዝግዬንም ፡ ለጆቸንም ፡ ጠብቂለኝ ።

'If there is aught that is missing I will in future
make it up to you,
Keep guard over my relatives and children for me.'

As I take all the grass and food out I hold a metal knife in one hand and throw away the rubbish, still holding the knife, and come back quickly. Then that is it. The *ch'ellé* has been honoured, the beads are put back in their basket and I continue with daily life.

In 1978, there was an attempt by the government to stop the payment of tribute to *ch'ellé* spirits. As well as giving speeches on the issue, representatives of Party officials came to people's houses to confiscate the beads and the baskets. Some women managed to hide their tokens, this action being rationalized by an order made to them by the spirits themselves in the form of a dream. Those who gave up their beads did not necessarily abandon the belief. Many bought new beads, whilst some resorted to celebrating their *ch'ellé* with coins, preferably old silver ones, including the Maria Theresa Thaler, but failing these, any coin in circulation.

Buda

Ayne t'ila, literally shadow of the eye, and *buda* are both forms of the evil eye, often but not always merged with *aganint* and *jinn*. Outsiders and people involved in crafts, such as potters, blacksmiths and weavers, are most likely to be identified as the ones inflicting the evil. These crafts-people (men, except in the case of potters) are the exception to a female-dominated scene, and come nearest to what might be described as sorcerers or witches. In the *buda* spirit belief three people are involved: the person causing the possession, or 'eating' as it is called in Amharic, the possessed or 'eaten', and the person called upon to cure the possessed. Appropriate, given the food image, is the belief that the *buda* offends dietary rules by eating carrion meat and other foods prohibited in the society, and that they transform themselves into hyenas by night.

The person inflicting the harm is usually male, and almost exclusively defined as an outsider.[18] Traditionally these came from the community of people who had emigrated into the area or for some other reason had not acquired rights to land and earned a living in craft production. Potters, blacksmiths and weavers were the most likely candidates. In Menz, a community of potters resides in a few locations, mainly in Keya Gebriel *wereda*. Their religion is said to be different from the Christian Orthodox one of their neighbours, and similar to that of *Felasha* Judaism practised in the north-west of the country, in Gonder. The population is known to have existed in the area for centuries. Thus the community of 'eaters' is, in all likelihood, as old as that of the 'eaten', yet they remain clearly distinct, their different beliefs, together with their skills, and the occasion for interactions through the market place, setting them up to be an identifiable group of transgressors. Increasingly, immigrant blacksmiths in towns such as Mehal Meda form another category.

The people who develop a reputation as healers are likewise male and also usually outsiders. In the past these would have been men with a church education who deviated from the mainstream belief and its preachings, or even priests in the fold of the Church who would be asked to exorcize the spirits with holy water. More recently they also include men without education or with a lay education, who manage to build a reputation on the grounds of personal knowledge and interaction with the spirits. The *buda* 'doctors' will also be referred to in the case of the other spirit-associated illnesses, in particular, that of *aganint*. Such practitioners are increasingly located in towns. Protection given by these 'doctors' against such dangers include various amulets. Many people also believe that individuals can take their own precautions: a stick of rue used as a toothpick, whole lentil seeds, and, some say, a piece of fresh dung hidden in your clothes. When possession takes place, the spirit is exorcized with spells, herbs and the smoke of particular types of incense.

The main actors, the possessed, are usually women who reside in the community. Anyone can be 'eaten', the cause usually being attributed to envy, to being 'seen'. Thus, beautiful, wealthy, powerful, lucky or even happy women are particularly prone, their basis of superiority being attacked by the envious spirit. The event can occur anywhere, although crowds and events such as markets are particularly feared as times when someone is likely to 'see and eat you'. Unlike the *zar* possession, which tends to be inherited and manifests itself periodically, the *buda* possession has a specific beginning, an occasion during which the spirit 'enters' the patient. The actual possession fit can occur immediately or at any time thereafter. It can then be completely exorcized after one fit or lie dormant, rather like the *zar* spirit, manifesting itself only periodically.

In general, men seem to 'eat' and women are 'eaten', though this gender division is far from rigid. Those with the knowledge both to do harm and to cure are outsiders, whilst those who suffer are insiders. Once again the picture is one in which the beliefs centre on women. In this case it even re-enacts the story of women's vulnerability to men, both their subordination to male power, the *buda*, and their dependence on male knowledge, the *buda* 'doctor'. It would also seem that it is not the most marginalized of women who are 'eaten', but, on the contrary, those with an advantage such as wealth or beauty. It could therefore be interpreted as an active response by women whose relative security is threatened, either a pre-emptive action or a *post hoc* manifestation of a change in fortune. Unlike the *zar*, the *wik'abï*, and the *ch'ellé* spirits, the *buda* illness is not inherited.

Aganint

The final category of spirits to be discussed here are *aganint* or *ganil*. Like the *buda*, they tend to be seen as evil, though in this case they are not personified, but external, non-human agents of mishap. They are usually described as water spirits and are believed to be the cause of most deaths in the vicinity of rivers. They can also be blamed for other misfortunes, such as madness. Most of the spirits are said to inhabit different kinds of water, such as lakes and rivers, although some live in forests and the very powerful *berak*'[19] comes from the sky. These latter forces were described to me as beings the size of chickens that come to burn houses and give people skin diseases. *Jinn*[20] are sometimes said to be the same as *aganint*, and at other times to be a different evil spirit, male or female, likely to be encountered on the road, who disconcerts people by appearing in human form and then suddenly disappearing.[21]

There are ways of pacifying the *aganint* spirits and keeping them at bay, such as the lighting of tobacco, *timbuho*, a strategy also used for the *adbar*. In the past, but hardly ever in recent years, there were also ways of making use of these spirits as oracles, calling them up and asking for advice. *Aganint gottach, aganint* 'pullers', were usually male shamans who had the power of communication with the spirits at night, once various offerings (food, drink, cut grass) had been prepared in their honour. One famous *aganint gottach* is said to have lived in Keya Gebriel, one of the *wereda* in Menz. It seems significant that the single form of spirit mediation perceived as being almost exclusively a male terrain had ceased to operate.

Links with Christianity

The power of these spirits and their hold on individuals, especially on women, spills over into the Christian religious culture, despite the Church's attempts to avoid contamination. For example, the ritual slaughtering of livestock which is then consumed is part of the Christian culture and a way of celebrating such festivals as Christmas. Even when the slaughtering is done in a Christian context, however, it is fitted into rituals more closely associated with spirit beliefs. Thus slaughtering is carried out inside the hut rather than outside, and there is a prohibition against entering the huts for three days after the event, applicable to all those not present at the time of the slaughtering. Finally, the specificities of colour and sex of the animals, a part of the spirit beliefs, is carried over into the colour traditions of the Orthodox Christian religion.[22]

To give other examples, *t'enk'way* (sorcerers), who can be male or female, offer predictions, advice and amulets. Male *t'enk'way* often start life learning to become priests and, even after moving away from the Church, continue to legitimate their knowledge by referral to and borrowings from the Bible and Orthodox Christianity. Even priests themselves are not averse to delving into the 'opposition spirits' for a greater influence on people's actions and beliefs. Finally, it is quite common for the wife of a priest to be particularly prone to involvement in spirit beliefs, a situation accepted by all, including her husband.

Summary

All forms of spirit beliefs currently vie for a hold on individuals – almost all women are captured by at least one spirit, usually by combinations of several. People interpret births and deaths, health and illness, wealth and poverty, temperament, and many other things besides, in terms of spirit 'interference', often in the same breath as making reference to the will of the Christian God and/or his enemy, Satan. In the eyes of many there is nothing contradictory about this cocktail of beliefs. When suggestions of incompatibility arise in people's minds, usually these can be traced to propaganda against spirit beliefs by the Church ('the devil's work') or the state ('backward practices'). This propaganda seems to have had the effect both of creating an increasingly internalized, private belief, and of encouraging people to have a negative attitude towards the beliefs that they hold. As yet, there are few signs of the beliefs themselves being superseded either by a straightforward Christian belief or by scientific, materialist explanations. The impact of impoverishment[23] and villagization are undoubtedly the factors that have triggered the most change, as was mentioned in Chapter 4. I often heard people observe that villagization had had at least one good result – it had released people from subservience to the 'place' and its 'habits', from the *timbuho*, tobacco, and the 'blood' of sacrificial animals.

There are differences in the degree to which different categories of women are involved in these beliefs.[24] Undoubtedly a happy, married, young woman, with children, in a relatively prosperous household, is less likely to be possessed by a *zar* spirit than a less fortunate woman. On the other hand, the former woman's very luck is likely to attract the evil, envious eye, and make her prone to being 'eaten' by the *buda*. A single woman who has lost several children, or is childless, is more likely to invest in *ch'ellé* and *zar* beliefs, especially if she has a sympathetic relative at hand able to foot the bill. Most women, regardless of their position and status, are likely to resort to *wik'abï* illnesses to vocalize some ailment and/or to justify expenditure on some luxury goods for themselves. Most women are also likely to honour the *adbar* spirit, paying special attention to the rituals if they have a particular problem on their minds.

Another distinction that could be made focuses on the expression of belief. There seems to be a difference between spontaneous, occasional celebrations of the spirit and regular, expected ones; between possession manifested through trance, and possession through varying kinds and degrees of illness. Once again, the different scenarios allow for distinctions in the expression of belief. This discussion should serve as a reminder of the heterogeneity of experiences, and the danger of treating women as an undifferentiated category.

I have argued that the spirit beliefs in which women predominate are viewed within the society as being of negligible importance as compared to legitimized Christianity. Yet they are a key component of women's lives, and throughout this book references have been made to the way these beliefs affect women's actions. The spirit manifestations can be seen as a way of justifying the celebrations and consumption of the society's luxury goods. In some senses it is a female consumption not unlike the male consumption of the other type of spirit – alcohol! Belief in the spirits can also function as an excuse – a rationale – for certain actions and decisions[25] and can serve as an outlet for expressing frustration, fear and pain.

The spirits can be interpreted as sources of support to the extent that they present an explanation of women's world view, and represent practically the only public sphere in which women have power. However, this phenomenon could also be seen as detrimental to women, to the extent that it channels their expression into this peripheral sphere, one which is not politically threatening to the mainstream ideology and culture, and one which instead of challenging male hegemony, seems to perpetuate women's subordinate position. This point is made about marginalized belief systems in general by Lewis, who writes:

It is possible for men to give in to them [women] without ostensibly deferring to their wives or jeopardizing their position of dominance. . . . neither sex loses face and the official ideology of male supremacy is preserved.[26]

The way people adapt to changing conditions is not uniform. Some women cling to long-held beliefs, others are quicker in discarding them as inappropriate and in taking up alternative modes of thought. Generally, however, it is my impression that these beliefs are increasingly perceived, from within the society, by both men and women, as a source of oppression and fatalism.

It would be interesting to pursue further the question of the sexual construction of these beliefs. In one way the spirits stand as a representation of female opposition to male dominance in Christian beliefs. The male prerogative is made use of, rather than shunted aside through the creation of a separate system of female valuation. Gender reversals in the language used during communication with spirits and in particular when addressing a woman being possessed are common practice. *Zar* possession is enacted in terms of *serg* marriage, the spirit representing a male penetration of the woman who is possessed. Likewise the *wik'abï* spirits are also male, exerting their power over their 'subject' women, and the *buda* is usually a man. This picture strongly suggests that women portray spirit possession in the same way as they construct their daily relationships: that is, with themselves in the subordinate position. However, not all the spirits have a male identity: *adbar, Atété, ch'ellé* are female, and even in the *zar* possession, in Menz at least, the central figure called for is that of the symbolic daughter 'Awgered'. Furthermore, in the course of my fieldwork it became apparent that enacting of possession was the exception. For the most common belief, *wik'abï*, there was no need to enter a trance or even to name the spirit.[27] Indeed, when referred to, the *wik'abï* was usually not personified; presents were needed for an ungendered *lewik'abïyé, lebeshitayé*, 'for my *wik'abï*, for my illness'. I would therefore suggest that there are a number of different constructions, the cross-sexual imagery used to re-enact women's subordination being but one, others being set within an all-female framework.

It is difficult to estimate both the rationale and the extent of the changes in progress. My interpretation would lean towards explaining developments in terms of a reduction in structural and regular activities, without a falling-off in the beliefs themselves. Thus, incidental events and expenses can and still do occur. As already hinted, I would also suggest that the reason for the reduction in material manifestations of the beliefs is impoverishment rather than a loss of belief. The parallel is with traditions such as the *mehaber* within mainstream Christian religion which many women abandoned because of worsening economic conditions. Perhaps derision directed at the spirit beliefs, in particular the label of 'backward superstition', the availability of scientific explanations of disease and the antagonism of the state will provide more than an outward justification for abandoning these beliefs. However, unless structural conditions change enough to allow women new outlets for frustration, or, more fundamentally still, unless conditions improve and women's material grievances are alleviated, it is more than likely that the spirit beliefs will survive.

Language

In Menz, men and women, children and adults all speak Amharic. It is the only language used in the area, an unusual situation in Ethiopia, where a mix of populations within each locality often results in multilingualism.

Writing and reading was traditionally almost completely restricted to the domain of those who progressed through the church schools – a small minority of the male population. Literacy tended to be looked upon negatively by much of the population, including the nobility. Modernization in Imperial Ethiopia introduced schools to a wider group of boys and girls, and, as we saw in Chapter 3, the literacy and educational drive of the *Derg* attempted to achieve mass literacy. I would now like to turn to the way Amharic is used in the society.

Levine, among others,[28] showed that the finer uses of Amharic were reserved for learned elders in the society, those trained in *k'iné*, a form of poetry often making use of *double entendre*, and this continues to be the case. Most of the verses quoted in this book, for example, are in the masculine voice and are likely to have been composed by men, though most of the verses were recited to me by women. The clear exceptions were the mourning dirges, the composers of which are often women.

In the more mundane daily use of language, the rule was that men spoke and women remained silent. This rule applied in most social and official settings, such as in peasants' association meetings. In legal terms, women had to be represented by men for any public transaction such as borrowing money. Even in law courts today, it is usually a man who speaks for a woman. If there are guests in a home, women are expected to provide food and drink, whilst men take charge of the talk and entertaining. If women want to communicate among themselves when there are men around, they 'whisper' or 'gossip'.

The rule that men have the greater right to speak is unquestioned; it is one that is also common in other societies.[29] Yet it is often broken by women who have enough security to do so. In particular, the more equal the marriage, the greater the woman's voice. Furthermore, though 'whispering' and 'gossiping' are conditions that imply constraint, this is not to say that women do not actively use the channels available to them to their own advantage.[30]

Cultural meanings and information are transmitted by language,[31] yet language itself is not a gender-neutral construct. The sexist nature of the English language, analysed in Spender's *Man Made Language,*[32] is probably paralleled in most other languages, including Amharic. However, it is not so much this dominant sexism that I wish to draw attention to here, but rather the exceptions to this bias.[33]

The following are separate extracts from my diary, giving examples of gender reversals in Amharic:

A group of men were sitting on some stones, not far from my hut. Work'u, the literacy teacher, addressed Mekonen, the secretary of the peasants' association, in the feminine. They had just come back from the market in town and were talking about their day. Soon after, Mekonen used the feminine to address Tizazu, a middle-aged man. Could there be a direction, a logic, to its use? In the first case, the person addressed was the younger, yet the one with the greater social status. In the second case, the person addressed was older and of lower social status.

I witnessed the following exchange between Tesfayé, a boy of about four, and a neighbour, Sindé, a middle-aged woman.

Tesfayé: *Na, tolo, na!*   'Come quickly, come!'
Sindé: *Teyi, irefi, met't'ahu.*   'Leave it, be still, I am coming.'

The boy addressed the woman in the masculine whilst she addressed him in the feminine. A double inversion.

I heard Tizazu speaking to an elderly male relative in the feminine, and being answered in the same form. Here the person addressed was an elder, deserving honour from a younger relative, yet the reversal worked both ways. This is confusing. The only conclusion I can come up with is that these uses cut across age and status and express a sense of closeness and friendship.

The phenomenon is curious; given that there is a sexual order to the language, why is this order sometimes broken? Can anything be said about these reversals, bearing in mind the debates about the relationship between language and culture? Are gender distinctions being used for other goals? The purpose of this discussion is to provide some information on this linguistic phenomenon, and to hazard some answers.

Amharic marks gender differences in pronouns, personal names and verbs. Articles are required only to qualify or emphasize the noun, in which case they too can be assigned a gender. Inanimate objects need not be gender-specific. The general framework is one of a language in which gender specifications are not always used to express a sexual distinction. In the realm of inanimate nouns, words such as *ts'ehay*, sun, do not have to be prefaced by a gendered article, nor do they carry an automatic gender specification. However, in any but the most mundane conversation, there is a high likelihood of the inanimate noun either being prefaced by a gendered article, e.g. *Echï ts'ehay*, ('this sun', f.), *yihé ts'ehay* ('this sun', m.) or having a qualifying article attached to the end of the word, e.g. *ts'ehayu* ('the sun', m.), *ts'ehaywa* ('the sun', f.). Thus, the masculine or the feminine can be used for inanimate objects. There are 'more likely' articles attached to many objects, but, preferences are often left open to the individual speaker and to the context.

Sometimes, however, a sexual distinction is conferred on an inanimate object which reveals the gender construction in society. Thus male soils, *yewend merét*, are rich and fertile whilst female soils, *yesét merét*, are light and relatively infertile. Size will also determine the gender, the feminine being used to suggest a smaller, the masculine a larger object. Nevertheless, even in this case the feminine for the diminutive is far from obligatory.

As we saw in the earlier references from my diary, it is not uncommon for people to reverse the biological gender when talking to each other. For example, *ante hid* ('you go', m. sing.) or *ante na* ('you come', m. sing.) might be substituted by the female, *anchï hïjï* ('you go', f. sing.) or *anchï ney* ('you come', f. sing.). The substitution could also take place the other way round, the biologically feminine being referred to in the masculine. The uses to which these reversals are put will be discussed in turn.

Gender reversal is most commonly applied to children and operates in the case of both females and males. From my diary:

> Zegene and Mammit have a daughter, Sintayehu, aged about five. She was sometimes addressed by both parents in the masculine, sometimes in the feminine. Sintayehu often goes to play with Tesfayé or Addisé, two boys in the neighbourhood. She is related to neither. The three children can be heard to mix the genders indiscriminately.

When applied to children, this blurring of gender identity is used as a strategy to defeat the evil eye, and other malignant forces conspiring against the life of the child. By referring to the boy as 'she' or the girl as 'he', people believe they can trick the 'death-wishers' and increase the likelihood of survival. In addition, the child is not usually named before it reaches the age of two. Until then, and often long afterwards, non-gender specific endearment terms such as Tinisé ('my little one') tend to be used for all infants. Even when the child is named, boys are sometimes given female names and vice-versa, whilst a large proportion of names are not gender-specific.

Among adults, gender reversal is also usual, though more context-specific. It is most frequently observed when men are referred to in the feminine. There are, in particular, three almost contradictory reasons for these reversals.

- As a term of rapprochement, or a term of endearment and closeness between friends. It is in this sense that the reversals are most common. This explanation seems satisfactory in the examples introduced at the beginning.
- As a term of insult, to belittle or express distancing from or superiority over someone; for example, an elderly person to a youngster, or as a way of referring to an enemy. It was often used to refer to the rebel groups as a put-down. Here language is used to express a feeling of social difference between people. This is also common usage in the context of an older man using the feminine to address a younger boy.
- As a way of honouring someone, a symbol of status differential in which the person addressed in the feminine is placed above the second person. This last use is referred to in the literature,[34] with examples of men using the feminine towards those they are elevating, though I have not heard this use of reversals. What is commonly heard, however, is the use of the masculine applied to women as praise, the implication being that they are acting 'like a man'.

Women use gender reversals among themselves. From my diary:

> Abeba, a young woman, lives alone with her mother. They often address each other in the masculine. Today Almaz, a friend of Abeba, came visiting. Almaz has recently given birth, and lives with her daughter and husband. Throughout the visit Abeba and Almaz referred to each other in the masculine. The two are distantly related.

> Dessita is a widow who lives with her three children. She uses the masculine form to refer to Asselefech, one of her neighbours, a young wife, and I have also heard her refer to Asselefech's husband, Bek'ele, in the feminine.

The use of the masculine for, or between, women can be explained predominantly in terms of the first of the categories earlier, as a form of attachment and closeness. In addition, as already mentioned, the reversals are applied to women, both by themselves and by men, in terms of the third explanation: as a form of honour, a way of looking up to some women who are acting 'like a man' or as an 'honorary man'.

It would seem as if, despite the existence of differences in Amharic, these can be used for other reasons than to specify sex. The flexible use of gender demarcations and the liberty people take with the language suggest that in the culture itself gender distinctions can be tampered with. The picture that emerges from this discussion on language is in keeping with the main theme of this book, that despite gender division of work and entitlements in an androcentric and patriarchal society, there is considerable negotiation with and subversion of the dominant scenario.[35] The message from the linguistic side seems to be that gender distinction can be put to different uses, that sexual differences in language are 'hijacked' for purposes other than to describe a gendered world. When used towards children, the reversals are a trick against evil forces. Ironically, sexual reversals among adults are used to give contradictory meaning: they distance and bring together, they aggrandize and belittle.

There remains, however, a dominant use of the reversals, namely as a form of endearment, between individuals of the same or different genders. The reasons are perhaps located in a connection with heterosexual love rather than a comment on relative power and status. In a society where homosexuality is taboo, terms of affection come more easily to people of opposite sexes. Thus by defining a woman as male, another woman can address her endearingly, and the same scenario applies for a man addressing another man in the feminine. In fact, these gender reversals are one of the few linguistic forms of endearment.

Whatever the use to which they are applied and irrespective of the speaker, the reversals subvert the accepted gender distinctions in language, appear to reinforce the notion of male supremacy, and, in contradistinction, cut across the gender hierarchy.

Conclusion

In the sections on religion and on language, the discussion in this chapter concentrated, not on the dominant scene, but on where the rules were broken. It was argued that there are times when the androcentric frame is not applied, or when it allows, or fails to disallow, space in which women can operate.

The rationale for the lengthy discussion on belief lies in its continuing importance to the society. The 'socialist' state failed to suppress religion, and was not even able to distance itself from it. I am not suggesting that the state was completely outmanoeuvred by the Church. The argument is that, although the coercive power of the state ensured its outward supremacy, the ideological influence of religion remained more central to the community and, in the case of Christianity, was even outwardly wooed by the local representatives of the state.

I have argued that there were two forms of religious belief in operation. The first, Ethiopian Orthodox Christianity, is overt and visible. It imposes work taboos, purification ceremonies and rules about fasting, and is present in the ceremonies of birth and death. In opposition to this, and in a more marginal social position, is a non-legitimated spirit belief. Symbolically, men rule on earth just as they do in the heaven of Christianity; nevertheless, we saw that, as well as finding support systems within the main Christian beliefs, in particular through the figure of the Virgin Mary and the organization of *mehaber*, women predominated in the alternative religious sphere which caters more specifically to them.

In the second part of this chapter we turned to language since the terms people use determine the kind of communication they achieve and the perceptions they hold. In many cultures, analysts of language have found that the spoken culture belongs to men more than to women. This is also the case in Amharic, the only language spoken in Menz. Nevertheless, we saw that gender differences in language were used for other purposes than sex differentiation and that reversals even obscured the standard distinction between the way men and women were addressed. As well as pointing to an element of flexibility within the framework of gender hierarchy, the contradictory ways in which reversals are used should act as a reminder of the untidiness of a reality which belies neat and simplistic generalizations.

The choice of a focus on religion and language is not coincidental. Religion is vocalized through language, and both are central ideological elements of the way men and women perceive each other, and the differences in their respective social identities. They both help to describe the co-existence of a dominant world view and a subordinate one. The male-controlled Church retains power over the Christian population through its exclusive rights and access to the religious language of Geez, whilst most of the spirit beliefs invent their own argot, and, when speaking in Amharic, often turn to gender reversals. Moreover, the spirit beliefs give women a voice, the space and time to clamour in a society which tends to demand their silence.

Notes

1 Lewis, 1975; in Ethiopia, Reminick, 1974.

2 Certain days of the month are associated with individual saints, for example, Saint George's day is on the 23rd of each month. In addition, one or two months in the year are particularly important, for example, in the case of Saint George it is 23 Miyazya.

3 Walker, 1933: 74. In addition, one of the national Christian holidays has an association with a female figure. Thus the story goes that *Mesk'el*, the Finding of the True Cross, originated in the early Christian era, when Queen Eléni [Helena] went in search of the cross of the crucifixion and announced the finding by lighting a torch that her people could see.

4 Natvig, 1987: 671.

5 'Women, otherwise limited in cultural participation among the Amhara, particularly in the Church institution where their expressive behaviour and opportunities for service are almost entirely rejected, constitute a considerable majority in the *zar* societies, even in the top leaderships'. Messing, 1957: 598. Also Tsehai Berhane Selassie, 1984: 14; Boddy, 1989.

6 Lewis, 1975: 31. Very similar comments are made in his more recent book, 1986: 39. See also March and Taqqu, 1986. For a similar interpretation in terms of stress in Eastern Transkei, see O'Connell, 1982; in Kenya, see Gomm, 1975; in Sudan, Boddy, 1989.

7 I am not arguing a simplistic functionalist view of the spirit or, for that matter, Christian beliefs. Women's involvement in religion is more than a simple compensatory action, a protection against the world or against male supremacy. It is an expression of culture and a belief system in which some actions can be explained this way. See Holmberg, 1983, for a critique of this type of analysis; also Van Binsbergen, 1979, for an explanation in terms of social formation and political change.

8 The term is pronounced *angel libs*, though it should probably be *anget libs*, literally neck-clothes, i.e., a scarf.

9 Lewis suggested that whereas mainstream religions, in this case Orthodox Christianity, are moral religions praising and blaming humans for their actions and thoughts, the peripheral religions are often amoral in nature: they treat the victim of possession as blameless with respect to actions and thoughts within the society, in essence because the religion plays no direct part in the structuring of society.

10 Trimingham, 1952: 27; Messing, 1958: 1120; Lewis, 1975: 96.

11 Natvig, 1987: 677.

12 In both cases, women afflicted with the possession sometimes display their condition outwardly by wearing a foot bracelet called *allo*.

13 For similarities with beliefs among the Gurage see Shack, 1966, 1971; among the Oromo, see Knutsson, 1975; among the Sidamo, Hamer and Hamer, 1966, Brøgger, 1975.

14 The term means something like 'a taster'. Honoured people are sometimes hand-fed a few times as a sign of friendship and as a symbolic gift.

15 The term Galla is a reference to the people now known as Oromo. *Ch'ellé* literally means beads in Amharic.

16 This is likely to be another Islamic influence, since the Muslim religious leaders do not drink *t'ella*, but only *buk'ri*, a form of non-alcohol beer.

17 For parallels from other countries, see Lewis, 1975: 63.

18 For an account of the origin of the *buda* belief, see Reminick, 1974.

19 These are also called *YeMedhané Alem fanta,* 'the share of the Saviour of the World', i.e., Christ. The descriptions of the spirit suggest an association between the sighting of the spirit and lightning; the word *berak'* also has this connotation in Amharic.

20 *Jinn* or *Jini* are prevalent in Islamic cultures. Describing this in the case of Somalia, Lewis writes: 'Anthropomorphic *jinns* lurk in every dark and empty corner, poised ready to strike capriciously and without warning at the unsuspecting passer-by. These

malevolent spirits are thought to be consumed by envy and greed, and to hunger especially after dainty foods, luxurious clothing, jewellery, perfume and other finery.' 1975: 75.

21 The presentation here stresses the belief as a serious one. However, there is a second level in which terms like *wik'abï, jinn* and *buda* are used, namely as insults or in jokes. The angry muttering '*mett'abet jinnïw*', 'his *jinn* has come upon him' towards a husband who is misbehaving in some way, or '*buda new*', 'he is a buda' referring to someone who is disliked, are common usages in Amharic.

22 There are a number of other ways in which the distinctions between spirit beliefs and Christianity are hard to draw. A good deal of ceremony is negotiated around food. The prayer below is recited in honour of St Gabriel; it is not far removed from ones sometimes recited to the *adbar*.

እንተ፡ነህ፡ቅዱስ፡ገብርኤል፡	You are Saint Gabriel,
ተዎc፡ለዎcህ፡	From month to month,
ታመት፡ለመትህ፡	From year to year,
ደህና፡እድርገኝ፡	Keep me well,
እስከ፡ዘመዴ፡	Together with my relative,
እስከ፡እዝግዴ፡	Together with my kin,
__እስከ፡ወደድኩት፡	Including those I love,
እስከ፡ወለድኩት፡ ፡፡	Including those I bore.

23 One women commented *ak'im yansenal, gin sïsay ayset'unim*, 'we cannot afford them, but they do not give peace (otherwise)'.

24 Note also that I am not making a clear distinction between what the anthropological literature might label witchcraft (*buda*) and different forms of possession (*zar, ch'ellé*, and so on). This is because no distinction is made along these lines at the diagnosis stage. Illness can be diagnosed in either of these terms and because even when labelled in distinct terms, it is still common for a woman to be under the influence of both *buda* and *ch'ellé*, i.e., both witchcraft and possession. For an attempt to argue against the validity of the conventional distinctions, see also Lewis, 1986.

25 For example, a woman can decide on a divorce, or ask for other major changes in her life, justifying her actions in terms of her *wik'abï*.

26 Lewis, 1975: 86.

27 I have a hunch that the enacting of possession is more common in urban settings, whilst the expression of possession in terms of malaise and specific ailments characterizes rural methods of drawing attention to possession. Alternatively, the distinction might be more closely correlated with wealth.

28 Levine, 1965.

29 Gilmore, 1978; Jabbra, 1980.

30 Harding, 1975, argues that in view of women's lack of formal access to information, gossiping provides an implicit way of finding out about decision-making processes. It is a political act which is made fun of because politics should not be a woman's prerogative. See also Wolf, 1974, for women's manipulation of gossip in China.

31 For an account of this in the context of sociological research, see Cicourel, 1964.

32 Spender, 1980.

33 A study by Teshome Demisse and Bender, 1983, on the argot of 'unattached girls' in Addis Ababa would also fit in this category. The authors argue that the argot is a personal language used by prostitutes, as a tool for self-defence and as a means of creating group cohesion.

34 Messing, 1957: 419.

35 These types of ritual exceptions occur in other societies in different forms. For example Mead, in her study of seven Pacific communities, points to times when dress conventions are reversed. 'In adult life elaborate rituals in which men dress as women, caricaturing their lesserness, and women dress as men, caricaturing their glorious bombast, are a frequent feature of ceremonial life.' Mead, 1962: 88. On the separation of biology from gender in the case of cross-gender females, *berdache*, see Blackwood, 1984.

9

Gender, Rural Poverty and the State: Towards a Synthesis

Two sets of issues were introduced in Chapter 1. The first concerned the peasant–state relationship; the second, the lives of women. The empirical work presented in this book has addressed in some detail the questions posed at the outset. In this concluding chapter, brief answers are highlighted by means of a summary of the consecutive chapters. Though many of the arguments can be taken out of the context of Gragn, Menz, or even Ethiopia, to form a more general commentary on the position of women and the peasantry, the attempt in this book has been to ground the arguments securely in the context of ethnographic research.

The structure of this book reflects how, in the course of my research, I came to a better understanding of the relationship between women and men, on the one hand, and the peasantry and the state on the other. I went to Menz to learn about the impact of state institutions and found that I was taking the state too much for granted, assuming radical transformation was taking place where in fact there was none. In the empirical chapters we therefore moved from a primary interest in the state to a perspective in which it becomes incidental, merely one of a number of factors to be taken into account. My search for an understanding of women's lives progressed along a similar trajectory. In the discussion of state institutions, women were incidental, their position unilluminated. In order to see women come to life, and to understand how their relations with men were constructed, I had to move entirely away from government policies.

I have argued that, in Menz, the state's economic contribution to society was marginal, while the ideological penetration of socialism was even less significant. We saw in Chapter 3 that the most fundamental of the policies undertaken was the land reform, which made land the property of the 'people', redistributed it within communities and abolished tenancy. Beyond this, the state succeeded in creating a number of administrative institutions. The peasants' associations provided, and even after the demise of the *Derg* continued to provide, an ongoing communication between state and society. They were the executive institutions of local government. These associations had their own local law courts and police, and the capability to command a regular workforce. Service cooperatives provided peasants' associations with services and were, at the same time, a channel of extraction. In Menz there were no state farms, and producer cooperatives were almost non-existent.

Literacy, education, agricultural and health extension services established in the early years of the revolution became less and less visible as time passed. Despite claims to the contrary, these services provided few inputs, and then only to a minority of the population. One of the more important, if not the most significant, form of support acknowledged by the population was the provision of aid, mostly channelled through aid agencies. The extractive arm of the state was most ruthless in the demand for men as military service recruits, in tax dues, and in regular, as well as occasional levies. Organizations such as the women's association and the youth association were viewed as little more than additional channels of government tax collection.

As to the position of women within the administrative organizations created, we find that women were relegated to the women's association, and participated only in literacy and, much less extensively, in education. Peasants' associations, service cooperatives and producer cooperatives were androcentric institutions, officials being ubiquitously male. In Menz, the Ministry of Agriculture failed to communicate with women and the Ministry of Health, though recognized in the community as being of potential value, had only a nominal presence. The result was that the relationship between women and the state was particularly tenuous and indirect. I argued that even judging the state on its own terms, where it created an institution with women in mind, the result was disappointing. The women's association was a token gesture. In practice it would have taken too much administrative commitment, money and time to carry through potentially emancipating programmes.

The same criticism underlies the failure of most administrative structures in Menz. The costs to the society were increased by the *tabula rasa* method of operation, which resulted in the rejection of existing structures in the attempt to build something 'modern' and socialist, and the campaign fixation which marshalled efforts suddenly, for a limited period, on a single policy. Finally, corruption and nepotism increased, in particular at the level of local peasants' association and service cooperative officials.

Chapter 4, on villagization, warned against too rigid and unified a perception of state policies and too simplistic a view of the implications of such policies. The general negative attitudes to the policy sprang from a host of reasons, including the problems which arose from accommodating livestock and humans at close quarters, and the reluctance to move from a well-established, 'warm' home to a bare hut, often smaller and less well-made. Nevertheless, despite the overall unfavourable reaction of the population to villagization, the move away from the more isolated homesteads of the past was appreciated by many children and some vulnerable households, such as those lacking adult men. Some services became easily available to more people than would previously have benefited. In addition, less time was wasted waiting for work campaigns to start, and travelling to and from meetings.

The complex decisions underlying the heterogeneous population's reacting to villagization were presented. For example, officials felt obliged to express nominal support for the campaign and have a hut allocated to them. However, as they belonged, for the most part, to the richer section of the population, they were more likely to remain in their old homes. The difficulties of controlling livestock in such close confines, and the greater distance from grazing land, proved to be particularly troublesome, notably for the comparatively wealthy who had significant livestock herds. More generally, people made different judgements about the costs and benefits of making the move, with such factors as distance from the existing homestead and the state of the existing hut being taken into account.

As we have seen, beyond the predominant antagonism between state and population, lay a more complicated reality. Some state policies, in particular military service, were feared and hated; some interventions had a mixture of welcome and unwelcome consequences (service cooperatives, for example, brought in goods but were also a means of extraction); some were disliked but benefited a section of the population, be it only a minority (thus villagization advantaged the young and some single women). Lastly, certain state policies met the desires of the majority of the population and were highly valued, such as the initial land reform and the provision of aid. A distinction can also be drawn between the planned outcome of a policy and its actual outcome, within a context in which different policies impact negatively or positively on each other. An example of the negative impact of one policy on another is the effect of villagization on the afforestation programme. Though deforestation was an acknowledged problem in the region and tree planting campaigns were organized, the policy of villagization, requiring a massive use of wood, resulted in a significant setback to afforestation campaigns. An example of the reinforcing impact of polices was the effect of villagization on the influence of spirit beliefs. We saw that, although direct attempts to reduce the influence of spirit beliefs, deemed a 'backward practice', had little effect, the villagization campaign resulted in reductions in spirit-related practices, as people abandoned customs, in order that the new place should not 'learn' them.

Overall, the peasantry remained suspicious of the state. The latter had the force to command because of its coercive apparatus, but also because power held by rulers – in this case Mengistu Haile Mariam's government – was perceived by the peasantry as legitimate. Fear of the costs of the relationship was tempered by fear of exclusion, given the expectation of present and future beneficial inputs by the state.[1] Because of the distribution of aid in particular, an element of patronage entered into the relationship. The population's attitude was one of taking maximum advantage of the state, doing as much as was necessary to reciprocate and then going their own way. Evidence of this attitude of paying lip service to the state was provided by those who built a hut in the new village, but, preferring not to live there, kept it shut or housed someone else in it. Summarized simply, a strategy of continuous adjustment between resistance and compliance characterized the unequal relationship between state and peasantry.[2]

If the perspective is widened from what the state attempted to achieve, to what it might have but did not attempt, it becomes clear how much people's existence was divorced from government influence. The issues of primary importance to the community remained, by and large, outside state involvement. In Chapter 5, on the household economy, the role of the state is seen to dwindle, its direct involvement virtually limited to crop cultivation. I argued that households were involved in a much wider set of concerns, with activities beyond crop cultivation, including livestock production and processing, fuel production, the wool economy and trade. These activities have become increasingly pivotal as a consequence of the recent succession of droughts. Moreover, in addition to their nurturing role, women's economic importance to the household lay in part in these other activities. The state's partial vision is focused on men's principal work domain. The visibility of cultivation contrasts with the more diverse tasks of women which tend to be socially hidden.

The reduction of all production to crop cultivation reflects women's subordinate social status, and fails to recognize women's economic significance. The reduction is a bias also adopted in the Boserup–Goody vision. It will be remembered that the literature separates the male–plough cultivation systems of Asia, in which women are often veiled and have few rights and a relatively low status, from the female–hoe cultivation systems in Africa, in which women are the main cultivators, have more control over economic aspects of the household and are comparatively better off. When applied to Menz, not only is there the problem that we have a plough economy in Africa, but the position of women in Menz does not fully accord with that predicted for plough economies. If a link is to be made between social position and economic contribution I would argue that, symbolically important though it is, men's control over cultivation is not the only factor to consider. Women's contribution outside this sphere of crop production must be taken into account before a correlation between social position and economic contribution can be attempted.

In the mixed economy of Menz, the spinning of wool, the production of fuel, the processing of butter, and the revenue from small-scale trade, for example in eggs, contribute to the domestic economy, and these activities provide an alternative to the importance in West Africa of women's role on the household plot. It is curious that in West Africa, in an area in which women were renowned for their role in marketing, they often maintain the household through subsistence activity, whilst men, increasingly involved in cash production, spend their earnings on imported luxuries. In the poorer, more subsistence-oriented society of Ethiopia, however, it is increasingly the women's small-scale involvement in the cash economy that provides the weekly contributions to subsistence. This is a reversal of the West African sexual division of labour and the subsistence/exchange spheres of the household economy.

When the role of livestock in the economy is examined, it is usually the largest, most visible, most expensive, male animal – the ox – that is highlighted. This is also the animal most closely associated with ploughing – the male task. Yet, as we have seen, the livestock economy is also reliant on sheep, pack animals, and chickens. Cows reproduce, provide milk and can be used to plough. Sheep are vital as a form of capital, a risk-spreading, faster-reproducing bank which can yield additional profit: the skin and wool can be processed, the meat can be eaten. But, to insiders and outsiders alike, sheep are smaller, more mundane forms of livestock than oxen. As for chickens, their importance to the day-to-day running of a household is trivialized, and is forgotten in accounts of production. It is perhaps no coincidence that they are the only form of livestock to which women have almost exclusive rights.

The picture drawn in Chapter 6, dealing with marriage (or rather, divorce and remarriage), shows a complex situation with various types of marriages and extra-marital relations. The position of both single women and independent women heads of household was discussed. Divorce, often instigated by women, is the rule rather than the exception, the average number of marriages per adult being 3.3. The unequal nature of gender relations emerged in the chapter; but it was also clear that women have the power to express dissatisfaction and to search for a better life. The same pattern emerged in Chapter 8 in the realms of religion and language.

Conditions surrounding, and attitudes to, motherhood and the first few years of a child's life were considered at the beginning of Chapter 7. It was shown that women were socially constructed as mothers, their reproductive role central to the definition of their identity and status. There coexist in the society positive and negative valuations of fertility. It is valued because it is life-giving, but women's blood is 'polluting' and contact with it needs to be mitigated through 'purification' by a priest. At least part of the negative associations, however, derive from a fear for mother and child. To increase the likelihood of survival, pregnant women have to be camouflaged and carry protective charms, while infants must be kept out of the sight of evil-wishers.

On a material level, the discomfort and pain of menstruation and the less frequent but more dramatic burden of pregnancy, childbirth and nurturing occupy women's thoughts and influence their actions. Impoverishment and the cold climate of Menz result in conditions that are particularly hard for women. Contraception is not openly practised, and the concept of controlled fertility is not considered an area of discussion between spouses, let alone an issue of women's rights. Nonetheless, arguments over sex and the possibility of repeated pregnancies are central elements in tensions and break-ups between partners. Furthermore, late menarche, extended weaning, high infant mortality and arrangements such as spouses sleeping separately, usually with a child, keep household sizes at a relatively low average for Africa of 4.4.

In parallel with the picture elsewhere, the activities of women in social and biological reproduction do not usually count as 'work', nor, more ironically, as 'labour'. Though the reproductive role of women is often undervalued by them and by others, it is this role which also defines them as the 'other' in a category complementary to men. The paradox is that, though undervalued, the reproductive role of women is, at the social level, that for which women are prized. The virgin girl is given a symbolic endowment of luxury items at her first marriage to symbolize her worth to her future husband, and her reputation is assessed primarily in terms of childbearing. A barren wife can expect her husband to give her notice to leave, a situation which is unlike the more common one of women initiating divorce, as seen in Chapter 6. Recognizing her vulnerability, however, she might try to pre-empt divorce by suggesting that they bring in another 'fertile' wife.

All women are considered to have expertise in the reproductive sphere. In addition, some women become known as 'women of knowledge', in the role of midwives, while others become circumcisers of both boys and girls. Associated with the reproductive role of women is an arena in which kinship networks can be reactivated or created. Thus, for example, an expectant mother, or one who has newly delivered, turns to her own mother during the *aras* recuperation period, and godparents are chosen at the time of the child's baptism.

We return now to the theory about the correlation between women's social status and their economic contributions. Merely considering the 'economic' role of women in various societies, and then plotting these differences to emerge with a theory about the comparative position of women, ignores the paradox of women's role in reproduction. Such a procedure also fails to take into account the ownership of resources and how this affects work and power. The Boserup–Goody theory does serious injustice to the complex way people think about their gendered world. Among researchers and policy makers, it reflects a male bias in priorities which downgrades reproduction.

The importance of life-cycles to society, acknowledged by the participation of the church therein, is contrasted with the non-involvement of the state which has taken little interest in health improvement or family planning. Socialism notwithstanding, birth and death are constructed in Christian terms and ceremonies. The state did not address the social relevance of expenditures associated with the life-cycle, let alone substitute or amend them through policy measures. In the case of burial, the costs were borne, in the past, with the help of informal support systems. In Gragn, the formalization of *iddir*, burial associations, was a new phenomenon, an internal adaptation to change rather than one instigated by the state.

An overall theme of the book has been the argument that to look at gender relations in Menz within the limited framework of women's subordination and the hardship of their daily existence would do serious injustice to their active negotiation of a position in all spheres of life. I suggested that there were similar implications to be drawn from the chapter on divorce and that on religion and language. What characterized the conclusions about the marital and religious issues, is that within the overall framework of male dominance, women have found means of expression and rebellion. Thus divorce was explained as action usually undertaken by women dissatisfied with their husbands. Yet, the fact that women initiated action is itself also a reflection of the virilocal norm giving men a greater control on the home. Furthermore, although women were the prime movers, the ones abandoning the joint home, this was, more often than not, a response to their husbands' unacceptable behaviour.

In the realm of the dominant form of religion, Ethiopian Orthodox Christianity, women are considered inferior to the male laity, themselves subordinate to the clergy. There is, nevertheless, support for women in the figure of the Virgin Mary, the protector of women, particularly during childbirth. Women's rotating socio-religious gatherings, the *mehaber*, are usually in her name. These provide a legitimate female-dominated forum, celebrated with food and drink and the chance to socialize. The *mehaber* also develop a socially created kinship network of 'sisters'. This is one of the rare occasions when women have time to sit down and talk, when they will be seen without a bundle of wool at their feet, or a spindle in their hands.

We saw that even within the male-dominant religion, there were ways in which women found a valued and legitimate support system. The alternative spirit religion that exists in the society provided another area of expression for women and, to a lesser extent, for marginalized men. We saw that there were a number of different spirits with specific characteristics; that the spirits involved women in a variety of regular and occasional outlays, that some beliefs included trance enactment, while others were displayed through complaints of illness. The beliefs provide a channel through which women can express dissatisfaction, seek attention, be made a fuss of, and receive material benefits and luxuries such as clothes, honey and coffee.

In Menz, as elsewhere, language was usually a male preserve. It was suggested that the gender reversals in daily language, in the *argot* of spirit-belief and the cross-sexual imagery of spirit possession, point to ways in which the social divisions according to which men were considered superior to women were challenged, or at least freed from their usual meaning.

In terms of the changes over time, I argued that impoverishment and the unexpected side-effects of state intervention resulted in a number of developments. These include a decrease in the importance of land cultivation and an increase in the importance of other resources, livestock, labour and access to state inputs. However, in the case of male labour, these other activities were in turn constrained by such policies as communal work campaigns. These campaigns were timed not to interfere with cultivation, but conflicted with other activities. The result was an increase in the comparative importance of women's income-earning activities, since the communal labour was predominantly male.

Worsening economic and environmental conditions, and the effects of some forms of state intervention, have contributed to an erosion of the material base of the culture. Many *mehaber* were discontinued because of the drought and, in the case of some male *mehaber,* because of hostility to the government's policy of hosting them in the church. *Serg* ceremonial marriages, and the celebrations associated with other life-cycle events, have been significantly reduced because of the cost of providing the attendant feasts. Even the convalescence time given to those who have newly given birth had, for similar reasons, been eroded. Villagization, together with increasing economic constraints, has also resulted in a marked decrease in offerings to spirits.

The discussion of poverty should not be taken to mean that all people in the community were equally impoverished. A local hierarchy clearly existed. Patronage networks, for example, were discussed in different contexts: they were mentioned in terms of local-level state representatives replacing feudal lords, in the selection of godparents for a child, and in the sphere of *ribbï,* livestock herding arrangements by which the poorer households looked after the animals belonging to richer households. Most women were in a more precarious position than most men, yet even within the category of women there were significant variations: those with secure and direct access to land, and those without; those who had entered into different forms of marriage and households; those at different stages in the life-cycle. Equally among women and men of Gragn, there was the significant distinction between the poor and those verging on destitution.

Notes

1 For parallels in the comparative and theoretical literature, see Rothchild & Chazan, 1988. Chazan, for example, notes: 'To many people in the countryside . . . the state . . . constitutes an intrusive device from which they can possibly reap benefits, but over which they have little influence' and 'Viewed from below, the state is seen as both a distributor of benefits and an intruder. It is simultaneously an oppressor and an ally. . . .' 1988: 137 and 333.
2 This idea is developed by Scott, 1985; the title of his book, *Weapons of the Weak: Everyday Forms of Peasant Resistance,* summarizes his arguments.

10

Epilogue: A Glimpse of Menz after Mengistu

While my study of Menz was being turned into a book, Mengistu's government was defeated and replaced by a 'Transitional' administration. In Menz, the Ethiopian People's Revolutionary Democratic Front, the EPRDF, captured Mehal Meda and then lost and regained it twice before taking control of Addis Ababa and the country as a whole, in May 1992.

Two years after finishing the fieldwork, in April 1992, I returned to Menz and spent a week trying to find out what had happened in Gragn in the interim. Approaching the villagized settlement I saw first a spectral ruin: huts collapsed, stones strewn around the old shell, thatched roofs and wooden doors all gone, not one tree in sight. Then I saw some huts still standing, and inhabited: 17 households scattered amidst the ruins.

Many of the remaining households had been amongst the most vulnerable in society; seven had been very poor, and five were female-headed. The proportion of female-headed households, at 30 per cent of those remaining compared with the 15 per cent expected from the fieldwork data, was twice the average. The rest were householders who had invested heavily in the new village. Twelve had destroyed their old homesteads to create the new dwelling; 14 had built an additional kitchen or cattle-shed.

In Menz, the peasants' associations still functioned as local administrative units. Former officials had been replaced; many chairmen and secretaries had been imprisoned, though some were later released. In Gragn, despite the changes, former leaders seemed to have retained their influence.

Land in many parts of Menz had been redistributed within existing peasants' association boundaries. It had been allocated to a couple jointly, on the understanding that the land should be divided equally between them if they divorced. A quarter of this basic allocation was added for each child after the first one and up to, and including, an eighth child. Women over 18 and men over 24 could be given land separately as independent householders. The former leadership had not been allocated land, and some of their wealth, in the form or livestock and grain, had been confiscated.

The redistribution of land seemed to have been appreciated by many, though the process of change resulted in social unrest, potential losers even managing to delay redistribution in some areas. Where implementation went ahead, more people became eligible, with a resulting reduction in an individual's share. Complaints of land shortage therefore continued. Communally held trees were also allocated to individual households.

In Gragn, people had not, as yet, been taxed, or summoned for *corvée* labour, lengthy meetings, or military service. The service cooperative, shop and mill had been closed, the sewing project abandoned, and the water taps and pump had ceased to function. Many of those who left for resettlement had since returned, and had been promised or given land. Schools had resumed after two years of disruption. In Gragn, the sixth form school under construction during fieldwork had finally opened, though literacy classes had not been organized.

People complained about increasing poverty, though the situation did not appear to me to have worsened significantly. This might be because, despite poor harvests, there had not been the annual collection of state dues and because people had more time for income-earning activities. However, continued soil degradation, together with the threat of rain failure, could quickly undermine the standard of living. The prices of grain which people had to buy when harvests failed had risen considerably over the period. Aid continued to reach the peasants' association through World Vision, which supervised the mother and child vaccination programme and was involved in various other projects. However, the more widespread programmes of food distribution and food-for-work had ceased.

There was a sense that people had been left to their own devices with the demise of the old régime. Attitudes to the new government mixed hostility to the 'otherness' of leadership perceived as coming from Tigray with appreciation of the lack of coercion, forced labour and taxation. As one friend put it, '*Sewu tenfiswal*', 'people can now breathe'. At the same time, there now appeared to be a lack of governance. This was expressed variously: '*Mastedader yellem; sine sirat yelewim; yelijoch ch'ewata yimeslal*'; 'There is no governing; it has no order; it looks like child's play.' Such comments gave the impression that the country, at that time, had moved from 'bad' to 'no' government. In a relatively homogeneous community, there was no evidence of the ethnic tension afflicting many other parts of the country. However, there was a fear that the lack of effective government would lead to an escalation of conflict between neighbours.

There is no reason to suppose that gender relations had altered in the intervening period. During my return visit I was brought up to date on events in the village and the peasants' association; I heard of births, deaths, marriages and, of course, divorces. In terms of state–peasant relations, the overall findings of the book remain true after the change of government. As I argued in earlier chapters, the revolutionary government had wrought no radical transformation in Menz. Since the fall of Mengistu, the peasants had had the opportunity to abandon policies which they had been obliged (or had pretended) to follow. In current perception, the 'transitional' government appeared to be less interventionist, and less powerful. Some of the data on the *Derg*'s agrarian policies are now a matter of historical record. However, the concerns of the peasantry, and especially of the women, remain as described in the book. People continue their own battle against an increasingly eroded, harsh and bleak environment, on the whole without any welfare system, economic support or development provisions.

APPENDICES

Appendix A: Reflections on the Research Process

Evolution

The work for this book started in October 1987, with nine months of preparatory study and reading at Edinburgh University. I then spent 14 months in Ethiopia, most of the time collecting data in the chosen peasants' association, the rest of the time inputting data on a computer, reading, and visiting other areas of the country to obtain a comparative perspective.

The questions which were, in the end, addressed by the book are set out in Chapter 1. These are not the enquiries with which I set out. During the course of the work, the initial research aims were modified both by changing opportunities and by my own understanding of the situation. The initial project was to study gender relations in the context of villagization. However, when my fieldwork began in May 1988, much of Menz, the area of my research, remained unvillagized. Moreover, even where some communities had been partly regrouped, I found that respondents were keener to talk about other factors which impinged more forcefully on their everyday lives. Furthermore, there was little variation in what people said about villagization, and though I could have set about measuring changes in resource use, I found it more meaningful to talk to people about the issues that they were discussing with each other, or which were a regular feature of their lives. An exclusive focus on villagization would have been depressing for both informants and myself, since the policy was generally disliked. Instead we talked about a range of issues which yielded more positive, meaningful, and lively debate. Thus the method adopted, participant-observation, combined with the population's preferences and my own, resulted in the decision to let the study evolve into a more general enquiry into women's lives and government structures.

Another change emerged as a result of the gradual realization that I had the choice between labelling my work as research on women, a study of gender relations, or an analysis of the state–peasantry relationship (leaving the women/gender issue implicit). The last of these options was attractive because it seemed important not to box in, and hence segregate, the study as dealing with what are considered by many as sideline issues, 'women and that kind of thing'.[1] I felt, for example, that simply having the word women in the title would limit interest. The second option was, moreover, sounder than the first in that it acknowledged that one could not look at women in isolation; that it was the relationship between men and women which was at issue. However, the fact remained that women were the key component of my fieldwork. With them I spent most time, and it was observations on their lives that I recorded in greatest depth. In the end, I decided to opt for an overt focus on women in the belief that honesty to my data was preferable, and in the perhaps naïve hope that the more numerous male-centred accounts of fieldwork would also explicitly state their androcentric angle. A less ambitious and realistic hope might be that, to those who read it, the data presented here would show how much male researchers and policy makers are missing with their almost exclusive focus on men.

The focus on women's issues is a starting point of gender analysis and of a study of the discrimination against women on the basis of sex. My aim was to elucidate on the one hand the cultural/social, political and economic elaborations of sexual distinctions which subordinate women, and, on the other hand, those forces that seemed to work towards gender equality. There is the inevitable problem that instead of working towards the abolition of the distinction, such approaches tend to return to a sexually based dichotomy between men and women, thus subordinating the divisions within each gender and the unions across gender. Thus, ironically, in attempting to argue that the biological difference between men and women is used to perpetuate a certain type of hierarchy, there is the danger of sex and the biological distinction themselves being reinstated as the dominant, or even the only issue. Nevertheless, this study focuses on women as a distinct category, stressing the inherent contradictions in their position. The heterogeneity of women's experiences and its context in terms of the position and work of men is, however, constantly reaffirmed.[2]

Furthermore, although the subject matter is women, the way this study presents their position is by making an analogy, based on the issue of subordination, between their relationship with men and that between the peasantry and the state. In the chapters on state policies, the approach was to examine the situation as it occurred on the ground, rather than as planned and publicized by the government. The interest was also in what the state does *not* do, as well as in what it attempts to achieve. I was thus concerned with a study of less obvious parts of the culture and economy. Not surprisingly, given that women are marginalized in most societies, the study of the less visible and often less valued is located primarily in women's spheres of the private and public world.

Associated with this is another difference between the study as first conceived and the final product, namely the incorporation of structures which existed prior to the Ethiopian revolution of 1974.[3] Initially, I was more interested in change, and in the impact of socialist transformation, but due to the very lack of such a transformation, I found myself focusing more and more on people's own efforts, 'traditional' beliefs and means of livelihood. This shift can also be justified by the criticism that the government was unaware of the constraints and potentials within existing structures. The state seemed to be working indiscriminately against some traditions, yet at the same time one noticed areas in which it put little emphasis on transformation, leaving traditional systems unchallenged. A study of state involvement was meaningless without a study of what was already in place, and how the two related to each other. As well as covering state and peasant actions and reactions, therefore, the study had to discriminate between spheres in which action was taken and those in which it was not. An analysis of the repercussions of 'non-action' became central.

Since this book is based on ethnographic research, it may seem to be an anthropological account. However, the study has not neglected the sociological, political and economic domains. Having decided to work beyond a single discipline, I must concede, however, that there are limits to what a researcher can usefully explore. In particular, in this study there is no attempt to consider the role of psychoanalysis or to look at the subconscious. The omission needs comment because Levine and Reminick,[4] two earlier researchers in Menz, relied heavily on psychological explanations, and because part of the literature on gender veers in the same direction. This omission is the result of a number of interrelated factors which can be listed briefly. Firstly, psychoanalysis has largely been conceived of and theorized by men in the West, using concepts and examples which are androcentric and Eurocentric in the extreme. It was the use of psychology which, in the view of Ethiopian readers amongst others, marred the accounts of the two aforementioned researchers.[5] Secondly, attempts to formulate analyses with more understanding of women seem biased in reverse, replacing the Freudian mother–son centrality with a mother–daughter one.[6] Finally, socio-economic and political considerations seemed far more immediate and relevant than the universalistic and fatalistic psychoanalytic approach.[7]

My position as a woman in many ways determined the kind of information I was privy to during the fieldwork period. Also important was the fact that I felt, and was seen to be, involved in the society. In many ways what I saw was not particularly alien to me, since I was brought up in Ethiopia. This situation of ambivalence and part-belonging was unlike the stereotype of traditional ethnography.[8] Furthermore, my political and social commentary on Ethiopia was supported by the knowledge that I was freer to express my views than many Ethiopians.

In terms of presenting myself to the peasants' association, my approach was to try not to fit too comfortably into any mould and in this way to encourage an ambivalent attitude towards me; an attitude which allowed me to talk to different groups of people without consciously putting on too much of a chameleon act.[9] I was seen as neither a proper foreigner nor a proper Ethiopian (being white but claiming to be born in the country, and speaking Amharic); I was not an outsider nor an insider (residing in the area, but new to it, temporary, and mobile within it); not young nor old (it was difficult to estimate my age since many of the things I did which might have given them an indication conflicted with each other). I was not important, yet had status amongst the population, the leadership and outsiders. I was not poor, yet not rich (I did not have the traditional forms of wealth, and was only a student). I was not part of the government yet communicated extensively with government agents. Finally, I was not a normal woman, because of my clothes and the things I was doing. My marital status was never clear since I encouraged conversations about sexual issues yet claimed to be 'still a girl', essentially for reasons of personal security.

From data to book

In addition to the perusal of archival and printed material, my data was collected in the form of diaries, questionnaires and life histories, a triangular strategy to widen the type of information received, the respondents questioned and the framework within which data was passed on.

Diaries
I always walked about with a small note-book and would scribble in it addictively. Respondents and subject matter would be considered before I decided whether to make visible and constant my addiction, to wait for pauses in the conversation or for the respondent to become occupied, or whether it was best to hold back until I was in my hut before writing up. In general, I quickly established my note-pads as necessary accoutrements. Many of the quotations were written down in these diaries. I would often translate there and then, with the exception of the odd significant Amharic expression or sentence which I noted in the original.

My visits to Addis Ababa after bouts of fieldwork were particularly useful, not only to consult the literature, but also for keying in data from these diaries into a computer. This form of data, most of which was accessible before I left Ethiopia, was the most interesting and qualitatively the richest. The subjects, often jotted down in the diary one sentence after another, ranged from adultery to *zemecha*, labour campaigns. I keyed in the information by subject matter into the computer, and by the end I had more than 300 files on different issues. In this way I sorted data as I went along and had opportunities to return to the peasants' association with new questions or requests for clarification.

Questionnaires
Most of my time was spent in the villagized area of Gragn and adjacent communities, with only the odd conversation and excursion to other parts of the peasants' association. Eight months into fieldwork, it seemed important to talk to a wider set of people in the peasants' association, and work on an overview of their lives. Perhaps more importantly, it was difficult to ask for quantitative and economic data once I started living as part of the community. Questionnaires seemed to provide a way out – a way of collecting a relatively large sample of necessary statistics.

I administered these myself, 97 of them, mainly to men, usually sitting with my respondents slightly apart from people working on communal labour tasks, busy building huts or installing water pumps. The interviews each lasted between half an hour and an hour, though when groups congregated, the interviewing would stop in favour of discussions, sometimes turning into arguments.

The data collected answered a diverse set of questions, such as household composition, educational background, use of services and structures both traditional and modern, amounts and yields from land and livestock, other income-earning activities, aid received, details on the sexual division of labour. An analysis of these questionnaires provides the source of most of the quantitative data in the book. The sample size varied for a number of reasons, including interruptions and unclear data. I have therefore indicated the size of the sample in Appendix C. I also administered a short questionnaire on students' backgrounds and aspirations.

Life histories

I gathered detailed qualitative data by spending whole days at a time with individual women. These sessions would often be organized beforehand so as to be on a convenient day, and would usually take place in the woman's hut, though we would sometimes go on errands together. Usually, the woman would get on with her tasks in and around the hut: food and drink preparation, cleaning the hut, watching livestock, spinning. Other people – household members, neighbours and friends – would be involved part of the time, and the conversations would shift accordingly. I carried with me a set of questions about marital history, childbirth, and so on, and used these to initiate conversations at various times during the day and as a checklist to try and maximize coverage of different issues. About 70 women were interviewed in this way, varying in age from the late teens to the seventies. Lengthy quotations usually have their origin in these interviews. As with the case of the diaries, much was translated immediately, though I also did some transcribing, particularly of interesting or apt expressions. Once when I started carrying the cards on which I recorded the life-histories in a rucksack, a friend commented that, these days, instead of my note-book in hand, I slung my rucksack on my back as a woman did her child, carrying it wherever I went. Another neighbour added, 'her writing is her child'.

A single written text is a highly unsatisfactory and artificial reduction of dynamic processes and complex relationships – in this case between men and women, people and the state. The book format, with the progression of chapters through headings and sub-headings to yield a linear, unidirectional account, with the odd themes woven in for variation, belies the chaos and intangibility of reality. The sense of frustration generated in the writing-up stage can best be illustrated by the questions I kept asking myself: How can I conceive of the individual life-cycle without bringing in, at the same time, issues of household structures, and vice versa? How can I evaluate state policies in isolation from the individual and household chapters, and how do I incorporate comparisons with traditional structures? How satisfactory is the term 'traditional' when it is the present manifestation of past phenomena that are being observed, when the present tends to be discussed in terms of the past and thus the clear distinction between 'modern' and 'traditional' begins to blur? In short, how can I mention one issue in isolation without mentioning its impact on a series of other factors? Even more fundamentally, what issues should I highlight, which explanations do I espouse?

To give an example of the dilemmas, here is an extract from my diary written in Menz, which comes at the end of a description of a christening:

> The christening of Almaz's child [the first I had been to since I arrived] was unimpressive. This is not because Almaz's father is poor for he is comparatively rich. I do not know whether the cause was the illegitimacy of the child, or perhaps the fact that the christening was organized by the father

of the young mother, or because the infant is a girl. Maybe it was on the small scale because that is the way things are now (poverty, drought) or because that's the way things have always been in the area. Perhaps foreigners, travellers, all outsiders, tend to build up a more colourful event than is actually warranted. Also, they are most likely to see the grandest celebrations since they have more access to the households of lords than to those of the peasantry.

The extract above points to a number of different leads. The key words could be: christening, illegitimacy, social stratification, traditions and observation – which one should be developed, which abandoned? How should I interpret and order casual happenings?

To lessen the constriction on the data, theory and practice would have to be presented in a variety of parallel accounts; stories creating a plethora of images and ideas, some of which are quickly or gradually rejected, others adding up to a clear picture, remaining unexplained, or proving inconclusive. Ethnographic work, in particular, seems ill-suited to the loaf presentation in which even the size of the result is more or less prescribed by the size of the tin – the 200 or so pages of the book. It would be easier to mould the data into a number of different rolls, numerous stories that do not necessarily fit neatly together. The need to tell one story involves an ironing out and tidying up process which is particularly unsatisfactory to the researcher, since it is the very variations and complexities, the intricacies of the particular case and the subtlety of patterns – almost the perversity of reality – which is so exciting.

To mention one last problem, the theoretical grounding and empirical knowledge of even the most conscientious researcher is patchy. One page of the final draft might represent findings from more than 100 observed events, or, at the other extreme, from the views incidentally expressed to the researcher by one respondent. Different kinds and quality of data are merged together because of the need to present one complete picture. Yet, to be constructive about the whole enterprise, its value lies in the unravelling of the respondents' world through the 'lens' of the researcher with the hope that, by the end, a view of their world will have been created, and a few of their problems elucidated and brought into a wider context. The rationale for the conventional book format lies in the value and necessity of simplifications, interpretations and generalizations.

Notes

1 See Robertson, 1987: 97; Moore, 1988: 1–11; Papanek, 1984.
2 'Explaining matters by sex may be both the most useful and the most dangerous manner of explanation imaginable. . . .The problem with most of the work in these areas is precisely that it over-extends the explanatory capacity of the variable sex.' Eichler, 1980: 122.
3 The research therefore became a study of continuity and change, themes that seem to appear and reappear in the literature on Ethiopia: Molvaer, 1980; Clapham, 1988.
4 Levine, 1963, 1965 and Reminick, 1973.
5 See the review of Levine's *Wax and Gold* by Gedamu Abraha, 1967.
6 See, for example, Eichenbaum and Orbach, 1982.

7 For a critique of the psychoanalytic contribution to understanding women's oppression, see Brenner and Ramas, 1984; Henley, 1985. For an attempt to integrate a psychoanalytic analysis with a materialist anthropological approach see Rubin, 1975.

8 For example, Lévi-Strauss, 1955, on the sense of alienation from the observed society and rejection of one's 'own' society. However, there are disadvantages to being at least a part-insider. For example, events, and attitudes might be taken for granted and therefore not considered for analysis.

9 See Agar, 1980: 88 for the different roles adopted by researchers.

Appendix B: A Personal Note

The author's personal background and interests are central to the conception of any study, yet these are often kept well out of sight. This is unfortunate since, to the reader, information on the directions taken and the choices made provide indications of the likely strengths, limitations and biases of the researcher. They are also of general value to readers in contextualizing and situating the work, since the whos and whys of the research process can be of interest in themselves. In this appendix such background details are presented in a narrative format that seemed in keeping with the nature of the subject.

My background is in development economics; this academic interest is itself the result of being born and brought up in Ethiopia. My mother was a librarian; my father a historian specializing in Ethiopia. As I grew up, other formative influences included the two 'isms' of socialism and feminism.

When it came to the question of whether to look for a job connected with development issues or continue my education, the most appealing option was to continue studying by undertaking empirical research. I found the possibility of fieldwork particularly attractive in that the conclusion of much of the development literature stressed the need for a micro-level understanding of conditions, rather than the ungrounded construction of macro theories. The interest in gender issues arose from my family background in the Suffragette movement, and from my own feminism. It was easy to recognize women as a vulnerable group in society. Compared with the position of the proletariat in class analysis, the oppression of women seemed relatively untheorized. In a course at Sussex University, I was introduced to, and intrigued by, the little theory there was on the role of women in rural production systems. Finally, I remember feeling that the feminist literature and that on women in development seemed to espouse a socialist alternative as a foil for criticism of existing oppression; this suggested the need to consider the condition of women in socialist countries and to evaluate what socialist feminism could contribute.

Having put together my interest in the position of women and in socialist developing countries, locating the study in Ethiopia seemed an obvious step. It was one, however, that I was reluctant to take, preferring to learn about a country I did not know. However, given the interest in development, Ethiopia's condition and in particular the outbreak of the famine, the facts that I had an entry into the society and spoke Amharic, the official language, were impossible to ignore. It made sense to study Ethiopia.

When I started composing the proposal for Edinburgh University and the funding body, the Economic and Social Research Council (ESRC), I considered doing a comparison with socialization policies in Cuba, a country with a longer history of socialist development and which seemed to have influenced the direction Ethiopia was taking. The knowledge that ESRC would most certainly be unwilling to fund such an ambitious project, especially given the increasing importance of completion rates, put an end to the idea. A combination of funding constraints and a feeling that an in-depth analysis was an approach that I valued, then prompted the focus on a single community.

The importance of agriculture for an almost exclusively rural population led me to consider tackling an agrarian issue. Villagization was at the time the most widespread recent policy undertaken in Ethiopia, one on which there was very little information available. At first, I assumed it would bring about a rapid and fundamental change in society. The components of my research proposal were thus brought together under the title: *Gender Relations in a Recently Villagized Peasant Community in Northern Ethiopia*. As mentioned in the previous appendix, the villagization component ceased to play a commanding role in my work, which expanded to take in the spheres of state action and inaction.

The selection of Menz as the region of analysis was based on a number of factors. The selection of an Amhara population was already taken as given, since knowledge of the language had been an important factor in choosing to work in Ethiopia. Given the political situation at the time, some regions were out of bounds, but at the beginning of the fieldwork period, northern Shewa seemed a safe choice. It was also a region on the edges, rather than in the heart of the area affected by recent and ongoing conditions of drought and famine. I felt that I would be unable to justify my research, however well-intentioned, with a population that was still traumatized by famine. However, there is no escaping the fact that, even in Menz, the region I finally chose, the land is increasingly becoming incapable of supporting the population.

Having arrived in Addis Ababa, and obtained all my letters of introduction, research papers and visas, the next step was to locate the exact area of research, to choose 'my' village. As I was beginning to ponder a 'reconnaissance' of the area, I heard that Save the Children Fund UK were about to start a cluster survey of randomly chosen peasants' associations in the area, for a nutrition study. I asked if I could accompany the team of four Ethiopians, and was welcomed. The two weeks I spent with them was a good introduction. We visited isolated communities, travelling by Landrover, by foot and by mule, across spectacular scenery which brought to mind the comment by a British soldier on the Napier Expedition of 1867–8: 'They tell us this is a table land. If it is, they have turned the table upside down and we are scrambling up and down the legs.'

Unfortunately for me, though we passed some villagized sites, none of the peasants' associations we visited were villagized, and I soon realized that my choice was quite limited. However, I stayed with the team, knowing that I was learning much that would be useful, including a rural vocabulary and, more generally, something of conditions in Menz. By the time we returned to Mehal Meda, the regional capital, the rains seemed imminent and it became important to concentrate on the immediate objective of locating the village for study and settling down before the weather inhibited communication and travel.

In Mehal Meda I asked about villagized communities within reach of the town. The first one I visited, Tsehay Sina, had been the location of an American Baptist Mission. They had set up a school, a clinic, a carpet factory and a generator providing electricity to some of the buildings. The Baptists had been forcibly moved out, and their projects abandoned, but the infrastructure remained. Meanwhile a villagized community had been built nearby. The whole sight looked impressive – too impressive to be representative, and its background set it apart from the villagization phenomenon I was hoping to study.

Others were ghost villages of a few huts, people still residing in their old settlements. Two villages were well inhabited, but seemed to me to be too near the town, and I had been taught to be wary of urban bias. As I continued with my selection procedure, I was soon left with two villages, in two different peasants' associations, and determined to choose one of them rather than waste any more time.

Having reached this decision, I begged a lift from a Ministry of Agriculture driver who was depositing some seedlings in the direction of the villages. He dropped me just above Gragn, the nearer of the two peasants' associations, and I walked towards the village. This was on a Saturday, mid-morning, and many people had gone to market. After some enquiries, I was told that the only official around was the women's association's secretary. She often retold the story in the following way.

> Remember? I was called to talk to you and as I approached with fear in my heart, I said to Teshome, 'How am I going to talk to her?' You laughed, and said, 'Do not worry, I speak Amharic.' You asked lots of questions about the peasants' association and those that were here answered as well as they could. I had invited you and everybody came with you to my hut; my mother was in bed with her monthly trouble. Remember, you asked what was hurting her and we said she had a headache!... You showed your letters of permission, and there was even one there with your photograph. I asked you if you would share some *injera* with us and you said yes, and from then on we were sisters.

The sense of goodwill was general that day, so much so that when I explained what I wanted to do, I was greeted all around with enthusiasm. 'Of course it would be all right, if you want to live with us and study our lives.' I then explained that I would be back after visiting the next village, and repeated that my plans were to choose between the two peasants' associations. The people in the hut would have nothing of it. 'Why do you want to walk to that village, it is far, why don't you just choose this one. It is a good place, it is an association that you will like.'

I was disconcerted by these arguments. In my mind, the need to visit another village before deciding had been important. Furthermore, this peasants' association did not have a school, whilst the next one did. I put forward these objections. Again they were not impressed. 'But we have a literacy programme that you could study, and why go to another place when you can come and stay with us?' Against such logic and persuasiveness I was powerless. 'All right then, this will be it.' I had chosen, correction: – the peasants' association had chosen me!

In retrospect I think there are numerous reasons why people wanted me there. Behind their enthusiasm was probably a calculation that some benefits would ensue, for, after all, foreigners are associated with aid of one kind or another; and there was probably also a rivalry with the neighbouring peasants' association. At the same time, they had my interest in mind, they wanted to save me a long walk, and indeed it was an impractical expedition, given that I wanted to return to the town by the evening. For my part, however, what swayed me was that it felt good talking to them, we 'hit it off'. This was visible in terms of the humour and interest on both sides, and was in marked contrast to the village I had visited the previous day in which I had felt distrust and lack of communication, my impressions not diminished by an early encounter with a none too friendly pack of dogs.

That this was to be the place in which I was to conduct my research had been decided without the knowledge of the peasants' association leadership, who now had to be found and convinced. An advance party was sent with the appropriate letters, while I walked back at a more leisurely speed. When I reached the town, after a few false starts I located the chairman and secretary in a drinking house. There followed an extended bowing and introduction session, after which we sat down, to be joined by a growing audience.

I explained that I had been given permission to do research whilst living in a village; that I was interested especially in the position of women, in the current conditions of the population and in the impact of villagization. I then told the story of how I had visited Gragn and that this seemed like a good site for my research. The chairman then took over and said that he had received the advance party with my letters, that all the permissions were in order, that I would be welcome. In turn I expressed happiness at his approval and then moved on to three requests.

The first of these was a hut: could one be built for me? The chairman consulted with the secretary and then, turning to me, asked whether it had to be a new one, built especially for me. No, I answered, any hut in the villagized location would do. In that case, this was not a problem: I would be given a hut on arrival. 'What is your second need?' I answered that my own things would be coming, but it would be useful if I could get a bed from the area, rather than try and bring one from town. More deliberations as the chairman and secretary consulted each other and sipped their drinks.

'Do you need one of these modern ones with springs, as you see in towns, or would a local leather and wood one do?' I gravely answered that I would be more than happy with a local one. The chairman relaxed, 'In that case, one will be ready for you, not to worry. What was your third request?' This, I explained, was somebody, a young girl or an elderly woman, to help fetch water, and help me with other domestic chores. I mentioned this from a totally unfounded fear that employing someone might be unacceptable. No objections to such an arrangement were stated and it was left that I would return the following week. We shook hands and separated; the following morning, I took the bus back to Addis Ababa.

Thanks to the kind help of a couple of friends in Addis Ababa and their Toyota four-wheel drive, I returned as planned with some belongings and more weighty fears and forebodings. The morning was spent in the market buying a few pieces of household equipment. We then drove to the village, the last vehicle to make the journey until after the end of the rains. When we arrived, the chairman turned out to be staying in his old house, some distance from the village. The secretary of the women's association suggested I stay the night in her house, since the chairman would not come until the following day. I accepted the sensible suggestion, my friends made their way back to Addis Ababa, and I prepared myself for a night on the floor. However, Ethiopian hospitality is such that the only bed was vacated for me, while mother and daughter slept on the floor.

The following morning the chairman and his entourage arrived. They proceeded to take me round the village, the chairman asking me which hut I wanted, and pointing out, among others, his own, and that of the secretary's. 'But', I said naïvely, 'I do not understand, don't you live here? I don't want to cause anybody problems!' I felt desperate, ideals of fitting in quietly, of fading into the background, being a fly on the wall, the whole methodology in ruins from the beginning. The chairman scratched his head and answered patiently, 'Do not worry about that, you choose where you want to be.'

While he was talking, I noticed nearby a hut that was locked. Making the calculation that this person perhaps had left the village, and that any disruption caused would thus be minimized, I asked, 'What about that one?' 'So be it', came the answer. Much to my dismay, the owner was found soon after and he unlocked the door. However, he was all smiles and would hear none of my apologies at having chosen his hut. It was only gradually that I came to understand what was going on, that many households had not destroyed their previous huts and still resided at least in part in their old homes, and that in general people were delaying occupation. By occupying a hut I was releasing its owner from an obligation to some kind of presence in the villagized location. I would probably have been greeted with even more enthusiasm had I required ten or twenty huts! As it was I had made one faithful friend.

To complete the story, on the question of having someone to help, the secretary of the women's association had already befriended me. We came to an informal arrangement whereby I would have supper with her and her mother and spend the evenings with them, and that they would also provide me with the water I needed. In exchange, I would buy them things on my trips to Addis Ababa, and give them some money for the market. On the question of the bed, soon after the hut selection, the chairman brought out one of his and donated it to me. Rumour had it that he had since bought himself one with springs, 'the kind you get in town'!

Appendix C :
Summary of Data from Questionnaires

I. The household

Household size and composition (sample 97)

	Total numbers	Range		Mean
		min	max	
Household size	430	1	10	4.4
Adults	226	0	5	2.3
Ad. male	108	0	3	1.1
Ad. female	118	0	3	1.2
Under 18	204	0	7	2.1
>18 Male	116	0	3	1.2
>18 Female	88	0	5	0.9
Under 5	61	0	3	0.6
>5 Male	35	0	2	0.4
>5 Female	26	0	2	0.3

Generations within the household

Generations	1	2	3	Total
Numbers	7	21	69	97
%	7	22	71	100

Adoption
Households included a child of a relative in at least 16 cases (16%), and an adopted child in at least 4 cases (4%).

II. Resources

The first section provides data on the village (both those who have moved and those who have built but not yet moved in), the second is based on the questionnaire administered more widely in Gragn.

Village resources
The sample size was 88. In most cases, household wealth is considered jointly. Where a man or a woman have separate resources from that of the household they are living in, these have been counted as separate households.

	Mean	Range min	Range max
Agricultural land	1.3 hectares	0	4
Fragmentation	4.7 plots	2	7
Grass land	106.0 m^2	1	450
Fragmentation	3.6 plots	1	12
Oxen	1.3	0	4
Cows	0.7	0	2
Steer/heifer	0.8	0	8
Sheep with lambs	13	0	72
Goats with kids	0.5	0	4
Horses	0.05	0	1
Mules	0.1	0	1
Donkeys	0.8	0	2
Chickens	4	0	7

Peasants' association resources

The data from questionnaires administered to the wider Gragn population.

	Sample	Mean	Range min	Range max
Agricultural land	94	1.4 hectares	0.75	3.25
Fragmentation	88	5.6 plots	2	13
Oxen	96	1	0	2
Cows	96	0.5	0	2
Steer/heifer	96	0.7	0	2
Sheep with lambs	96	7.4	0	50
Goat with kids	96	0.8	0	6
Horses	96	0.2	0	1
Mules	96	0.1	0	1
Donkeys	96	1	0	2
Chickens	96	5	0	29
Bees	97		1 household only	
Dogs	97	0.7	0	3
Cats	97	0.3	0	2

Yields from the land in sacks (approximately 1/2 quintal)
Sample 40

Good year	Range 5–30	Mean 20
1988	Range 1–18	Mean 6.38

Yield from the land in months of food
Sample 36

Good year	Range 3–24	Mean 12.47
1988	Range 0–12	Mean 7.35

III. General questions

• *Do you keep some land fallow ?*

Sample 91	76 No	15 Yes
	83.5%	16.5%

• *How much of your land is flat/at a gradient?*

Flat	∑Flat 197	%Flat=75
Sloping	∑Sloping 64	%Sloping=25

Where ∑ is the notation for the sum.
Of a sample of 44, there were 28 people (64%) with at least one plot on sloping land.

• *Have you planted any trees?*

Sample 95	37 No	58 Yes
	37%	63%

For a sample of 65 households, the number of trees they had planted ranged from 0 to 600. The sum was 1261 and the average 19.4.

• *Are these trees located next to your residence ?*

Sample 27	2 No	25 Yes
	7.4%	92.6%

• *Do you regularly grow some vegetables during the rainy season?*

Sample 92	24 No	26 Very little	42 Yes
	26%	28.3%	45.7%

• *Do you accumulate ash?*

	15 No	79 Yes
Sample 94	16%	84 %

• *Have you ever used chemical?* 47 No   47 Yes

Sample 94	50%	50%

• *If you have used chemical fertilizer, when did you start doing so?*

Sample 47   1988/9 = 45   Before 1988 = 2

• *How many of your plots can you see from your homestead?*

Sample 41. The number of plots that could be seen ranged from 0 to 7 out of a range of 3 to 10 plots owned. The ratio of plots visible from the homestead over total number of plots owned gives a figure of 164/232, i.e., 70%.

• *Do you or any member of your household do any weeding on your land?*

Sample 40	38 No	2 Yes

• *Do you or any member of your household spend time guarding the land, protecting it against wild animals, etc ?*

Sample 38	37 No	1 yes

• *Is your household involved in ribbï systems of looking after livestock?*

Sample 94	66 No	70 %
	11 Own livestock looked after	12 %
	17 Look after the livestock of others	18 %

• *Is your household involved in Gwassa Tera, communal herding schemes?*

Sample 85	Only cattle	52	61.2%
	Only sheep	0	0%
	Both cattle and sheep	11	13%
	No	22	25.9%

• *Have you ever been a migrant labourer?*

Sample 48	No	31	64.6%
	Yes	17	35.4%

All those who had been labourers had gone to the Debre Berhan area, to help in harvesting and/or to shear sheep. The duration of their stay was between one and six months. Most went for two months, usually once or twice rather than on a regular basis. None of them had gone since 1986/7, many of them just around the time of the 1985/6 famine.

• *How much tax plus membership fees did your household pay last year?*

Sample 51	24 *birr*	2
	33 *birr*	48
	96 *birr*	1

• *Has your household received aid donations in the past?*

Sample 93	No 24	Yes 69

• *During the years when donations were in dollars, how much did your household receive in one year?*

Sample 67	Range 20-70 *birr*	Mean 43.2 *birr*

• *Do you currently owe money to anybody, if so, by how much are you indebted to them?*

Sample 90	No 66	Yes 24

Of those who are indebted, sample 23
Range 8–100 *birr*   Mean 39.6 *birr*
• *What does your household use as source of fuel?*
Sample 63

Dung	Mainly dung	Wood	Mainly wood	Wood&dung
3	56	1	2	1
4.8%	88.9%	1.6%	3.1%	1.6%

• *Has your household ever bought fuel?*
Sample 63   No   44   69.8%
                         Yes   19   30.2%
The fuel in all these cases was dung rather than wood. The amount spent in one year by those who did buy, sample size 17, ranged from 5 to 40 birr, with a mean of 17.8 birr.
• *Do you have close relatives who have been resettled?*
Sample 92   No 58   Yes 34
                         63%   37%
• *Numbers of close relatives resettled per household*
Sample 34   Range 1–14   Mean 3.1   Total 104
• *Do you have any close relatives who have migrated away from Gragn?*
Sample 50   No 21   Yes 29
                         42%   58%
• *Numbers of close relatives who have migrated away from here*
Sample 29   Range 1-3   Mean 1.6   Total 47
• *Do you have any close relative who has or is undertaking military service?*
Sample 93   No 38   Yes 55
                         40.9%   59.1%
• *Numbers of close relatives who have, or are undertaking military service*
Sample 55   Range 1-6   Mean 1.6   Total 86

IV. Education and literacy

The data in this section is divided into three, for three different sources. The first gives the overall picture based on the answers from the general questionnaires. The second gives data on the nearest school, and the third on the village literacy site.

Overview
Of the total population (370) the number of those who had at some stage attended at least one year of school was 51, or 14% of the sample. A significant proportion, approximately a quarter, had some education many years ago and had become illiterate since then.

The population which had never attended school, and was above five years of age was 319, or 86% of the sample.
    Of those attending school, boys= 36, or 71%
                              girls= 15, or 29%
Of children that are of school age, i.e., 5 to 20, the population was 160.
Of that age group, 81 boys (86%) of the boys were not attending.
Of that age group, 62 girls (94%) of the girls were not attending.
Of the total sample (370) , 13 people have been educated to sixth grade or above (3.5% of the population).
Of the 13, 3 (23%) were girls and 10 (77%) were boys.

Church education
In the sample (370), 19 boys had an Ethiopian Orthodox Church education.

Literacy
Of the sample, which considered only those who had not attended school and were above 4 years of age, 231 had attended at least one round of literacy, and 86 had never attended. This gives a 73% attendance rate.

However, the figures below show the results. The first column, entitled Nothing, gives the number and the percentage of people who cannot write their name. Column I refers to those who can write their name but little else, and column II to those who can also read and write a little. The percentage figures refer to the total population over 4 years old.

	Nothing		I		II	
	No.	%	No.	%	No.	%
Men	84	27	35	11	36	11
Women	101	32	45	14	16	5
Total	185	59	80	25	52	16

Data from the nearest school to Gragn

Grade	Male	Female	Total	Female as %
1	11	6	17	35
2	4	3	7	42
3	20	4	24	17
4	5	4	9	44
5	3	4	7	57
6	12	1	13	8
Total	55	22	77	35

Data from the village literacy site
Adults defined here as those over 20 years old.

Beginners				
Adults	Children	Male	Female	Total
M F T	M F T			
0 34 34	32 33 65	32	67	99
Middle level				
Adults	Children	Male	Female	Total
M F T	M F T			
24 0 24	0 0 0	24	0	24
Advanced level				
Adults	Children	Male	Female	Total
M F T	M F T			
6 12 18	0 1 1	6	13	19
Grand total				
Adults	Children	Male	Female	Total
M F T	M F T			
30 46 76	32 34 66	62	80	142

Bibliography

Note: *All Ethiopian names are entered, as is traditional practice, in alphabetical order of the author's first name followed by the father's name.*

Abebe Zegeye & S. Isheno (eds). 1989. *Forced Labour and Migration: Patterns of Movement within Africa*, London: Hans Zell

Abercrombie, Nicholas, Stephen Hill & Bryan Turner. 1980. *The Dominant Ideology Thesis*, London: Allen & Unwin

Abrahams, Ray. 1987. 'Sungusungu: village vigilante groups in Tanzania', *African Affairs*, Vol. 86, No. 343

Afework Abraham. 1989. 'Excerpts from the Draft National Population Policy for Ethiopia', paper prepared for the Conference on Population Issues in Ethiopia's National Development, 20–22 July, 1989, Population and Development Planning Unit, Office of the National Committee for Central Planning, Addis Ababa

Afshar, Haleh. (ed.). 1987. *Women, State and Ideology: Studies from Africa and Asia*, London: Macmillan

Agar, Michael. 1980. *The Professional Stranger: An Informal Introduction to Ethnography*, New York: Academic Press

Agarwal, Bina. 1986. 'Women, poverty and agricultural growth in India', *Journal of Peasant Studies*, Vol. 13, No. 4

Alemayehu Lirenso. 1985. 'Rural Service Cooperatives in Ethiopia: tasks and performances', *Northeast African Studies*, Vol. 7, No. 2

Alpern-Engel, Barbara. 1987. 'Women in Russia and the Soviet Union', *Signs*, Vol. 12, No. 4

Alula Abate, Moira Hart, Ian Watt & Justin Maeda. 1988. 'Quick assessment: cash-for-food program UNICEF/RRC emergency intervention', Unpublished report, Addis Ababa

Amadiume, Ifi. 1987. *Male Daughters, Female Husbands*, London: Zed Books

Amin, Samir. 1974. 'Accumulation and development: A theoretical model', *Review of African Political Economy*, No. 1

Amin, Samir. 1976. *Unequal Development*, Hassocks: Harvester

Amsden, Alice (ed.). 1980. *The Economics of Women and Work*, Harmondsworth: Penguin

Anderson, Dennis. 1986. 'Declining tree stocks in African countries', *World Development*, Vol. 14, No. 7

Anderson, Perry. 1974. *Lineages of the Absolutist State*, London: New Left Books.

Angola, Organization of Angolan Women. 1984. *Angolan Women: Building The Future*, London: Zed Books

Ardener, Shirley. 1964. 'The comparative study of rotating credit associations', *Journal of the Royal Anthropological Institute*, Vol. 94

Ardener, Shirley 1973. 'Sexual insult and female militancy', *Man*, Vol. 8

Ardener, Shirley (ed.). 1975. *Perceiving Women*, London: Dent

Ardener, Shirley. (ed.). 1978. *Defining Females*, London: Croom Helm

Arnesson, Gunne. 1986. *Documentation of the role of women in integrated rural development in Arsi, Ethiopia*, Working Paper 40, International Rural Development Centre, Swedish University of Agricultural Sciences

Arnfred, Signe. 1988. 'Women in Mozambique: Gender struggle and politics', *Review of African Political Economy*, No. 41

Assefa Mehretu. 1987. 'Regions under stress: catastrophic collapse of the subsistence base in Ethiopia's geographic margins', *Northeast African Studies*, Vol. 9, No. 2

Aster Akalu. 1982. *The Process of Land Nationalization in Ethiopia: Land Nationalization and the Peasants*, Lund: Bloms Boktrycheri

Atkinson, A. 1983. *The Economics of Inequality*, Oxford: Clarendon

Axinn, George & Nancy. 1969. 'An African village in transition: research into behaviour patterns', *Journal of Modern African Studies*, Vol. 7, No. 3

Azarya, Victor. 1988. 'Reordering State-society relations: incorporation and disengagement', in D. Rothchild & N. Chazan (eds), *The Precarious Balance: The State and Society in Africa*

Bailey, Glen. 1980. *An analysis of the Ethiopian Revolution*, Papers in International Studies, African Series No. 40, Centre for International Studies, Ohio University

Bain, J. 1976. 'Less Than Second-Class: Women in Rural Settlement Schemes in Tanzania', in N. Hafkin & E. Bay, *Women in Africa* (eds), Stanford: Stanford University Press

Baker, Jonathan. 1986. *The Rural-Urban Dichotomy in the Developing World: A Case Study from Northern Ethiopia*, London: Norwegian University Press

Baran, Paul. 1978. *The Political Economy of Growth*, Harmondsworth: Penguin

Bardhan, Pranab. 1974. 'On life and death questions', *Economic and Political Weekly*, Vol. 9, No. 32, 33 & 34

Barnes, J. A. 1967. 'The frequency of divorce', in A. Epstein (ed.), *The Craft of Social Anthropology*

Barnes, J. A. 1977. *The Ethics of Inquiry in Social Science*, Delhi: Oxford University Press

Basset, René (ed.). 1897. *Histoire de la conquête de l'Abyssinie (XVI Siècle)* Paris: Leroux

Baster, Nancy (ed.). 1972. *Measuring Development: The Role and Adequacy of Development Indicators*, London: Cass

Bauer, Dan. 1973. 'Land, leadership and legitimacy among the Inderta Tigray of Ethiopia', Ph.D. thesis in Anthropology, University of Rochester

Bauer, Dan. 1977. *Household and society in Ethiopia: an economic and social analysis of Tigray social principles and household organisation*, Occasional Papers Series, Committee on Ethiopian Studies, African Studies Centre Monograph 6, East Lansing: Michigan State University

Baumann, Hermann. 1928. 'The division of work according to sex in African hoe culture', *Africa*, Vol. 1, No. 3

Beauchamp, Tom, Ruth Faden, Jay Wallace, Jr. & Leroy Walters (eds). 1982. *Ethical Issues in Social Science Research*, Baltimore: Johns Hopkins University

Beauvoir, Simone de. (1949) 1972. *The Second Sex*, London: Cape

Becker, Howard. 1970. *Sociological Work: Method and Substance*, Chicago: Alire

Beckstrom, John. 1969. 'Divorce in urban Ethiopia, ten years after the civil code', *Journal of Ethiopian Law*, Vol. 6, No. 2

Beechey, Veronica. 1979. 'On patriarchy', *Feminist Review*, No. 3

Belov, Gennady. 1986. *What is the State?*, Moscow: Progress

Beneria, Lourdes. 1981. 'Conceptualizing the labour force: the underestimation of women's economic activities', in N. Nelson (ed.), *African Women in the Development Process*

Beneria, Lourdes & Gita Sen. 1981. 'Accumulation, reproduction, and women's role in economic development: Boserup revisited', *Signs*, Vol. 7, No. 2

Bengelsdorf, Carollee & Alice Hageman. 1979. 'Emerging from underdevelopment: women and work in Cuba', in Z. Eisenstein (ed.), *Capitalist Patriarchy and the Case for Socialist Feminism*

Bengelsdorf, Carollee. 1985. 'On the problem of studying women in Cuba', *Race and Class*, Vol. 28, No. 2

Bennholt-Thomsen, Veronika. 1981. 'Subsistence production and extended reproduction', in K. Young *et al.* (ed.), *Of Marriage and the Market*

Berihun Teferra. 1988. 'An economic study of the Villagization Programme in Ethiopia: the case of a village in Selale *awraja* of Shewa Region', in partial completion for a B.A. in Economics, Addis Ababa University

Bernstein, Henry. 1977. 'Notes on Capital and peasantry' *Review of African Political Economy*, Vol. 10

Bernstein, Richard. 1976. *The Restructuring of Social and Political Theory*, Oxford: Blackwell

Blackwood, Evelyn. 1984. 'Sexuality and gender in certain native American tribes: The case of cross-gender females', *Signs*, Vol. 10, No. 1

Boddy, Janice. 1989. *Wombs and Alien Spirits*, Madison: University of Wisconsin

Boserup, Ester. 1970. *Woman's Role in Economic Development*, London: Allen & Unwin

Bossen, Laurel. 1988. 'Towards a Theory of Marriage: the economic anthropology of marriage transactions', *Ethnography*, Vol. 27, No. 2

Bowen Smith, Elenore. 1954. *Return to Laughter*, London: Gollancz

Bowles, Gloria & Renate Duelli Klein (eds). 1983. *Theories of Women's Studies*, London: Routledge & Kegan Paul

Bradby, Barbara. 1977. 'Research Note: the non-valorisation of women's labour', *Critique of Anthropology*, Vol. 3, No. 9/10

Brenner, Johanna & Maria Ramas. 1984. 'Rethinking women's oppression', *New Left Review*, No. 144

Brett, April. 1987. 'Changing the approach? The Wello water experience', GADU, *Oxfam's Gender and Development Unit*

Brøgger, Jan. 1975. 'Spirit possession and the management of aggression among the Sidamo', *Ethnos*, Vol. 40, No. 1-4, 1975

Brown, Judith. 1970. 'A note on the division of labor by sex', *American Anthropologist*, Vol. 72

Brown, Susan. 1975. 'Love unites them and hunger separates them: poor women in the Dominican Republic', in R. Reiter (ed.), *Toward an Anthropology of Women*

Bubner, Rüdiger. 1982. 'Habermas's concept of critical theory'. in J. Thompson & D. Held (eds), *Habermas: Critical Debates*

Buckley, Mary. 1981. 'Women in the Soviet Union', *Feminist Review*, Vol. 8

Burgess, Robert. 1984. *In the Field: An Introduction to Field Research*, London: Allen & Unwin

Bystydzienski, Jill. 1989. 'Women and Socialism: a comparative study of women in Poland and the USSR', *Signs*, Vol. 14, No. 3

Cantarero, Rodrigo & Forrest Colburn. 1986. 'The structural basis of rural employment in post-revolutionary Nicaragua', *Journal of Developing Areas*, Vol. 21

Cassiers, Anne. 1974. 'Eléments pour une étude sur le rôle de la femme dans la société Éthiopienne', unpublished report, Addis Ababa

Cassiers, Anne. 1988. 'Mercha: an Ethiopian woman speaks of her life', in P. Romero, *Life Histories of African Women*, London: Ashfield

Cesara, Manda. 1982. *Reflections of a Woman Anthropologist: No Hiding Place*, London: Academic Press

Chambers, Robert, Richard Longhurst & Arnold Paley (eds). 1981. *Seasonal Dimensions to Rural Poverty*, London: Pinter

Chazan, Naomi. 1988. 'Patterns of state-society incorporation and disengagement in Africa' and 'State and society in Africa: images and challenges', in D. Rothchild and N. Chazan (eds), *The Precarious Balance: The State and Society in Africa*

Cicourel, Aaron. 1964. *Method and Measurement in Sociology*, New York: Free Press of Glencoe

Clammer, John (ed.). 1978. *The New Economic Anthropology*, Basingstoke: Macmillan

Clammer, John (ed.). 1987. *Beyond the New Economic Anthropology*, Basingstoke: Macmillan

Clapham, Christopher. 1987. 'Revolutionary Socialist development in Ethiopia, *African Affairs*, Vol.86, No.343

Clapham, Christopher. 1988. *Transformation and Continuity in Revolutionary Ethiopia*, Cambridge: Cambridge University

Clark, Ronald. 1979. 'Terminal project report of adviser in Land Reform settlement and administration', Rome: Food and Agriculture Organisation

Cliffe, Lionel, *et al*. 1975. *Rural Cooperation in Tanzania*, Dar es Salaam: Tanzania Publishing House

Cliffe, Lionel & R. Moorsom. 1979. 'Rural class formation and ecological collapse in Botswana', *Review of African Political Economy*, No. 15/16

Cohen, Anthony. 1985. *The Symbolic Construction of Community*, Chichester: Horwood

Cohen, John. 1974. 'Ethiopia: a survey on the existence of a feudal peasantry', *Journal of Modern African Studies*, Vol. 12, No. 4

Cohen, John. 1981. 'Foreign involvement in the formulation of Ethiopia's land tenure Policies, Part I & Part II', *Northeast African Studies*, Vol. 7, No. 2 & 3

Cohen, John. 1984. *Agrarian reform in Ethiopia: the situation on the eve of the Revolution's tenth anniversary*, Development Discussion Paper No. 164, Institute of International Development, Cambridge: Harvard University

Cohen, John & Ingvar Jonsson. 1987. 'The size of Peasant Association holdings and Government policies: questions raised by recent research in Arsi region, Ethiopia', *Northeast African Studies*, Vol. 9, No. 1

Cohen, John & Nihls-Ivar Isaksson. 1987. *Villagization in the Arsi region of Ethiopia*, Uppsala: Report prepared by SIDA Consultants to the Ethio-Swedish Mission on Villagization in Arsi

Cohen, John & Nihls-Ivar Isaksson. 1988. 'Food production strategy debates in Revolutionary Ethiopia', *World Development*, Vol. 16, No. 3

Constable, M. & Derik Belshaw. 1985. Unpublished Report 'A summary of major findings and recommendations from the Ethiopian Highlands Reclamation Study 1983/85'

Cook, Rebecca & Deborah Maine. 1987. 'Spousal veto over family planning services', *American Journal of Public Health*, Vol. 77, No. 3

Copans, Jean and D. Seddon. 1978. 'Marxism and anthropology: a preliminary survey', in D. Seddon (ed.), *Relations of Production: Marxist Approaches to Economic Anthropology*

Coquery-Vidrovitch, Catherine. 1975. 'An African Mode of Production', *Critique of Anthropology*, Vol. 1, Nos. 4 & 5

Coulson, Andrew. 1977. 'Agricultural policies in mainland Tanzania', *Review of African Political Economy*, No. 10

Coulson, Andrew. (ed.). 1979. *African Socialism in Practice: The Tanzanian Experience*, Nottingham: Spokesman

Coulson, Andrew. 1982. *Tanzania: A Political Economy*, Oxford: Clarendon

Crane, Julia & Michael Angrosino. *Field Projects in Anthropology: A Student Handbook*, Morristown: General Learning

Croll, Elizabeth. 1981. (a) *The Politics of Marriage in Contemporary China*, Cambridge: Cambridge University

Croll, Elizabeth. 1981. (b) 'Women in rural production and reproduction in the Soviet Union, China, Cuba and Tanzania', *Signs*, Vol. 7, No. 2

Croll, Elizabeth. 1983. *Chinese Women Since Mao*, London: Zed Books

Croll, Elizabeth. 1984. 'Research methodology appropriate to rapid appraisal: a Chinese experience', *Institute of Development Studies Bulletin*, Vol. 15, No. 1, Sussex University

Croll, Elizabeth. 1985. *Women and Rural Development in China*, Geneva: International Labour Organisation, Women, Work and Development No. 11

Crummey, Donald. 1981. 'State and society: 19th-Century Ethiopia', in D. Crummey & C. Stewart (eds), *Modes of Production in Africa: The Precolonial Era*, London: Sage

Daniel Gamachu. 1988. 'Environment and development', in Angela Penrose (ed.) *Beyond the Famine*

Daniel Teferra. 1987. 'Subsistence production behaviour and famine in Ethiopia', *Northeast African Studies*, Vol. 9, No. 2

Davin, Delia. 1987. 'Gender and population in the People's Republic of China', in H. Afshar (ed.), *Women, State and Ideology*

Dawit Bekele. 1982. 'Peasant Associations and Agrarian Reform in Ethiopia', *Institute of Development Studies Bulletin*, Vol. 13, No. 4, Sussex University

Deere, Carmen. 1976. 'Rural women's subsistence production in the Capitalist periphery', *Review of Radical Political Economy*, Vol. 8, No. 1

Dejene Aredo. 1990. 'How holy are holidays in rural Ethiopia? An enquiry into the extent to which Saints' Days are observed among followers of the Orthodox Christian fChurch', in R. Pankhurst, Ahmed Zekaria & Taddese Beyene (eds), *Proceedings of the First National Conference of Ethiopian Studies*

Denzin, Norman. 1978. *The Research Act: A Theoretical Introduction to Sociological Methods*, New York: McGraw-Hill

Dessalegn Rahmato. 1984. *Agrarian Reform in Ethiopia*, Uppsala: Scandinavian Institute of African Studies

Dessalegn Rahmato. 1988 (a). 'Peasant survival strategies', in Angela Penrose (ed.), *Beyond the Famine*

Dessalegn Rahmato. 1988 (b). 'Some notes on settlement and resettlement in Mettekel awraja (Gojjam province)', in *Proceedings of the Ninth International Congress of Ethiopian Studies, Moscow, 26–29 August, 1986*, Moscow: Nauka

Dessalegn Rahmato. 1991. 'Rural women in Ethiopia: problems and prospects', in Tsehai Berhane-Selassie (ed.), *Gender Issues in Ethiopia*

de Vries, James & Louise Fortmann. 1979. 'Large-scale villagization: operation Sogeza in Iringa region', in A. Coulson (ed.), *African Socialism in Practice*

Diamond, Norma. 1975. 'Collectivization, kinship, and the status of women in rural China' in R. Reiter (ed.), *Toward an Anthropology of Women*

Donham, Donald. 1981. 'Beyond the domestic mode of production', *Man*, Vol. 16

Donham, Donald. 1985. *Work, Power and History in Maale, Ethiopia*, Ann Arbor: UMI Research

Donham, Donald & Wendy James (eds). 1986. *The Southern Marches of Imperial Ethiopia: Essays in History and Social Anthropology*, Cambridge: Cambridge University

Dore, Ronald. 1971. 'Modern cooperatives in traditional communities', in P. Worsley (ed.), *Two Blades of Grass*

Douglas, Mary. 1966. *Purity and Danger: an Analysis of Concepts of Pollution and Taboo*, London: Routledge & Kegan Paul.

Draper, Patricia. 1975. '!Kung women: contrasts in sexual egalitarianism in foraging and sedentary contexts', in R. Reiter (ed.), *Towards an Anthropology of Women*

Duncan, Margaret. 1982. 'A Prospective Clinico-Pathological Study of Pregnancy and Leprosy in Ethiopia', M.D. Dissertation, Edinburgh University

Dunning, Harrison. 1970. 'Land Reform in Ethiopia: a case-study in non-development', *UCLA Law Review*, Vol. 18, No. 2

du Toit, Brian. 1988. 'Menstruation: attitudes and experiences of Indian South Africans', *Ethnology*, Vol. 27, No. 3

Edholm, F., Olivia Harris & Kate Young. 1977. 'Conceptualising women', *Critique of Anthropology*, Vol. 3, No. 9/10

Eichenbaum, Luise, & Susie Orbach. 1982. *Outside In-side Out: Women's Psychology: a Feminist Psychoanalytic Approach*, Harmondsworth: Penguin

Eichler, Margrit. 1980. *The Double Standard: a Feminist Critique of Feminist Social Science*, London: Croom Helm

Eisenstein, Zillah (ed.). 1979. *Capitalist Patriarchy and the Case for Socialist Feminism*, New York: Monthly Review

Engels, Friederich. (1884). 1972. *The Origin of the Family, Private Property, and the State.* New York: Pathfinder

Epstein, A. (ed.). 1967. *The Craft of Social Anthropology*, London: Tavistock

Epstein, T. 1967. 'The data of economics in anthropological analysis', in A. Epstein (ed.), *The Craft of Social Anthropology*

Eshetu Chole. 1988. 'The Ethiopian economy', in Angela Penrose (ed.), *Beyond the Famine*

Ethiopia, Constitution Drafting Commission. 1986. *The Draft Constitution of the PDRE*, June 1986, Addis Ababa

Ethiopia, Ethiopian Mapping Authority. 1988. *National Atlas of Ethiopia*, Addis Ababa

Ethiopia, Ministry of Agriculture and Settlement. 1978. 'Agrarian reform and rural development in Ethiopia', Addis Ababa

Ethiopia, Ministry of Agriculture/UNICEF. 1988. 'Baseline survey - Yifat -Timuga, in calf heifer project, Yedi - Angawa, sheep breeding project', November 1988

Ethiopia, National Villagization Coordinating Committee. May 1987. *Mender*, Addis Ababa

Ethiopia, National Villagization Coordinating Committee. *Myazia ' 79. Mender* Vol. 2, Amharic Edition, Addis Ababa

Ethiopia, National Villagization Coordinating Committee. *Hedar '81. Mender* Vol. 2, Amharic Edition, Addis Ababa

Ethiopia, Negarit Gazeta (Official Gazette). 1975. Proclamation 31/1975. 'Proclamation to provide for the public ownership of rural lands' and Proclamation 71/1975. 'Peasant associations organization and consolidation proclamation'

Ethiopia, Office of the National Committee for Central Planning. 1987. 'Agricultural pricing and marketing policy of Ethiopia: a synopsis', Pricing Policy Study Committee, Addis Ababa

Ethiopia, Office of the Population and Housing Census Commission, *1984 Population and Housing Census of Ethiopia, Analytical Report at National Level*, 1991

Ethiopia, Revolutionary Ethiopia Women's Association. 1982. *Women in Ethiopia*, Addis Ababa

Ethiopia, Revolutionary Ethiopia Women's Association. 1984 (a). *Ethiopia: Women in Revolution*, Addis Ababa

Ethiopia, Revolutionary Ethiopia Women's Association. 1984 (b). *Review and Appraisal of the Status of Women in Revolutionary Ethiopia, 1975-1984*, Addis Ababa

Ethiopia, Revolutionary Ethiopia Women's Association. 1987. *The Women of Ethiopia*, Addis Ababa

European Economic Commission. 1987. 'Ethiopia: Volume I. North Shewa rural reclamation and development project appraisal report', Addis Ababa

Evans, Peter, Dietrich Rueschemeyer & Theda Skocpol (eds). 1985. *Bringing the State Back In*, Cambridge: Cambridge University

Faithorn, Elizabeth. 1975. 'The concept of pollution among the Kafe of the Papua New Guinea highlands', in R. Reiter (ed.), *Toward an Anthropology of Women*

Fassil Gebre Kiros. 1976. 'An estimate of the proportion of the potential work-year allocated to socio-cultural observations in rural Ethiopia', *Ethiopian Journal of Development Research*, Vol. 2

Fassil Gebre Kiros. 1980. 'Agricultural land fragmentation: a problem of land distribution observed in some Ethiopian peasant associations', *Ethiopian Journal of Development Research*, Vol. 4

Fay, Brian. 1975. *Social Theory and Political Practice*, London: Allen & Unwin

Fellows, Ruth. 1987. 'Background information on the status of women in Ethiopia', unpublished report prepared for the Canadian International Development Agency, Addis Ababa

Fetenu Bekele. 1990. 'Women, employment, credit and appropriate technology: an overview', draft paper, Addis Ababa

Forrest, J. 1982. 'Defining African peasants', *Peasant Studies*, Vol. 9, No. 4

Foster-Carter, Aidan. 1985. *The Sociology of Development*, Ormskirk: Causeway

Foster-Carter, Aidan.1987. 'Knowing what they mean: or, why is there no phenomenology in the sociology of development?', in J. Clammer (ed.), *Beyond the New Economic Anthropology*

Gamst, Frederick. 1986. 'Feudalism in Abyssinia? Further commentary on the on-going controversy', in *Proceedings of the Ninth International Conference of Ethiopian Studies, Moscow, 26–29 August 1986*, Moscow: Nauka

Gavrilov, N., *et al. (eds)*. 1986. *Ten Years of the Ethiopian Revolution*, Moscow: Progress

Gedamu Abraha. 1967. 'Wax and Gold', *Ethiopia Observer*, Vol. 11, No. 3

Geertz, Clifford. 1962. 'The rotating credit association: a 'middle rung' development', *Economic Development and Cultural Change*, Vol. 10, No. 3

Giddens, Anthony. 1976. *New Rules of Sociological Methods: A Positive Critique of Interpretative Sociologies*, London: Hutchinson

Gilkes, Patrick. 1975. *The Dying Lion: Feudalism and Modernization in Ethiopia*, London: Friedman

Gilkes, Patrick. 1988. 'Ethiopia: recent history', in *Africa South of the Sahara i*, London: Europa

Godelier, Maurice. 1978. 'Objects of economic anthropology', in D. Seddon (ed.), *Relations of Production: Marxist Approaches to Economic Anthropology*

Golde, Peggy (ed.). 1970. *Women in the Field: Anthropological Experiences*, Chicago: Aldine Publishing

Gomm, Roger. 1975. 'Bargaining from weakness: spirit possession on the South Kenya Coast', *Man*, Vol. 10, No. 4

Goody, Jack. 1976. *Production and Reproduction: A Comparative Study of the Domestic Domain*, Cambridge: Cambridge University

Griffin, Keith & Roger Hay. 1985. 'Problems of agricultural development in Socialist Ethiopia: an overview', *Journal of Peasant Studies*, Vol. 13, No. 1

Guyer, Jane. 1980 (a). 'Female farming and the evolution of food production patterns amongst the Beti of South-Central Cameroon', *Africa*. Vol.50, No.4

Guyer, Jane. 1980 (b). 'Food, cocoa, and the division of labour by sex in two West African societies', *Comparative Studies in Society and History*, Vol. 22, No. 3

Guyer, Jane. 1984. 'Naturalism in models of African production', *Man*, Vol. 19, No. 3

Hafkin, Nancy. & Edna Bay (eds). 1976. *Women in Africa: Studies in Social and Economic Change*, Stanford: Stanford University

Haggis, Jane, *et al.* . 1986. 'By the teeth: A critical examination of James Scott's *The Moral Economy of the Peasant*', *World Development*, Vol. 14, No. 7

Halliday, Fred & Maxine Molyneux. 1981. *The Ethiopian Revolution*, London: Verso

Hamer, John. & Irene Hamer. 1966. 'Spirit possession and its socio-psychological implications among the Sidamo of Southwest Ethiopia', *Ethnology*, Vol. 5, No. 4

Hanna Kebede. 1978. 'Improving village water supplies in Ethiopia: a case study of socioeconomic implications', United Nations, Economic Commission for Africa, (ECA/5DD/ATRCW/VTW ATER/78)

Harbeson, John. 1988. *The Ethiopian Transformation: The Quest for the Post-Imperial State*, Boulder: Westview

Harding, Susan. 1975. 'Women and words in a Spanish village', in R. Reiter (ed.), *Toward an Anthropology of Women*

Harris, William. 1844. *The Highlands of Aethiopia*, London: Longman, Brown, Green, and Longmans

Harris, Olivia. 1978. 'Complementarity and conflict: an Andean view of women and men', in J. La Fontaine (ed.), *Sex and Age as Principles of Social Differentiation*

Harriss, Olivia. 1984. 'Households as natural units', K. Young *et al.* (eds), *Of Marriage and the Market*

Hartmann, Heidi. 1979. 'The unhappy marriage of Marxism and feminism: towards a more progressive union', *Capital and Class*, Vol. 8

Hartsock, Nancy. 1979. 'Feminist theory and the development of revolutionary strategy', in Z. Eisenstein (ed.), *Capitalist Patriarchy and the Case for Socialist Feminism*

Hay, Margaret & Sharon Stichter (eds). 1984. *African Women South of the Sahara*, London: Longman

Hedlund, Hans (ed.). 1988. *Cooperatives Revisited*, Uppsala: Scandinavian Institute of African Studies

Held, David *et al.* . 1985. *States and Societies*, Oxford: Blackwell

Henley, Nancy. 1985. 'Psychology and gender', *Signs*, Vol. 11, No. 1

Henn, Jeanne. 1983. 'Feeding the cities and feeding the peasants: what role for Africa's women farmers?', *World Development*, Vol. 11, No. 12

Henn, Jeanne. 1984. 'Women in the rural economy: past, present and future' in J. Henn & S. Stichter (eds), *African Women South of the Sahara*, London: Longman

Hill, Frances. 1979. 'Village Socialism: Dodoma 1969-71' in A. Coulson (ed.), *African Socialism in Practice*

Hill, Polly. 1963. *Migrant Cocoa Farmers of Southern Ghana*, London: Cambridge University

Hirschon, Renée (ed.). 1984. 'Property, Power and Gender Relations', in R. Hirschon (ed.), *Women and Property - Women as Property*, London: Croom Helm

Hirut Terefe, & Lakew Woldetekle. 1986. 'Study of the situation of women in Ethiopia', Research Project No. 23, Institute of Development Research, Addis Ababa

Hoben, Alan. 1973. *Land Tenure among the Amhara of Ethiopia*, Chicago: University of Chicago

Holmberg, David. 1983. 'Shamanic soundings: femaleness in the Tamang ritual structure', *Signs*, Vol. 9, No. 1

Homberg, John. 1977. 'Grain marketing and Land Reform in Ethiopia', Research Report No. 41, Scandinavian Institute of African Studies, Uppsala

Huffnagel, H. 1961. *Agriculture in Ethiopia*: Rome: United Nations Food and Agriculture Organisation

Huntingford, G. 1989. *The Historical Geography of Ethiopia*, Oxford: Oxford University Press

Hyden, Goran. 1980. *Beyond Ujamaa in Tanzania: Underdevelopment and an Uncaptured Peasantry*, London: Heinemann.

Hyden, Goran. 1983. *No Short Cuts to Progress: African Development Management in Practice*, London: Heinemann

Inter-African Committee on Traditional Practices Affecting the Health of Women and Children. 1988. *Report on the Regional Seminar on Traditional Practices Affecting the Health of Women and Children in Africa, 9–10 April 1987, Addis Ababa*, Uppsala: Amqvist & Tryckeri

International Bank for Reconstruction and Development/World Bank. 1988. *World Development Report*

Irvine, John *et al.* (eds). 1979. *Demystifying Social Statistics*, London: Pluto Press

Jacobs, Susie & Tracy Howard. 1987. 'Women in Zimbabwe: State policy and State action', in H. Afshar (ed.), *Women, State and Ideology*

Jeffery, Patricia, Roger Jeffery & Andrew Lyon. 1987. 'Contaminating states: midwifery, childbearing, and the State', in H. Afshar (ed.), *Women, State and Ideology*

Jeffery, Patricia, Roger Jeffery & Andrew Lyon. 1989. 'Taking dung-work seriously: women's work in rural development in Northern India', *Economic and Political Weekly*, Vol. 24, No. 17

Jeffery, Patricia, Roger Jeffery and Andrew Lyon. 1990. *Labour Pains and Labour Power*, London: Zed Books

Johnston, Charles. (1844). 1972. *Travels in Southern Abyssinia*, Westmead: Gregg International

Juncar, Barbara. 1978. *Women under Communism*, Baltimore: Johns Hopkins University

Kahn, Robert & Charles Cannell. 1983. *The Dynamics of Interviewing: Theory, Techniques, and Cases*, Malabar: Krieger

Kasfir, Nelson. 1986. 'Are African peasants self-sufficient?', *Development and Change*, Vol. 17, No. 2

Kay, Diana. 1982. 'Public and private experiences: Chilean men and women from Popular

Unity to exile', Ph.D. thesis, Edinburgh University

Knutsson, Karl. 1975. 'Possession and extra-institutional behaviour - an essay in anthropological micro-analysis', *Ethnos*, Vol. 40, Nos 1-4.

Kruse, Stein-Erik. 1987. 'Ethiopia: a strategy for assistance to women in development', a report for the World Bank, Addis Ababa

Kuhn, Annette & Ann-Marie Wolpe (eds). 1978. *Feminism and Materialism: Women and Modes of Production*, London: Routledge and Kegan Paul

La Fontaine, Jean (ed.). 1978. *Sex and Age as Principles of Social Differentiation*, London: Academic

Lal, Deepak. 1985. 'Nationalism, Socialism and planning: influential ideas in the South', *World Development*, Vol. 13, No. 6

Lamphere, Louise. 1974. 'Strategies, cooperation, and conflict among women in domestic groups', in M. Rosaldo & L. Lamphere, (eds.), *Woman, Culture, and Society*

Lane, Julia & Michael Angnosino. 1974. *Field Projects in Anthropology*

Last, Geoffrey. 1988. 'Ethiopia: physical and social geography', in *Africa South of the Sahara*, London: Europa

Last, Jill. 1981. *Ethiopians and the Houses they Live In*, Addis Ababa: Artistic

Leis, Nancy. 1974. 'Women in groups: Ijaw women's associations', in M. Rosaldo & L. Lamphere (eds), *Woman, Culture, and Society*

Leon, Magdalena. 1984. 'Measuring women's work: methodological and conceptual issues in Latin America', *Institute of Development Studies Bulletin*, Vol. 15, No. 1, Sussex University

Lefort, René. 1983. *Ethiopia: An Heretical Revolution*, London: Zed Books

Levine, Donald. 1963. 'On the history and culture of Manz', paper presented to the Second International Conference of Ethiopian Studies, Manchester University, July 1963; *Journal of Semitic Studies*, Vol. 9, No. 1, 1964

Levine, Donald. 1965. *Wax and Gold: Tradition and Innovation in Ethiopian Culture*, Chicago: University of Chicago

Levine, Donald. 1974. *Greater Ethiopia: The Evolution of a Multiethnic Society*, Chicago: University of Chicago

Lévi-Strauss, Claude. (1955). 1978. *Tristes Tropiques*, Harmondsworth: Penguin

Lewis, Herbert. 1974. 'Neighbours, friends and kinsmen: principles of social organization among the Cushitic-speaking people of Ethiopia', *Ethnology*, Vol. 13, No. 2

Lewis, Ioan. 1971. *Ecstatic Religion*, Harmondsworth: Penguin

Lewis, Ioan. 1986. *Religion in Context: Cults and Charisma*, Cambridge: Cambridge University

Lipton, Michael. 1968. 'The theory of the optimizing peasant', *Journal of Development Studies*, Vol. 4

Lukes, Steven. 1974. *Power: A Radical View*, London: Macmillan

Lundstrom, Karl. 1976. 'Northeastern Ethiopia: society in famine', Research Report No. 34, Scandinavian Institute of African Studies, Uppsala

McCann, James. 1984. *Household Economy, Demography, and the 'Push' Factor in Northern Ethiopian History 1916-1935*, African Studies Centre, Working Papers No. 97, Boston: Boston University

McCann, James. 1988a. 'History, drought and reproduction: dynamics of society and ecology in Northeast Ethiopia', in Douglas Johnson & David Anderson (eds), *The Ecology of Survival*, Boulder: Westview

McCann, James. 1988b. 'Towards a history of modern highland agriculture in Ethiopia: the sources' in *Proceedings of the Ninth International Conference on Ethiopian Studies, Moscow, 26–29 August 1986*, Moscow: Nauka

MacCormack, Carol. 1976. 'The compound head: structure and strategies', *Africana Research Bulletin*, Vol. 6, No. 4

MacCormack, Carol. 1977. 'Biological events and cultural control', *Signs*, Vol. 3, No. 1

MacCormack, Carol & Marilyn Strathern. (eds). 1980. *Nature, Culture and Gender*, Cambridge: Cambridge University Press

McDonough, Roisin & Rachel Harrison. 1978. 'Patriarchy and Relations of Production', in A. Kuhn & A. Wolpe (eds.), *Feminism and Materialism: Women and Modes of Production*

MacKintosh, Maureen. 1986. 'Economic policy context and adjustment options in Mozambique', *Development and Change*, Vol. 17

Malik, S. & R. Hauspie, 1986. 'Age and menarche among high-altitude Boar of Ladakh, India', *Human Biology*, Vol. 58

Maloney, Clarence. 1976. 'Don't say 'Pretty Baby' lest you zap it with your eye - the evil eye in South Asia', in C. Maloney (ed.), 1976. *The Evil Eye*

Maloney, Clarence (ed.). 1976. *The Evil Eye*, New York: Columbia University

March, Kathryn & Taqqu, Rachelle. 1986. *Women's Informal Associations in Developing Countries: Catalysts for Change?*, Boulder: Westview

Markakis, John. 1974. *Ethiopia: Anatomy of a Traditional Polity*, Oxford: Clarendon

May, Jacques & Donna McLellan. 1970. *The Ecology of Malnutrition in Eastern Africa and Four Countries of Western Africa*, Studies in Medical Geography, Vol. 9, New York: Hafner

Mbilinyi, Marjorie. 1979. 'Contradictions in Tanzanian education reform', in A. Coulson (ed.), *African Socialism in Practice*

Mead, Margaret. (1943). 1981. *Coming of Age in Samoa: A Study of Adolescence and Sex in Primitive Societies*, Harmondsworth: Penguin

Mead, Margaret. (1949). 1962. *Male and Female: A Study of the Sexes in a Changing World*, Harmondsworth: Penguin

Meillassoux, Claude. 1972. 'From production to reproduction' *Economy and Society*, Vol. 1

Meillassoux, Claude. 1981. *Maidens, Meal and Money*, Cambridge: Cambridge University

Mengistu Lemma. 1964. 'Snatch and Run or Marriage by Abduction', *Ethiopia Observer*, Vol. 7

Mengistu Woube. 1986. *Problems of Land Reform Implementation in Rural Ethiopia: A Case Study of Dejen and Wolmera Districts*, Geografiska Regionstudier No.16, Department of Human Geography, Uppsala University

Mencher, Joan & K. Saradamoni. 1982. 'Muddy feet, dirty hands: rice production and female agricultural labour', *Economic and Political Weekly*, Vol. 17, No. 52

Mesfin Wolde Mariam. 1984. *Rural Vulnerability to Famine in Ethiopia: 1958-1977*, New Delhi: Vikas

Messing, Simon. 1957. 'The highland-plateau Amhara of Ethiopia', Ph.D. thesis in Anthropology, University of Pennsylvania

Mies, Maria. 1983. 'Towards a methodology for feminist research' in G. Bowles & R. Klein (eds), *Theories of Women's Studies*

Mittelman, James. 1981. *Underdevelopment and the Transition to Socialism: Mozambique and Tanzania*, New York: Academic Press

Molvaer, Reidulf. 1980. *Tradition and Change in Ethiopia: Social and Cultural Life as Reflected in Amharic Fictional Literature ca. 1930-1974*, Leiden: Brill

Molyneux, Maxine. 1977. 'Androcentrism in Marxist anthropology', *Critique of Anthropology*, Vol. 3, Nos 9/10

Molyneux, Maxine. 1981. 'Socialist societies old and new: progress towards women's emancipation', *Feminist Review*, Vol. 8

Molyneux, Maxine. 1985. 'Family Reform in Socialist States: the hidden agenda', *Feminist Review*, Vol. 21

Moore, Henrietta & Megan Vaughan. 1987. 'Cutting down trees: women, nutrition and agricultural change in the Northern province of Zambia, 1920-1986', *African Affairs*, Vol. 86, No. 345

Moore, Henrietta. 1988. *Feminism and Anthropology*, Cambridge: Polity

Mulatu Wubneh & Yohannis Abate. 1988. *Ethiopia: Transition and Development in the Horn of Africa*, Boulder: Westview

Murray, Colin. 1977. 'High bridewealth, migrant labour and the position of women in Lesotho', *Journal of African Law*, Vol. 21, No. 1

Murray, Nicola. 1979. 'Socialism and feminism: women and the Cuban Revolution', part I & part II, *Feminist Review*, Vol. 2 & Vol. 3

Murray, Robin. 1975. 'Class, State and the world economy: a case-study of Ethiopia', conference on New Approaches to Trade, Institute of Development Studies, University of Sussex

Mwapachu, Juma. 1979. 'Operation Planned Villages in rural Tanzania: a revolutionary strategy for development', in A. Coulson (ed.), *African Socialism in Practice: The Tanzanian Experience*

Nash, June & Helen Safa (eds). 1980. *Sex and Class in Latin America: Women's Perspectives on Politics, Economics, and the Family in the Third World*, South Hadley: Bergin

Natvig, Richard. 1987. 'Oromos, slaves and the zar spirits: a contribution to the history of the zar cult', *International Journal of African Historical Studies*, Vol. 20, No. 4

Nazzari, Muriel. 1983. 'The "woman question" in Cuba: an analysis of material constraints on its solution', *Signs*, Vol. 9, No. 2

Negussie, Birgit. 1988. *Traditional Wisdom and Modern Development: A Case Study of*

Traditional Peri-Natal Knowledge Among Elderly Women in Southern Shewa, Ethiopia, Studies in Comparative and International Education No.13, Institute of International Education, University of Stockholm.

Nekby, Bengt. 1971. *CADU: An Ethiopian Experiment in Developing Peasant Farming: a summary of the work of the Chilalo Agricultural Development Unit during the period of the First Agreement*, Stockholm: Prihna

Nelson, Nici (ed.). 1981. *African Women in the Development Process*, London: Cass

Ninsin, Kwame. 1988. 'Three levels of state reordering: The structural aspects', in D. Rothchild and N. Chazan (eds), *The Precarious Balance: The State and Society in Africa*

Oakley, Ann. 1981. 'Interviewing women: a contradiction in terms', in H. Roberts (ed.), *Doing Feminist Research*

Oakley, Ann & Robin Oakley. 1979. 'Sexism in official statistics', in J. Irvine *et al.* (eds), *Demystifying Social Statistics*

O'Laughlin, Bridget. 1974. 'Mediation of contradiction: why Mbum women do not eat chicken, in M. Rosaldo & L. Lamphere (eds), *Woman, Culture and Society*

Oppong, Christine, Christine Okali & Beverly Houghton. 1975. 'Woman Power: retrograde steps in Ghana', *The African Studies Review*, Vol. 18, No. 3

Ortner, Sherry. 1974. 'Is female to male as nature is to culture?', in M. Rosaldo & L. Lamphere (eds), *Woman, Culture, and Society*

Pacey, Arnold & Philip Payne (eds). 1985. *Agricultural Development and Nutrition*, London: Hutchinson

Pankhurst, Alula. 1989(a). 'The administration of resettlement in Ethiopia in Abebe Zegeye & S. Isheno (eds), *Forced Labour and Migration : Patterns of Movement within Africa*

Pankhurst, Alula. 1989(b). 'Settling for a New World: people and the State in an Ethiopian resettlement village', Ph.D. thesis in Social Anthropology, Manchester University.

Pankhurst, Helen. 1988. 'Villagization in Menz', unpublished report for the Canadian International Development Agency, Addis Ababa

Pankhurst, Helen. 1989(a). 'Peasants' Associations in Harerge', unpublished report for the Canadian International Development Agency, Addis Ababa

Pankhurst, Helen. 1989(b). 'What change and for whom?', in S. Pausewang (ed.), *Ethiopia : Rural Development*

Pankhurst, Helen. 1989(c). 'The value of dung', in *Proceedings on Peasant Production Systems and Development in Ethiopia*, 28-29 August, Trondheim University, Trondheim

Pankhurst, Helen. 1990. 'Contrasting forms of women's groups in Menz' paper for the African Studies Association, Birmingham 11-13 September

Pankhurst, Richard. 1961. *An Introduction to the Economic History of Ethiopia from Early Times to 1800*, London: Lalibela House

Pankhurst, Richard. 1965. *State and Land in Ethiopian History*, Addis Ababa: Faculty of Law and Institute of Ethiopian Studies, Haile Sellassie I University

Pankhurst, Richard. 1966(a). 'Some factors depressing the standard of living of peasants in traditional Ethiopia', *Journal of Ethiopian Studies*, Vol. 4, No. 2

Pankhurst, Richard. 1966(b). 'The Great Ethiopian Famine of 1888-1892: a new assessment', *Journal of the History of Medicine and Allied Sciences*, Vol. 21

Pankhurst, Richard. 1968. *Economic History of Ethiopia, 1800-1935*, Addis Ababa: Haile Sellassie I University

Pankhurst, Richard. 1969-70. 'A preliminary history of Ethiopian measures, weights and values', *Journal of Ethiopian Studies*, Vol. 7, Nos 1 and 2, Vol. 8, No. 1

Pankhurst, Richard. 1990(a). 'The role of women in Ethiopian economic, social and cultural life from the Middle Ages to the rise of Tewodros,' in R. Pankhurst, Ahmed Zekaria & Taddese Beyene (eds), *Proceedings of the First National Conference of Ethiopian Studies*, Institute of Ethiopian Studies, Addis Ababa

Pankhurst, Richard, Ahmed Zekaria & Taddese Beyene (eds). 1990(b). *Proceedings of the First National Conference of Ethiopian Studies, Addis Ababa, 11-12 April 1990*, Addis Ababa: Institute of Ethiopian Studies, Addis Ababa University

Pankhurst, Richard. 1990 (c) *A Social History of Ethiopia*, Institute of Ethiopian Studies, Addis Ababa University.

Pankhurst, Rita. 1981. 'Women in Ethiopia today', *Africa Today*, Vol. 28, No. 4

Papanek, H. 1984. 'False specialisation and the purdah of scholarship', *Journal of Asian Studies*, Vol. 44, No. 1

Parkin, Frank. 1979. *Marxism and Class Theory: A Bourgeois Critique*, London: Tavistock

Parkyns, Mansfield. (1868) 1966. *Life in Abyssinia*, London: Cass

Parpart, Jane. 1988. 'Women and the state in Africa', in D. Rothchild and N. Chazan (eds), *The Precarious Balance: The State and Society in Africa*

Passmore-Sanderson, Lilian. 1981. *Against the Mutilation of Women: The Struggle to End Unnecessary Suffering*, London: Ithaca

Pausewang, Siegfried. 1973. *Methods and Concepts in Social Research in a Rural Developing Society: A Critical Appraisal based on Experience in Ethiopia*, Munich: Weltforum

Pausewang, Siegfried. 1978. 'Peasants and local society in Ethiopia: Land Reform and social structure', Working Paper, No. 105, Development Economics Research and Advisory Project,Chr. Michelson Institute Bergen

Pausewang, Siegfried. 1986. 'Peasants, organisations, markets: ten years after the Land Reform, *Derap Working Papers* A359, Chr. Michelson Institute, Bergen

Pausewang, Siegfried (ed.). 1987. 'Participation in social research: experience in rural Ethiopia', *Derap Working Papers* A370, Chr. Michelson Institute, Bergen

Pausewang, Siegfried. 1991. *Ethiopia: Rural Development Options*, London: Zed Books

Pelzer White, Christine. 1984. 'Rural women: issues for research, policy and organisation', *Institute of Development Studies Bulletin*, Vol.15, No.1, Sussex University

Pelzer White, Christine. 1987. 'State, culture and gender: continuity and change in women's position in rural Vietnam', in H. Afshar (ed.), *Women, State and Ideology*

Penrose, Angela. 1988. *Beyond the Famine*, Geneva: International Institute for Relief and Development, Food for the Hungry International

Peters, Pauline. 1983. 'Gender, development cycles and historical process: a critique of recent research on women in Botswana', *Journal of Southern African Studies*, Vol. 10, No. 1

Pettigrew, Joyce. 1981. 'Reminiscences of fieldwork among the Sikhs', in H. Roberts (ed.), *Doing Feminist Research*

Phillips, Anne. 1987. *Divided Loyalties: Dilemmas of Sex and Class*, London: Virago

Poluha, Eva. 1980. 'A study in two Ethiopian *woredas* on the economic activities of peasant women and their role in rural development', unpublished paper, Addis Ababa

Poluha, Eva. 1987 (a). 'The current situation of women in Ethiopia', unpublished report for the World Bank, Addis Ababa

Poluha, Eva. 1987 (b). 'The Producers Cooperative as an option to women - a case study from Ethiopia', paper presented at the seminar 'Cooperatives Revisited', Scandinavian Institute for African Studies, November

Poluha, Eva. 1988. 'Beddedo: A Peasant Association in the Red Cross Project Area, Wello, Ethiopia', draft report

Poluha, Eva. 1989. *Central Planning and Local Reality: The Case of a Producer Cooperative in Ethiopia*, Stockholm Studies in Social Anthropology, No. 23, Stockholm University

Popkin, Samuel. 1979. *The Rational Peasant: The Political Society in Vietnam*, Berkeley: University of California

Poulantzas, Nicos. 1973. *Political Power and Social Classes*, London: Macmillan

Powers, Marla. 1980. 'Menstruation and reproduction: an Oglala case', *Signs*, Vol. 6, No. 1

Radcliffe-Brown, A. (1950). 1987. 'Introduction' in A. Radcliffe-Brown & D. Forde (eds), *African Systems of Kinship and Marriage*, London: Kegan Paul International

Reeves Sanday, Peggy & Ruth Gallagher Goodenough (eds). 1990. *Beyond the Second Sex*, Philadelphia: University of Pennsylvania Press

Reiter, Rayna (ed.). 1975. *Toward an Anthropology of Women*, New York: Monthly Review

Reminick, Ronald. 1973 (a). 'The Evil-Eye belief among the Amhara of Ethiopia', *Ethnology*, Vol.13, No.3

Reminick, Ronald. 1973 (b). 'The Manze Amhara of Ethiopia: a study of authority, masculinity and sociality', Ph.D. thesis in Anthropology, University of Chicago

Rey, P. 1975. 'The lineage mode of production', *Critique of Anthropology*, Vol. 3.

Rezene Habtemariam, Tesfaye Seyoum & Sergei Boyadijev. 1987. 'Mental illness treated in Ethiopian hospitals 1977-1981', *Ethiopian Journal of African Studies*, Vol. 4, No. 2, Institute of African Studies, Asmara University

Richards, Audrey. 1961. *Land, Labour and Diet in Northern Rhodesia*, London: Oxford University

Roberts, Helen (ed.). 1981. *Doing Feminist Research*, London: Routledge & Kegan Paul

Roberts, Pepe. 1987. 'Bearers of labour: gender, divisions and development in Africa', paper presented to the African Futures Conference, Centre for African Studies, Edinburgh University

Robertson, Alexander. 1984. *People and the State: An Anthropology of Planned Development*,

Cambridge: Cambridge University

Robertson, Claire. 1987. 'Developing economic awareness: changing perspectives in studies of African women, 1976-1985', *Feminist Studies*, Vol. 13, No. 1

Rosaldo, Michele & Louise Lampher (eds). 1974. *Woman, Culture, and Society*, Stanford: Stanford University

Rothchild, Donald & Naomi Chazan (eds). 1988. *The Precarious Balance: The State and Society in Africa*, Boulder: Westview

Rubin, Gayle. 1975. 'The traffic in women: notes on the political economy of sex' in R. Reiter (ed.), *Toward an Anthropology of Women*

Rudebeck, Lars. 1988. 'Kandjadja, Guinea-Bissau 1976-1986' *Review of African Political Economy*, No.41

Sacks, Karen. 1975. 'Engels revisited: women, the organization of production, and private property', in R. Reiter (ed.), *Toward an Anthropology of Women*

Saith, Ashwani. 1983. 'The distributional dimensions of Revolutionary transition: Ethiopia', Working paper No. 15, The Hague Institute of Social Studies

Saith, Ashwani. 1985. 'Primitive accumulation, agrarian reforms and socialist transitions: an argument', *Journal of Development Studies*, Vol. 22

Schwab, Peter. 1985. *Ethiopia: Politics, Economics and Society*, London: Pinter

Scott, James. 1985. *Weapons of the Weak: Everyday Forms of Peasant Resistance*, New Haven: Yale University Press

Seddon, D. (ed.). 1978. *Relations of Production: Marxist Approaches to Economic Anthropology*, London: Cass

Seldon, Mark. 1982. 'The crisis of collectivization: Socialist development and the peasantry', *Institute of Development Studies Bulletin*, Vol. 13, No. 4, Sussex University

Sender, John. & Sheila. Smith. 1986. *The Development of Capitalism in Africa*, London: Oxford University .

Shack, William. 1966. *The Gurage, A People of the Ensete Culture*, London: Oxford University

Shack, William. 1971. 'Hunger, anxiety and ritual: deprivation and spirit possession among the Gurage of Ethiopia' *Man*, Vol. 6, No. 1

Sharma, Ursula. 1980. *Women, Work and Property in North-West India*, London: Tavistock

Sjostrom, Margareta & Rolf Sjostrom. 1983. *How Do You Spell Development?*, Uppsala: Scandinavian Institute of African Studies

Sjostrom, Rolf. 1986. 'A pilot study of effects of primary schooling in a rural community of Ethiopia', Stockholm: Swedish International Development Authority, Ethiopian Ministry of Education

Spender, Dale. 1980. *Man Made Language*, London: Routledge and Kegan Paul

Stacy, Judith. 1979. 'When patriarchy kowtows: the significance of the Chinese family revolution for feminist theory', in Z. Eisenstein (ed.), *Capitalist Patriarchy and the Case for Socialist Feminism*

Stacy, Judith. 1983. *Patriarchy and Socialist Revolution in China*, Berkeley: University of California

Stacy, Judith. 1988. 'Can there be a feminist ethnography?', *Women's Studies International Forum*, Vol. 2, No. 1

Stack, Carol. 1974. 'Sex roles and survival strategies in an urban black community', in M. Rosaldo & L. Lamphere (eds), *Woman, Culture, and Society*

Stahl, Michael. 1974. *Ethiopia: Political Contradictions in Agricultural Development*, Uppsala: Political Science Association

Stahl, Michael. 1977. *New Seeds in Old Soil: A Study of the Land Reform Process in Western Wollega, Ethiopia 1975-76*, Uppsala: Scandinavian Institute of African Studies

Stavis, Benedict. 1985. 'Some initial results of China's new agricultural policies', *World Development*, Vol. 13, No. 12

Survival International Report. 1988. *For their own good... Ethiopia's Villagisation Programme*, London: Survival International

Tadesse Beyene. 1989. 'Terms of endearment in Amharic, their morphological structures and sociolinguistic norms', *Journal of Ethiopian Studies*, Vol. 22

Tegegne Teka. 1988. 'The State and rural cooperatives in Ethiopia', in H. Hedlund (ed.), *Cooperatives Revisited*

Teshome Demisse & Lionel Bender. 1983. 'An argot of Addis Ababa unattached girls', *Language and Society*, Vol. 12, No. 3

Thiele, Graham. 1986. 'The Tanzanian villagisation programme: its impact on household productivity in Dodoma', *Canadian Journal of African Studies*, Vol. 20, No. 2

Thompson, John & David Held. 1982. *Habermas: Critical Debates*, London: Macmillan

Trimingham, J. 1952. *Islam in Ethiopia*, London: Oxford University

Tsegai Welde-Ghiorgis. 1989. 'Problems of traditional energy supply in two villages of Northern Ethiopia', *Ethiopian Journal of African Studies*, Vol. 5, No. 2

Tsehai Berhane-Selassie. 1981. 'Man's world, woman's position: the case of the darasa widow', *Journal of Research on North East Africa*, Vol.1, No. 1

Tsehai Berhane-Selassie. 1984. *In Search of Ethiopian Women*, International Reports: Women and Society, No. 11, London: Change

Tsehai Berhane-Selassie (ed.). 1991. *Gender Issues in Ethiopia: Proceedings of the First University Seminar on Gender Issues in Ethiopia. Addis Ababa, December 24-26, 1989*, Addis Ababa, Institute of Ethiopian Studies, Addis Ababa University

United Nations, Economic Commission for Africa/International Labour Organization/Swedish International Development Agency. 1980. 'Report of the Workshop on the Participation of Women in Development Through Co-operatives with Special Emphasis on Handicrafts and Small-Scale Industries', Addis Ababa: UN/ECA

Urdang, Stephanie. 1984. 'The last transition? women and development in Mozambique', *Review of African Political Economy*, Vol. 27/28

van Binsbergen, Wim. 1979. *Religious Change in Zambia*, Haarlem: University of Amsterdam

Vaughan, Megan. 1987. *The Story of an African Famine: Gender and Famine in Twentieth-Century Malawi*, Cambridge: Cambridge University

von Freyhold, Michaela. 1979. 'Kitumbi-Chanika and Kitumbi-Tibili: two Ujamaa villages that refused to become one', in A. Coulson (ed.), *African Socialism in Practice*

Walker, Craven. 1933. *The Abyssinian at Home*, London: Sheldon

Weissleder, Wolfgang. 1965. 'The political ecology of Amhara domination', Ph.D. thesis in Anthropology, University of Chicago

Weissleder, Wolfgang. 1974. 'Amhara marriage: the stability of divorce', *Canadian Review of Sociology and Anthropology*, Vol. 11, Part I

White, Benjamin. 1984. 'Measuring time allocation, decision-making and agrarian changes affecting rural women: examples from recent research in Indonesia', *Institute of Development Studies Bulletin*, Vol. 15, No. 1, Sussex University

Whitehead, Ann. 1984. 'Women's solidarity - and divisions among women', *Institute of Development Studies Bulletin*, Vol. 15, No. 1, Sussex University

Wipper, Audrey. 1975. 'The Madaleo ya Wanawake movement: some paradoxes and contradictions', *African Studies Review*, Vol. 18, No. 3

Wolde Michael Kelecha. 1987. *A Glossary of Ethiopian Plant Names*, Addis Ababa: published by author

Wolf, Margery. 1974. 'Chinese women: old skills in a new context', in M. Rosaldo & L. Lamphere (eds), *Woman, Culture, and Society*

Wolpe, Harold (ed.).1980. *The Articulation of Modes of Production*, London: Routledge and Kegan Paul

Wood, Adrian. 1983. 'Rural development and national integration in Ethiopia', *African Affairs*, Vol. 82, No. 329

Woods, Roger. 1975. 'Peasants and peasantries in Tanzania and their role in socio-political development', in L. Cliffe *et al.*, *Rural Cooperation in Tanzania*

Worsley, Peter (ed.). 1971. *Two Blades of Grass: Rural Cooperatives in Agricultural Modernization*, Manchester: Manchester University

Wrong, Dennis. 1979. *Power: Its Forms, Bases and Uses*, Oxford: Blackwell

Yeraswork Admassie, Mulugetta Abebe & Markos Ezra. 1983. 'Ethiopian highlands reclamation study: report on the sociological survey and sociological considerations in preparing a development strategy', Addis Ababa: Institute of Development Research, UTF/ETH/037/ETH Working Paper 4, Addis Ababa University

Yeraswork Admassie & Solomon Gebre. 1985. *Food for Work in Ethiopia: A Socio-Economic Survey*, Research Project No. 24, Institute of Development Research, Addis Ababa University

Young, Allan. 1975. 'Magic as a "quasi-profession": the organization of magic and magical healing among Amhara', *Ethnography*, Vol. 14, No. 3

Young, Kate, Carol Wolkowitz & Roslyn McCullagh (eds). 1984. *Of Marriage and the Market: Women's Subordination internationally and its lessons*, London: Routledge and Kegan Paul

Zalkin, Michael. 1987. 'Food policy and class transformation in Revolutionary Nicaragua, 1979-86', *World Development*, Vol. 5, No. 7

Index